3 9

9 0   178 50

5 0   20   39 25
                                 90
45   51 32   50 36
    4 28 28   48 57
                                   4 44

‡131   16   30   0 ں

      65 38 00   2 amis

          22   4 23   107

     2   48   15) 26 5 17   33

          4   2   15
                                  115

         13

‡182 8 4   30   ‡114 50 30
    4   17   37 25
    90   90
  48   42   49   3 2 35
  5 2   37   34   2 8 20
                            4
      3 5 5 0 9

R Kanagunke

فى الحجة دار عم

ماجسير

ھھاारवि

في الحجة دار عم

David Livingstone and the Victorian Encounter with Africa

Lichtenstein

David Livingstone and the
Victorian Encounter with Africa

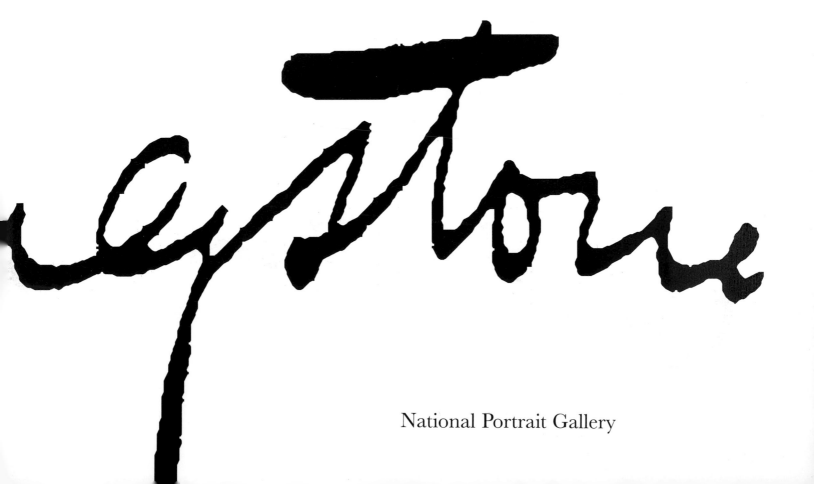

National Portrait Gallery

Published for the exhibition *David Livingstone and the Victorian Encounter with Africa,* held at the National Portrait Gallery, London, from 22 March to 7 July 1996, and at the Scottish National Portrait Gallery, Edinburgh (Royal Scottish Academy), from 26 July to 6 October 1996.

Published by National Portrait Gallery Publications
National Portrait Gallery
2 St Martin's Place
London WC2 0HE.

Hardback ISBN 1 85514 177 9
Paperback ISBN 1 85514 185 X

A catalogue record for this book is available from the British Library.

Advisory editor: John M. MacKenzie
Project editor: Joanna Skipwith
Printed in Italy by Amilcare Pizzi

End-papers:
Envelope with Livingstone's observations and journal entries for March–September 1871 (detail) (cat. no. 5.33)

Contents

Foreword

When I became Director of the National Portrait Gallery in January 1994, there was a proposal to hold a small-scale educational exhibition devoted to the life and work of the great Scottish explorer and missionary, David Livingstone, as part of the programme for the Studio Gallery downstairs. I felt, however, that Livingstone was particularly deserving of a major exhibition, for there are few other people who so conspicuously exemplify the idea of the individual as hero. Single-minded, determined and self-disciplined, he was treated as a creature of myth from the moment he died. In 1855, the year before the foundation of the National Portrait Gallery, he won acclaim as the first European to see the Victoria Falls. Yet now, like so many Victorian heroes, he has been forgotten, and, as someone who has never studied Victorian history in any depth, I was not sure whether it was legitimate to admire him or whether he had been debunked as a colonialist.

There were other, more contingent reasons for holding a major exhibition on Livingstone. We have for a long time enjoyed a close working relationship with the Scottish National Portrait Gallery. They were planning a small exhibition to commemorate the bicentenary of Robert Moffat's birth in 1795, and, through them, we were put in touch with Jeanne Cannizzo, an anthropologist with special knowledge of missionaries and their contacts with African peoples. It seemed a pity to have two small-scale exhibitions devoted to the work of African missionaries, rather than one large one devoted to the whole subject of African exploration. So we decided to collaborate. The exhibition will open in London and then travel to Edinburgh to coincide with the Edinburgh Festival.

Much of the burden of administration has fallen on Peter Funnell, the Gallery's nineteenth-century curator, who has worked tirelessly to ensure an appropriate selection of objects and pictures for the exhibition and of authors for the catalogue. He has been assisted at all stages by John Cooper, the Gallery's Head of Education. Jeanne Cannizzo has been a brilliant special advisor, contributing her great knowledge and enthusiasm to the project. And we were fortunate to have the assistance of a remarkable group of contributors to the catalogue, under the advisory editorship of Professor John MacKenzie. Together, they have illuminated the whole subject of African exploration and have done so while following the dictates of a tough schedule.

Charles Saumarez Smith
Director, National Portrait Gallery, 1996

Acknowledgements

It became apparent at an early stage of this project that we had the opportunity of putting together an exhibition of great diversity and of producing a book that would bring recent scholarship in the field to a wider readership. In so far as this has been achieved, Jeanne Cannizzo and I have been reliant on the help and expertise of a great many people. It is a pleasure to be able to acknowledge their assistance here and to extend our warmest thanks.

Many individuals and institutions responded sympathetically to our request for loans and acted as patient guides to their collections. We are most heartily grateful to Janet M. Backhouse and Shelley M. Jones (The British Library); Alan Jesson (Cambridge University Library); the Earl of Clarendon; Geoffrey Duncan, Richard Huthwaite and Sylvia Robinson (The Council for World Mission); Rosemary Seton (School of Oriental and African Studies); David O'Neill and Sheila Watt (The David Livingstone Centre); Elizabeth Allen (Hunterian Museum, The Royal College of Surgeons of England); John and Virginia Murray (John Murray Ltd); Antonia Lovelace (Art Gallery and Museum, Kelvingrove); Quentin Keynes; Mary Leitch; Dr John Mack (Museum of Mankind); Michael Baldwin and Ian Robertson (National Army Museum); Ian Cunningham, Ann Matheson and Elspeth Yeo (National Library of Scotland); David Alston and Oliver Fairclough (National Museums & Galleries of Wales); Paula Jenkins, Christopher Mills, Dr Robert Prys-Jones, John Thackray and Kathie Way (The Natural History Museum); Clare Brown and John Pinfold (Rhodes House Library); Dana Josephson and Toby Kirtlee (Bodleian Library); Kate Edmundson, Cheryl Piggott, Naomi Rumball, Bernard Vercourt and Marilyn Ward (Royal Botanic Gardens, Kew), Dr Andrew Tatham, Karen Gee, Francis Herbert, Paula Lucas, Rachel Rowe and Joanna Scadden (Royal Geographical Society); Linda Wigley (Bath Royal Literary and Scientific Institution); Rosalyn Clancey, Briony Crozier and Dale Idiens (Royal Museum of Scotland); Pam Roberts (Royal Photographic Society); Dr Robert Bud and Tim Boon (Science Museum); Sara Stevenson and Julie Lawson (Scottish National Portrait Gallery); Peter Speke; and Michael F. Stanley (Wilberforce House).

Others who have given invaluable help and advice include Terry Barringer, Hugh Bett, Oliver Crimmen, Alexander Maitland, Richard Ovendon, Judith Prendergast, James Ryan, Mrs J. Stanley and Dr David Livingstone Wilson. It has been a great pleasure to work with our colleagues at the Scottish National Portrait Gallery and I am especially grateful to James Holloway for ensuring that this has been another successful collaboration.

David Livingstone and the Victorian Encounter with Africa raises complex issues that cannot be dealt with in the form of an exhibition. A book of essays, closely tied to the exhibition through captioned illustrations and an exhibition list but providing different views of Livingstone's role in Africa, seemed essential. Our warmest thanks go to the authors of the essays, who agreed to write to a rigorous deadline and who have been a source of much free advice. We are especially grateful to John MacKenzie for acting as Advisory Editor.

Both the exhibition and the book have involved a number of colleagues at the National Portrait Gallery. Charles Saumarez Smith recognised the potential of the subject at an early stage in his directorship and has been an invaluable supporter of the project. I am also enormously grateful to John Cooper, Head of Education, who helped shape the exhibition in its formative stages, selected items for the Stanley section of the show, and has created an impressive programme of educational events to accompany it. In the exhibitions office, Kathleen Soriano has shown her usual remarkable levels of energy and efficiency and she has been ably assisted by Stephanie Hopkinson and Kate Holden. The book could not have been produced without the foresight and tenacity of Robert Carr-Archer and his colleagues in the Gallery's Publications Department, Louisa Hearnden and Lucy Clark. Joanna Skipwith performed the task of editing an unusually complex text, working to tight deadlines, with exceptional skill and patience. Others who I would like to thank are Lesley Bradshaw, Honor Clerk, Emma Floyd, Robin Gibson, Sarah Kemp, Janine Learner, Tim Moreton, Carole Patey, Terence Pepper, David Saywell, Jill Springall, Lisi Streule and Kai Kin Yung. A final word of thanks must go to Caroline Brown, designer of the exhibition. This is the last exhibition Caroline has designed at the Gallery; after thirty-five years of distinguished work here, I hope she feels that we have provided the right ingredients to make it a fitting climax to her career at the NPG.

Peter Funnell
Curator of the Nineteenth-Century Collection,
National Portrait Gallery

7

The National Portrait Gallery is most grateful
to the following for their support:
Baillie Gifford & Company
The John Ellerman Foundation
The Mrs Harryhausen Trust
Harpers & Queen

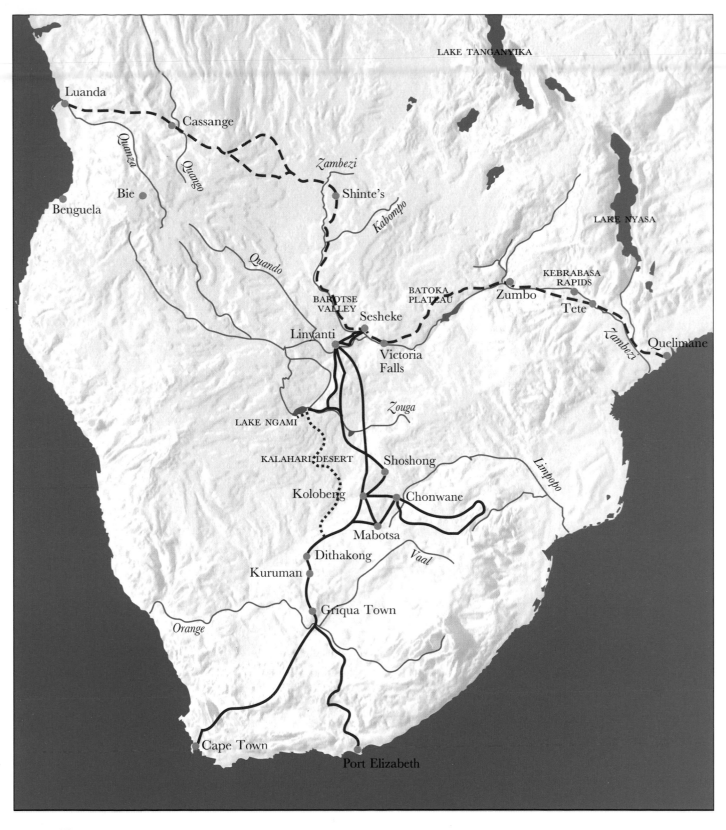

9

Sketch Map of Livingstone's Journeys, 1841–1856

—— Journeys in Southern Africa 1841–1853	● Towns and places
– – – Coast-to-coast journey 1853–1856	—— *Rivers*
······ Lake Ngami journey 1849	

0   100   200   300   400 miles

**Livingstone's pocket
surgical instrument case**
21 x 26.1 cm (open)
THE DAVID LIVINGSTONE CENTRE
(cat. no. 5.52)

IO

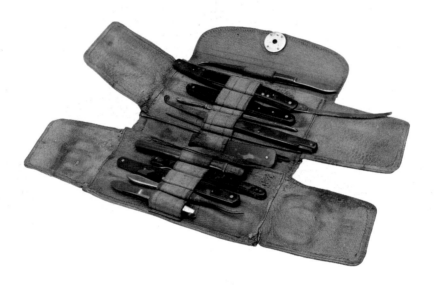

Tim Jeal

David Livingstone:
A Brief Biographical Account

I

David Livingstone
By Henry Wyndham Phillips, 1857
Oil on canvas
76.2 x 61 cm oval
PRIVATE COLLECTION
(cat. no. 1.1)

David Livingstone:
A Brief Biographical Account

Commissioned by Livingstone's publisher, John Murray, Phillips' portrait was engraved by William Holl for *Missionary Travels and Researches in South Africa*, 1857. In a letter to Murray of 12 November 1857 Livingstone reported that his friends 'all call out against the portrait', one of them remarking that 'it will do for any one between Captain Cook & Guy Fawkes'. Nevertheless, it is one of the few oil portraits of Livingstone done from life.

The skies above Southampton were overcast on the morning of 15 April 1874. Despite the wind and rain crowds had been gathering along the docks and quays since dawn. Shortly before 9 a.m. a battered and insignificant-looking steamer was sighted. By now the mayor and aldermen of the town had assembled in their fur-trimmed robes and a company of the Royal Horse Artillery began to fire a twenty-one gun salute at one-minute intervals. Through binoculars it was possible to see on the steamer's deck a coffin draped in the Union flag. Later a small black boy stepped forward on to the quay and lifted up a placard decorated with sable rosettes. It read: 'To the memory of Dr Livingstone, Friend of the African'. A band struck up the 'Dead March' from *Saul* and telegraph operators started to tap out the news.

Livingstone, more than any other famous Victorian, had become a mythical figure in his own lifetime. His road to fame from child factory worker to national hero, through determination and hard work, was seen as a triumph of 'self-help'. His three decades in Africa as missionary and explorer spanned an era when the 'Dark Continent' seemed more romantic and mysterious than space travel does today. Adulation was only to be expected; Livingstone was, after all, the first European to have made an authenticated crossing of the continent from coast to coast.

Today Livingstone's exceptional fame is harder to understand. Other explorers made important discoveries but were not singled out for such reverence, and Livingstone can be said to have failed in all he most hoped to achieve. He failed as a conventional missionary, converting only one African, who subsequently lapsed. The two missions that went to Africa at his behest ended in fiasco and heavy loss of life. He was considered a great geographer, but one series of miscalculations scuppered his government-sponsored Zambezi expedition and, on his last journey, he believed that he had found the source of the Nile when he was, in fact, on the upper Congo.

Livingstone's fame, however, was due not so much to what he had done but to what he had come to represent. In the eyes of the public he owned all the virtues they most wished to possess: bravery, philanthropic zeal and selflessness. By praising him, his countrymen could take pride in their exploration of foreign territories without guilt, reconciling contradictory motivation in a soothingly self-righteous combination of patriotism and Christianity. Livingstone assured the British that they were not simply the richest and most powerful people on earth but the

Blantyre
By Bruce Cameron, *c.* 1920
Etching
18.6 x 26.5 cm
SCOTTISH NATIONAL GALLERY OF
MODERN ART, EDINBURGH
(cat. no. 2.7)

This twentieth-century etching of
Shuttle Row, Blantyre, shows
where Livingstone was born and
brought up. Twenty-four families
occupied the building, each
crammed into one tenement room.

most moral, too – a people chosen by God to bring
progress and liberty to the benighted of the world.

David Livingstone was born on 19 March 1813 in Blantyre,
Lanarkshire. His father was a travelling tea-salesman
whose slender income obliged him to put his three sons to
work in the nearby cotton mill. From the age of ten,
between six in the morning and eight at night, David
worked as a 'piecer', crawling around under the spinning
frames, twisting together broken threads, and often
covering twenty miles a day. The air was steam-heated to
90°F, and the boys were beaten if they fell asleep.

At the end of the working day Livingstone and a handful
of other children would defy exhaustion and aching limbs
and spend two hours at the company school learning to
read and write. At home, a tenement room that he shared
with his parents and their four other children, he often
read until midnight (teaching himself Latin, mathematics
and botany) or until his mother took his book away from
him. He took books into the mill and balanced them on
the spinning frames in order to catch a sentence or two as
he passed. Not suprisingly, the other children pitched
bobbins at them to knock them off.

The picture that emerges from the few existing letters
written by his father, and from his sister Janet's
reminiscences, is of an over-earnest boy, exceptional more
for his obsessive determination to learn than for his
intelligence.[1] 'When I was a piecer,' he wrote many years
later, 'the fellows used to try to turn me from the path I
had chosen, and always began with, "I think you ought
etc.", till I snapped them up with a mild, "You think!
I can think and act for myself; I don't need anyone to
think for me."' [2]

The dominant figure in David's early life was his
formidable self-taught father Neil, who rarely did things
by halves. He disapproved strongly of alcohol and 'bad
language' – he had given up tailoring because his
workmates' profanities had become unendurable – and
labelled all non-religious literature as 'trashy novels'. As
a tea-salesman he enlarged his sphere of influence by
distributing religious tracts to his customers. Members of
his family were also expected to read these dry doctrinal
pamphlets, but young David preferred travel books and
scientific manuals. He was beaten as a result.

Fear of physical blows was nothing compared with fear of
divine punishment. By the time Livingstone was twelve his
father's Calvinist beliefs had left the boy terrified by the
prospect of eternal damnation. Looking back on this time,
he wrote, 'I found neither peace nor happiness, which

caused me (never having revealed my state of mind to anyone) to bewail my sad estate with tears in secret.'[3] His predicament was made worse by his father's disapproval of his interest in science, even though this manifested itself as a natural boyish curiosity about animals and plants. In Neil's opinion religious faith was undermined by science, and science was therefore ungodly.

At the age of nineteen Livingstone purchased a book that was to change his life. The arguments advanced in *The Philosophy of a Future State* by Dr Thomas Dick, a Scottish Nonconformist minister and amateur astronomer, brought immediate solace to Livingstone. Science, the elderly astronomer assured his readers, posed no danger to Christian belief, and, far from rendering God obsolete, confirmed His existence by establishing the complexity and variety of the natural world. No less significant for Livingstone was Dick's insistence that salvation was not limited to the Elect, but was freely given to all who were able to receive it. His release from fear brought religious revelation to Livingstone, who was soon writing:

> I saw the duty and incstimable privilege immediately to accept salvation by Christ. Humbly believing that through sovercign mercy and grace I have been enabled to do so . . . it is my desire to show my attachment to the cause of Him who died for me by devoting my life to His service.[4]

In 1832, the same year in which Livingstone overcame his doubts and vowed to devote his life to Christian service, his father also underwent a change of heart. On hearing a young Canadian preacher, Henry Wilkes, deliver a well-argued attack on the Calvinist theology of the Established Presbyterian Church, Neil Livingstone was so favourably impressed that he decided to apply for membership of the independent Congregational church where he had heard the sermon. The church at Hamilton, near Blantyre, maintained regular links with liberal theologians and churches in America, and members of the congregation supported missionary work abroad. In 1834 Neil brought home a pamphlet from the Hamilton Church; it had been written by Karl Gutzlaff of the Netherlands Missionary Society and was an appeal for missionaries to be sent to China from Britain and America.

In David Livingstone's view 'the salvation of men ought to be the chief desire and aim of every Christian', and he had already resolved to make regular donations to foreign missions.[5] Only when he learnt that Gutzlaff wanted to recruit missionaries who had been trained in medicine did

Title-page and flysheet, with Livingstone's signature, from *An Introduction to Arithmetic*
By James Gray
Published in Edinburgh, 1825
THE DAVID LIVINGSTONE CENTRE
(cat. no. 2.46)

Livingstone's childhood arithmetic book shows the earliest example of his signature.

15

Livingstone's certificates from the Andersonian University, Glasgow, 1836–1837
Printed cards with manuscript additions, each 7.6 x 11.3 cm
THE DAVID LIVINGSTONE CENTRE (cat. no. 2.52)

Livingstone's certificates from the Andersonian University, Glasgow, were signed by his tutors and confirm his attendance at courses on the medical sciences and chemistry between 1836 and 1837.

16

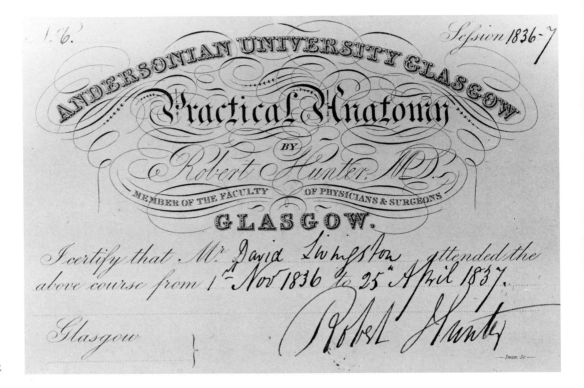

Livingstone consider becoming a missionary himself. In Gutzlaff's view the possession of medical knowledge made missionaries more effective in securing conversions, since gratitude invariably followed the relief of physical suffering. It may also have occurred to Livingstone that by becoming a medical missionary he would at last be able to combine an interest in science with a religious vocation. And, although it was clearly going to be more expensive to get a medical education than to obtain the theological training required by an ordinary missionary, Livingstone and his father agreed that the effort should be made. With factory wages of four shillings a week, it would take Livingstone a year and a half to save the £12 needed to meet the fees for his first term at the medical school of the Andersonian University in Glasgow.

David Livingstone was twenty-three-years old when he left the mill to begin studying for his medical degree. Since only ten per cent of child factory workers achieved partial literacy, he had already proved himself a rarity.

During his second year at medical school Livingstone applied to and was accepted by the directors of the London Missionary Society (LMS), an independent and unsectarian organisation and therefore acceptable to Neil as well as to David. The Foreign Secretary of the LMS, who had written an introduction to Gutzlaff's most recently published book,[6] was actively recruiting missionaries for the East. Livingstone's reasons for choosing to work in China are not fully known. China was considered by Victorian readers of travellers' tales to be among the strangest and most exotic countries in the world, and, given Livingstone's subsequent career, it seems likely that the challenge of bringing Christianity to an alien society with a vigorous and ancient culture appealed to his passion for overcoming difficulties.

Livingstone began his missionary training at Chipping Ongar, in Essex, in the autumn of 1838. His tutor, the Reverend Richard Cecil, prescribed a rigid diet of Greek, Latin, Hebrew and theology that was wholly inappropriate for men hoping to convert Indians, Africans and Chinese. Cecil considered the young Scot 'worthy but remote from brilliant' and hoped that he 'might kindle a little'.[7] Having had no formal education, Livingstone was at a disadvantage in comparison with the other students. His thick, indistinct voice was another handicap for an aspiring preacher. Descriptions of Livingstone by fellow students show him to have been an awkward and rather sullen young man. 'I have to admit,' wrote Walter Inglis, 'he was "no bonny". His face wore at all times the strongly marked lines of potent will. I never recollect him relaxing into the

17

Robert Moffat (1795–1883) with John Mokoteri and Sarah Roby
By William Scott, 1842
Oil on canvas, 53.4 x 45.7 cm
SCOTTISH NATIONAL PORTRAIT GALLERY
(cat. no. 2.4)

At the time this portrait was painted, Moffat was one of the most famous missionaries working in Africa and was soon to become Livingstone's father-in-law. The two Africans depicted were once part of his entourage. In 1826 Moffat's wife, Mary, found an abandoned infant whom she named Sarah Roby after the Manchester preacher William Roby, who had inspired her husband to become a missionary. John Mokoteri is said to have been rescued as a child by Moffat after the battle of 'Lattakoo' in 1823. He accompanied him to Britain where this picture was painted. Stories of 'saving' Africans, physically and spiritually, are common in missionary accounts.

abandon of youthful frolic or play.'[8] But Joseph Moore, another student, liked him in spite of 'all his rather ungainly ways and by no means winning face', and said that he possessed 'an indescribable charm'.[9] Even Richard Cecil came to acknowledge that Livingstone had 'sense and quiet vigour' and that 'his character was substantial'.[10]

In 1839, when Livingstone was still at Ongar, Britain and China drifted into the inglorious Opium War that would last three years. The directors of the LMS decided not to send missionaries to China until the war was over and suggested that Livingstone go to the West Indies instead. He declined on the grounds that the islands had been too long settled and that the work would therefore be 'too like the ministry at home'. Many other doctors, he argued, would be practising there, and his skills were surely required more urgently in a remote territory such as South Africa.[11]

In choosing South Africa Livingstone must have been influenced by the example of the LMS's outstanding propagandist for missions in southern Africa, John Philip, and by John Campbell and Robert Moffat, who had both established mission stations beyond the confines of the Cape Colony. David Livingstone met Moffat in London early in 1840 when the latter was in England fund-raising for the LMS and publicising his book, *Missionary Labours and Scenes in Southern Africa*. The great man's enthusiasm for African missions confirmed Livingstone in his determination to begin his life's work in that continent.

In 1840 the LMS arranged for Livingstone to live in London to gain practical medical experience at Charing Cross Hospital and at Moorfields, and to enlarge his knowledge of anatomy at the Hunterian Museum. In November he travelled to Glasgow to take his medical degree in the Faculty of Physicians and Surgeons, and shortly afterwards he returned to London to be ordained a Nonconformist minister in the Albion Congregational Chapel, Finsbury. By December he was ready to leave England and set sail for Cape Town from London on 8 December 1840.

When Livingstone landed in Simon's Bay on 15 March 1841 the geography of the African interior was still as much of a mystery to Europeans as it had been to the Greeks and Romans. The existence of the great lakes was not suspected, and the whereabouts of the sources of the Nile and Congo were subjects of unproductive speculation. That Africa was still a continent of fringe coastal settlements a thousand years after the establishment

Left

John Campbell (1766–1840)
By Thomas Hodgetts
(after John Renton), 1819
Mezzotint, 35.5 x 25.5 cm
NATIONAL PORTRAIT GALLERY
LONDON
(cat. no. 2.17)

An experienced minister and philanthropist, Campbell was appointed by the London Missionary Society in April 1812 to conduct an inspection of its southern African missions. He spent two years there, travelling into southern Tswana territory on a journey of over 2,000 miles. He returned to Africa on another tour of inspection in 1819, again visiting the Tswana people in the area of Dithakong, this time accompanied by the young Robert Moffat. It was among these people that Moffat established his successful mission station at Kuruman, where Livingstone himself was posted by the LMS in 1841.

Below left

Frontispiece and title-page from *Travels in South Africa*
By John Campbell, volume 2
Published by the London Missionary Society, London, 1822
QUENTIN KEYNES
(cat. no. 2.43)

Campbell's account of his second visit to southern Africa, between 1819 and 1821, is distinguished by its colour plates based on his own drawings. The frontispiece to volume 2 shows Mmahutu, Queen of the Tlhaping people, whom he visited at 'Lattakoo' (also known as Dithakong).

Southern African Sketches
By John Campbell, June 1813
Watercolour over pencil on paper
16.5 x 21 cm open
COUNCIL FOR WORLD MISSION
ARCHIVE, SCHOOL OF ORIENTAL
AND AFRICAN STUDIES
(cat. nos. 2.11)

These two sketches, now bound together with others from June 1813, date from Campbell's first period of travelling in southern Africa. Campbell was an astute observer, and although simply executed his drawings are remarkable on-the-spot records of areas barely visited by Europeans before his time.

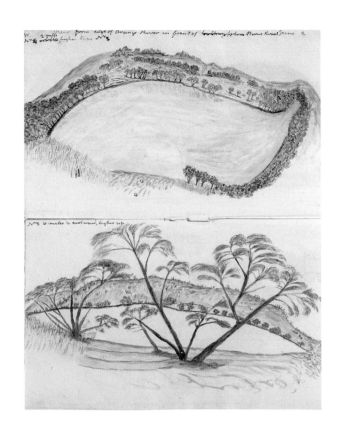

**'A View in the Town
of Litakun'**

From *Travels in the Interior of
Southern Africa*
By William John Burchell, volume 2
Published by Longman & Co.,
London, 1824
QUENTIN KEYNES
(cat. no. 2.42)

Burchell's plate shows a
panoramic view of 'Litakun'
(Dithakong), where he stayed in
August 1812. According to John
Campbell, who visited the town
the following year, it covered 'a
great deal of ground, perhaps five
miles in circumference'. Drawn and
engraved by Burchell, the colour
plates in *Travels in the Interior of
Southern Africa* make it one of the
finest books in the early literature
on southern Africa.

Right

**William John Burchell
(?1782–1863)**

By Mrs Dawson Turner
(after John Sell Cotman), 1816
Etching, 17.6 x 14.2 cm
NATIONAL PORTRAIT GALLERY
LONDON
(cat. no. 2.25)

A pioneer of southern African
exploration, Burchell travelled
extensively between 1811 and 1815.
His route penetrated far into
Tswana territory, where he spent a
period in August 1812 with the
Tlhaping people at Dithakong,
north of the eventual site of
Robert Moffat's Kuruman mission.
A distinguished naturalist,
Burchell stated that his African
collections amounted to no less
than 63,000 specimens, as well as
500 drawings and a mass of notes.

21

A View in the Town of Litakun

Published by Longman & Co. May 1 1824

David Livingstone
By Sarah Newell, 1840
Watercolour on ivory, 7.5 x 5.4 cm
COUNCIL FOR WORLD MISSION
ARCHIVE, SCHOOL OF ORIENTAL
AND AFRICAN STUDIES
(cat. no. 2.23)

It was the practice of the London Missionary Society to record the likenesses of their missionaries, before their departure abroad, in the form of miniatures. This, the earliest known portrait of Livingstone, is preserved with over a hundred similar portraits of missionaries, most of whom are now barely remembered.

of Arab stations along its eastern seaboard, and three centuries after the Portuguese built trading forts on the lower Zambezi, is best explained by describing the conditions that defeated early efforts to penetrate far inland.

The Zambezi's surf-beaten sandbars and lack of a natural harbour at the estuary were drawbacks that the river shared with most African waterways. In addition to this there were the cataracts, the intense heat and the inexplicable and sudden deaths. Malaria might carry off entire expeditions of several hundred men (the Portuguese at first suspected that their men had been poisoned by Arabs or Africans), and during the rains country that had been easily traversable several days earlier became impassable swamp. Tropical forests obstructed wheeled transport and the tsetse fly killed horses and oxen, leaving human porterage as the sole means of conveyance for goods and stores. Worst of all, the black inhabitants clearly possessed neither wealth nor an easily exploitable land. All interest in Africa might have died away in the sixteenth century but for the use of one African commodity: the African himself.

While some Portuguese were struggling up the Zambezi, their fellow countrymen were settling in Brazil, and the Spanish in the Caribbean, Mexico and Peru. The New World's population was proving too sparse to provide labour for the development of mines, sugar plantations and cotton fields; but, at that very moment, thousands of strong, hardy black men were known to be living lives of apparent idleness on the other side of the Atlantic. The transatlantic slave trade was the inevitable consequence. With most European countries soon joining in, and the European settlement of North America providing a vast new market for slaves, the trade was still flourishing more than two centuries later when William Wilberforce and the Abolitionists began a thirty-year campaign that culminated in 1833 with legislation banning slavery and setting a timetable for its implementation throughout the British Empire.

Slaves were employed in the Cape Colony until 1834, and when Livingstone arrived the slave-owning Boer farmers, who were descended from the earliest seventeeth-century Dutch settlers, were trekking north-east, beyond the colony's borders, to escape the authority of the Cape's British Governor. Britain had taken the Cape Colony from the Dutch during the Napoleonic Wars and had made their possession formal in 1806. With a clement climate, no malaria, and, in the Cape Colony at least, no tsetse fly, South Africa seemed set to rival Canada and Australia as a successful European colony.

On the last day of July 1841 Livingstone arrived at Moffat's mission station in Kuruman after a 600 mile journey from Cape Town by ox-waggon. At the time Kuruman was the most remote mission in southern Africa and Livingstone immediately disliked the flat and arid veldt that surrounded it. He was shocked to find that in twenty years of missionary labour only forty converts had been made in the region, and that half of these were showing signs of changing their minds. To attract funds from the public, missionary societies invariably claimed to be making more conversions than was actually the case, and Livingstone was enraged to find that he, like thousands of others, had been duped.

Within months Livingstone was writing of his missionary colleagues as men with 'contracted minds' and 'a really bad set', in whom only a fool would have 'the least confidence'. An inability to get on with white colleagues would be an oft-repeated motif in Livingstone's story, and it is not surprising that shortly after leaving Kuruman, to set up a mission station of his own 250 miles to the north-east, he fell out with Roger Edwards, the missionary who had been sent to run the station with him. The trouble initially arose from an article written by Livingstone for publication in the *Missionary Chronicle* in which he made no mention of Roger Edwards as co-founder of the Mabotsa mission. Without acknowledging the true cause of Edwards's hostility, Livingstone wrote a 9,000 word letter to the directors of the LMS representing Edwards as a small-minded idiot who constantly worked himself into a frenzy over trivialities. Mrs Edwards considered Livingstone to be 'shabby, ungentlemanly and un-Christian',[12] and in his dealings with her and her husband he certainly showed himself capable of hypocrisy and double-dealing.

Livingstone had also declared that the daughters of missionaries had 'miserably contracted minds' and had written to a friend that he would have to advertise for a wife in England: 'And if I get very old it must be for some decent sort of widow'.[13] But he had met Robert Moffat's compliant and good-natured daughter, Mary, while at Kuruman, and by July 1844 he had decided that a man in his position could not afford to be fussy. His announcement of the engagement in a letter to the LMS directors could not have been more impersonal.

Various considerations connected with this new sphere of labour, and which to you need not be specified in detail, having led me to the conclusion that it was my

Mary Livingstone, née Moffat (1821–1862)
Photogravure after an earlier photograph (photographer unknown, late 1850s)
36 x 29 cm
THE DAVID LIVINGSTONE CENTRE
(cat. no. 2.33)

23

The eldest daughter of Robert Moffat, Mary married Livingstone on 9 January 1845 and accompanied him on his early travels. She returned to Britain with their children in April 1852. By all accounts her remaining years were tragic. She was isolated and desperately poor during Livingstone's absence in the mid-1850s, apparently turning to drink. She returned with him to southern Africa in 1858 but could not travel beyond Cape Town and, after eventually joining the Zambezi expedition in January 1862, died of fever on 27 April. This photogravure is based on a photograph, probably taken in 1857.

24

duty to enter into the marriage relation, I have made the necessary arrangements with Mary, the eldest daughter of Mr Moffat.[14]

Livingstone's descriptions of Mary were extraordinarily unromantic. He described her to one correspondent as 'a little thick black-haired girl, sturdy and all I want'; while to another he confided, 'She is a good deal of an African in complexion with a stout stumpy body.'[15] Had Mary known Livingstone's views on marriage before her wedding, she might have had second thoughts. 'I have never found two agreeing,' Livingstone would later tell his brother-in-law, J. S. Moffat, 'unless one were a cypher.'[16]

In 1845 Livingstone and his wife set up a mission station forty miles north of Mabotsa at a place called Chonwane. Their move had been motivated in part by animosity towards Edwards but owed as much to Livingstone's belief that Sechele, chief of the Kwena (then settled at Chonwane), was a more likely candidate for conversion than the chief of the Kgatla at Mabotsa.

When the wells dried up at Chonwane Livingstone moved with the Kwena to Kolobeng, fifty miles further north. His initial optimism about Sechele's religious intentions would be shortlived, for although Sechele was very intelligent and learnt to read and write his own language within months, he still considered it 'highly meritorious to put all suspected witches to death'.[17] Sechele believed that witches could injure and even kill people, and it is to Livingstone's credit that he understood that the chief's actions were intended to protect his people.

Unlike his missionary colleagues, Livingstone recognised that Christianity appeared to Africans as subversion aimed at 'reducing them and their much-loved domestic institutions',[18] and he saw that this lay at the heart of their resistance to conversion. His tolerance astonished other missionaries when he asserted that polygamy could not be called adultery and that the *boguera*, or tribal initiation rites, were not black magic but a ceremony ensuring tribal unity. Unbelieving Africans were not stupid, he said, but 'showed more intelligence than is to be met with in our own uneducated peasantry'.[19] Although Livingstone also wrote of the degradation and sinfulness of Africans, his positive statements were more numerous. 'With a general opinion they are wiser than their white neighbours . . . They go direct to the point, and in so doing shew a more philosophic spirit than the Germans . . . They have few theories but many ideas.'[20] On another occasion he declared that, 'Africans are not by any means unreasonable. I think unreasonableness is more a hereditary disease in Europe than in this land.'[21]

No rain fell during Livingstone's first two years at Kolobeng. Trees died, the corn failed, the 'river dwindled to a dribbling rill', and food had to be transported from Kuruman. Such indignities could be tolerated but Sechele's continuing rejection of the gospel was harder to bear. At one point Livingstone suggested that the chief's eagerness to own European artefacts proved that he was 'desirous of civilisation'.[22] Sechele, however, the proud possessor of a Duke of Wellington jug, a pair of military boots and a hartebeest suit of European cut, still showed no inclination to be baptised.

Then, quite suddenly, when Livingstone had all but given up hope, Sechele agreed to send three of his wives back to their families and to keep only his first. Livingstone had not made their rejection a precondition for baptism since he knew and liked all the women and considered that 'they had sinned in ignorance'. Their misery distressed him, as did the tribe's anger with Sechele, who faced many threats and insults. The chief was baptised in September 1848 in front of hundreds of spectators, many of them in tears. Three months later Sechele was still standing up to his people's displeasure and finding consolation in Robert Moffat's Tswana version of *The Pilgrim's Progress*, for, as Livingstone observed, 'some parts of the pilgrim's experience and his are exactly alike'.[23]

In March 1849, however, Livingstone learnt that Sechele had resumed sexual relations with one of his rejected wives and that she was pregnant. Sechele's confession, wrote Livingstone, 'loosened all my bones. I felt as if I should sink to the earth or run away'. He sent the chief a note: 'My heart is broken . . . I can no longer be a teacher here.'[24] Livingstone had in fact already thought of moving on. Over a year earlier he had decided that he would stay with the Kwena only for a few more years and would then 'move on to the regions beyond'.[25] And earlier still, while at Kuruman, he had written, 'I would never build on another man's foundation. I shall preach the gospel beyond every other man's line of things.'[26]

Livingstone had wanted to make a series of journeys to the north before Sechele's lapse. To convince the LMS directors, and perhaps himself, that he would not be abandoning missionary work for mere travelling, he argued that his recent experience had proved it 'imperatively necessary to extend the gospel to all the surrounding tribes. This . . . is the only way which permits the rational hope that when people do turn to the Lord it will be by groups.'[27] The hope was, of course, anything

Snuff box of Tswana design collected by Robert Moffat in South Africa
Ivory, wood and (?)leather
20.3 cm (high)
LENT BY KIND PERMISSION OF THE TRUSTEES OF THE BRITISH MUSEUM
(cat. no. 2.58)

The head may be meant as a depiction of Moffat by the African artist, who has carefully shown a European male with a thick beard – Moffat habitually wore a long black beard. The colour black was associated with rainmaking by the Tswana, who also used parts of the body as ingredients in powerful medicines. It is possible that they thought Moffat was using his beard to compete with local ritual specialists.

25

The Slave Trade
By François-Auguste Biard,
c. 1840
Oil on canvas, 162.5 x 228.6 cm
WILBERFORCE HOUSE MUSEUM,
HULL CITY MUSEUMS, ART
GALLERIES AND ARCHIVES
(cat. no. 3.3)

Biard's painting representing the
horrors of the African slave trade
was exhibited at the Royal
Academy in 1840 and later
presented to Sir Thomas Fowell
Buxton, a leading abolitionist and
an important influence on
Livingstone. Biard's effective
indictment of slavery was noted in
the *Athenaeum* in 1840. In 1847 a
critic in the *Art Union* went so far
as to assert that Biard 'made the
"slave trade", by a single picture,
more infamous than it had been
depicted by a score of advocates
eloquent for its suppression'.

but rational; if years of residence had not produced one reliable convert, why should flying visits suddenly lead to groups becoming Christians?

The idea of an eternal salvation that was individual, rather than collective, was not easy for tribal people to grasp since their day-by-day salvation was achieved by sharing their resources and pooling their labour. Livingstone understood, far better than his colleagues, why Africans considered Christianity antithetical to their customs. He began to think that if more traders were to arrive and if better communication could be established with the outside world, Africans might become more respectful towards the white man's religious ideas. But unless he could show them ships and machinery and other glories of civilisation, why should they want to change their society or their beliefs? 'As there is no pressing necessity apparent to those whose wants are few, they take the world easy,' he observed glumly.[28] In 1840, while studying in London, Livingstone had attended a meeting in Exeter Hall, sponsored by the Society for the Extinction of the Slave Trade and for the Civilisation of Africa. At that meeting Thomas Fowell Buxton, Wilberforce's successor, had expounded his dream of Africans abandoning their participation in the slave trade as a result of Christian traders seeking goods like wax, ivory and ostrich feathers in exchange for the guns and cloth the Africans coveted. Commerce and Christianity together could achieve this miracle, not Christianity alone, had been Buxton's over-optimistic theme on the eve of the ill-fated Niger expedition.

Between 1849 and 1851 Livingstone spent much less time with the Kwena, instead making three journeys of more than 300 miles to the north-west of Kolobeng. From June to October 1849 and April to August 1850 he travelled as far as Lake Ngami. On the third and crucial journey he reached the upper Zambezi in the area of the Barotse valley. On 4 August 1851 he stood on the banks of the upper Zambezi, close to tears. At the very heart of the African continent, in an unusually dry year, he had found an expanse of rapidly flowing water.

A few months before reaching the Zambezi, Livingstone had written enthusiastically about rivers 'opening the prospect of a highway capable of being quickly traversed by boats to a large section of well-peopled territory'.[29] Now, on the banks of the Zambezi, he imagined large steamers plying up this mighty river from the coast to the very point at which he was standing. Hitherto he had held very mixed views about whether traders benefited

Boat's compass used by Livingstone on his first journey down the Zambezi
Manufactured by Dubas, Nantes
24 cm (diameter)
ROYAL GEOGRAPHICAL SOCIETY
(cat. no. 2.56)

This boat's compass was used by Livingstone when navigating the Zambezi on the eastward leg of his coast-to-coast journey between November 1855 and May 1856.

27

28

AETAT 32.

Africans. 'If natives are not elevated by their contacts with Europeans,' he had warned, 'they are sure to be deteriorated . . . All the tribes I have seen lately [1847] are undergoing the latter process.'[30] It was illogical to expect traders to become philanthropic simply because he, David Livingstone, would be leading them into virgin territory, but his recent experience with Sechele had convinced him that unless the whole basis of African culture were undermined, there would be no large-scale conversions.

Livingstone's journeys between 1849 and 1851 were dependent on the generosity of William Cotton Oswell, a young man of independent means who had left the Indian Civil Service for a life of big-game hunting and travel. Oswell had accompanied Livingstone on the first and third trips, but on the second journey north from Kolobeng in 1850 Livingstone had decided, most unwisely, not to wait for Oswell and had instead travelled with his family to the River Zouga, a tributary of the Zambezi.

In the space of five years Mary had given birth to three children and she would shortly have a fourth, Livingstone dubbing her frequent pregnancies 'the great Irish manufactory'. Mary had been pregnant in 1850 when she accompanied Livingstone across the waterless Kalahari Desert. She lost her baby as a result and suffered partial paralysis for several months. 'The affliction', Livingstone confessed, 'causes considerable deformity, especially in smiling.'[31] What Mrs Livingstone could have had to smile about is hard to imagine since her surviving children (aged four, three and one) had come home too weak to stand and were still suffering from the after-effects of malaria. Livingstone had fortunately had the foresight to take quinine with him. Four decades before the role of the anopheles mosquito was understood, Livingstone wrote confidently, 'The source [of the illness] is no doubt marshy miasmata,' and added, 'I could not touch a square half-inch on the bodies of the children unbitten after a single night's exposure.'[32]

Astonishingly, in spite of anguished opposition from Mary's parents, Livingstone took his wife with him on his 1851 journey. Heavily pregnant once more, she suffered for a second time the stifling heat, the jolting waggon, the rationed water and the lack of vegetables. Her baby son survived, but Livingstone at last acknowledged that his family would have to be sent to Britain. In April 1852 they sailed from the Cape, entrusted to the care of the LMS although Livingstone was still ignorant of the funds the LMS intended to grant for their support. His family's departure, Livingstone wrote, was 'like tearing out my entrails'.[33] For his wife and children a succession of

29

Mzilikazi with Ndebele warriors
By William Cornwallis Harris
1836
Watercolour over pencil on paper
27.8 x 37.5 cm
QUENTIN KEYNES
(cat. no. 2.14)

This striking drawing by the traveller and big-game hunter Captain (later Sir) William Cornwallis Harris (1807–1848) shows the powerful Ndebele king, Mzilikazi, whom Harris met in October 1836. Harris had been directed to Mzilikazi by the missionary Robert Moffat, who had already visited the king on two occasions. One of the most interesting early encounters between missionaries and Africans, that between Moffat and Mzilikazi, was notable for its intimacy, the king insisting on riding in Moffat's wagon, sleeping near him and stroking his beard. Harris, too, found Mzilikazi friendly, handsome and dignified.

rooming houses and the erosive pains of poverty lay ahead.

With his family on the high seas, Livingstone set out on the journey that would rank him among the greatest explorers in history, although thoughts of future glory as an explorer were not uppermost in his mind at the outset. It distressed him that the directors of the LMS would probably think he was abandoning static mission work for exploration because he had failed to convert the Kwena. He denied this vehemently at the time but later admitted that, of all his reasons for leaving Bechuanaland, 'the principal one was [the Kwena's] determined hostility to the requirements of the gospel'.[34] Dislike of his fellow missionaries was another reason for his peripatetic future, as was the nature of missionary work itself, which was often dull, usually disappointing and never very successful. Opening up the continent and leading the way for others, be they missionaries, traders or even colonists, was a far more attractive role.

At the beginning of his great transcontinental journey Livingstone had two main aims: first, to find a malaria-free site on the upper Zambezi, which would serve as a trading centre and mission station; second, to open a viable route to the east or west coast of the continent along the Zambezi. Before undertaking this, Livingstone had to travel the 1,500 miles from the Cape to the area between the Zambezi and Chobe rivers. There, in 1851, he had encountered the Kololo tribe and their chief, Sebitwane, who, for thirty years, had been fighting a losing battle against the neighbouring Ndebele. Since Sebitwane had imagined that Livingstone's teaching was 'chiefly the art of shooting' he had been very friendly, more so on learning that Livingstone's wife was Robert Moffat's daughter. Moffat had visited Mzilikazi, the chief of the Ndebele, in 1829 and 1835, and the old autocrat had developed such an extraordinary affection for the founder of Kuruman that, years later, Sebitwane was in no doubt that if he could only persuade Livingstone and Moffat's daughter to live with him, the Ndebele would make peace with the Kololo rather than risk harming a member of the Moffat family.

When Livingstone returned to the Kololo in the spring of 1853 he found that Sebitwane had died, but that the new chief, nineteen-year-old Sekeletu, was just as eager for the Livingstones to settle in the Barotse valley. Travelling without European companions (with whom he might otherwise have had to share the credit for his journey) and accompanied by only three native drivers and a West Indian half-caste trader, Livingstone needed to obtain men

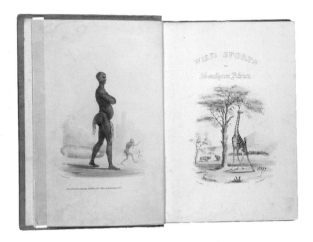

32

to act as porters on his expedition, and he needed to
obtain them cheaply. Not surprisingly he gave the young
chief the impression that he and his wife would indeed
come and live with the Kololo after he had achieved his
other objectives.[35] Livingstone also assured the chief that if
the Kololo could give him the free labour of a number of
men for two years, they would later reap the immense
benefits of a wonderful influx of trade.

At the end of June Livingstone, accompanied by Sekeletu
and 200 men, headed north from Linyanti (Sekeletu's
town) to the Zambezi. There they embarked in a fleet of
thirty-three canoes and headed north-west up river, bound
for the Barotse valley. Between June and September 1853
Livingstone travelled widely in Barotseland but failed to
find any place that was either free of malaria or immune
from the corrupting effects of the slave trade. 'The slave
trade seems pressed into the very centre of the continent
from both sides,' he lamented.[36] It tormented him that he
had led the directors of the LMS to expect that he would
find a healthy centre for trade and mission work within
this very area. To go on now and, at great risk to himself,
open a path from the coast regardless of whether anybody
(slave traders apart) would ever follow it to this malarial
region was not at all the outcome he had envisaged. 'I am
at a loss to know what to do,' he wrote unhappily.[37]

Because he believed that he was closer to the Atlantic
coast than to the Indian Ocean (he was in fact almost
exactly in the middle) and because he had recently
received advice from the Portuguese slave trader and
traveller, Silva Porto, Livingstone decided to travel west.
He had already suffered many bouts of fever and was
weak and thin, but he would not abandon his plan. The
early explorers Park, Lander and Clapperton had all died
in Africa, as had sixty per cent of the men on the four
expeditions sent from Britain between 1816 and 1841 to
explore the Congo, Niger and Zambezi. But Livingstone
seemed to find courage and determination in the severest
adversity. 'If God has accepted my service,' he wrote, 'my
life is charmed till my work is done.'[38]

On 11 November 1853 Livingstone left Linyanti with
twenty-seven men, several oxen and a canoe, all furnished
free by the chief. An inventory of Livingstone's possessions
included a rifle and a double-barrelled smooth-bore gun,
spare shirts and trousers, a nautical almanac, Thomson's
Logarithm Tables and a Bible. He had a tiny tent, a
sheepskin blanket and a rug but 'no nicknacks advertised
as indispensable for travellers'. Edible provisions were
carried separately, as were his most precious pieces of
equipment: a sextant made by Troughton & Sims of Fleet

Overleaf
**Manuscript map of
Livingstone's route from
Sesheke to Luanda** (detail)
By David Livingstone, 1854
Pencil and ink on paper laid on to
card and backed with linen
74.8 x 46 cm
ROYAL GEOGRAPHICAL SOCIETY
(cat. no. 2.18)

Livingstone's map shows the
westward leg of his epic coast-to-
coast journey. His route can be
traced from near its beginning at
Sesheke (lower right), reached on
19 November 1853, to Luanda on
the Angolan coast (upper left), where
he arrived on 31 May 1854. In all he
covered approximately 1,200 miles.

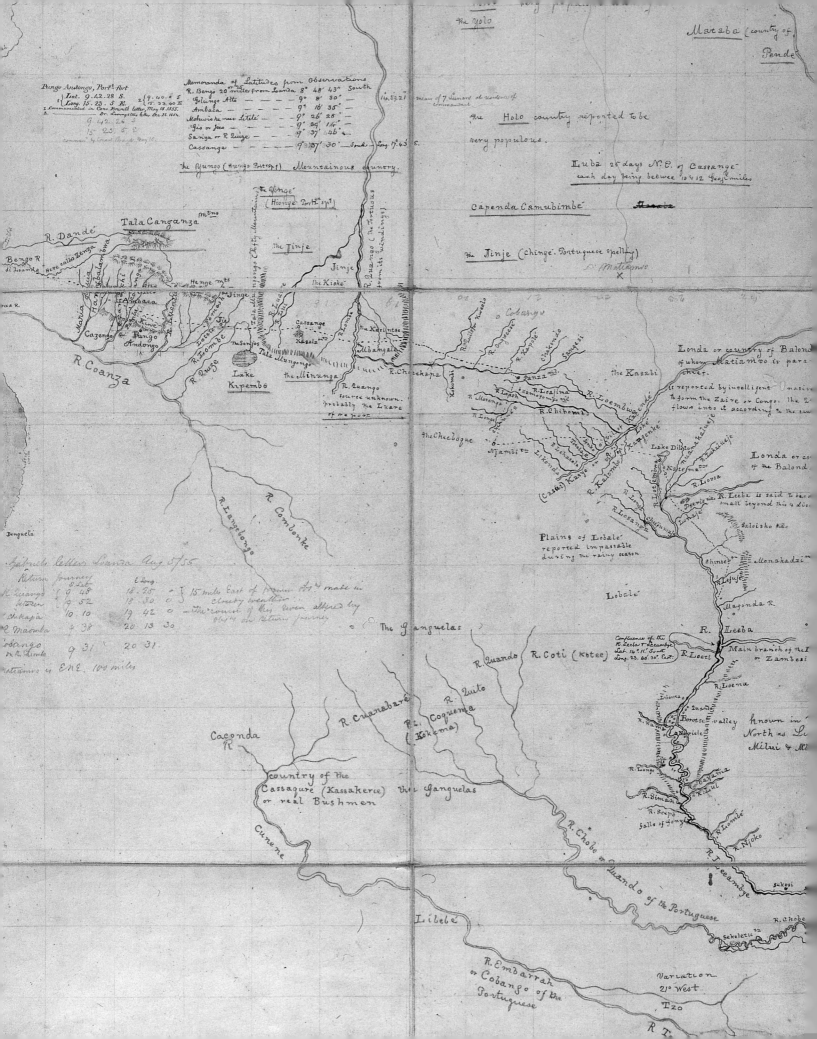

the Yolo

Mataba (country of
Pende

Pungo Andongo, Port.ᵉ fort
  Lat. 9.42.28 S.   2 {9.40.0 5
  Long. 15.23.5 E.   {15.33.40 E
1. Communicated in Cons Branch letter, May 18.1855.
2.   Dr. Livingstons letter Dec 21.1854.
           9.42.28 S
           15.23.5 E

Memoranda of Latitudes from Observations
R. Bengo 20 miles from Loanda 8° 48′ 43″ South
Golungo Alto ――― 9° 8′ 30″ ―――
Ambaca ――― 9° 16′ 35″ ―――
Motuvishe near Lilelé ――― 9° 26′ 28″ ―――
Gio or Jeca ――― 9° 39′ 14″ ―――
Sanza or R. Quize ――― 9° 37′ 46″·₄ ―――
Cassange ――― 9° 37′ 30″ South ― Long. 17.43 E.

14.57.21   mean of 7 Lunars at residence of commandant

The Holo country reported to be
very populous.

Iluba 25 days N.E. of Cassange
each day being between 10 & 12 Geog. miles

Capenda Camubimbé

The Ryungo (Huengo Port.ˢᵖ ?) Mountainous country.

The Jinje (Chinge Portuguese spelling)

Dr Matiamvo
X

Tala Canganza mtⁿˢ

R. Dande

Bengo R
di Loanda   Here calld Zenza

Henge mᵗˢ

The Jinje

Jinje

The Kioke

Londa or country of Balond
of whom Matiamvo is para-
chief.

is reported by intelligent natives
to form the Zaire or Congo. The 2
flows into it according to the same

The Cheeboque

Londa or co
of the Balond

R. Leeba is said to beco
small beyond this 4 Lie

Plains of Lobale
reported impassable
during the rainy season

Spabrielo letter Loanda Aug 5/55

Return Journey   S. Lat   E Long.
R. Quango   {9 48   18.25   • } 15 miles East of Bruun it.ᵈ made in
             {9 52   18.30   •} Cloudy weather
Chikapa   10.10   19 42   • The course of this River altered by
R. Maomba   9 38   20 13 30   this & on Return Journey
Cosango   9 31   20 31
or the Chombe
Matiamvo is E.N.E. 100 miles

Benguela

R. Combonke

R. Lungilongo

The Guanguelas

Lobale

Caconda
R.

country of the
Cassagure (Kassakerie)
or real Bushmen

the Guanguelas

R. Cuanabaré

R. Coti (Kotee)

R. Quando

R. Quito

R. Coquema
(Kokema)

Cunene

R. Chobe or Quando of the Portuguese

Libebé

R. Embarrah
or Cobango of the
Portuguese

Variation
21° West

Confluence of the
R. Leeba & Leeambye
Lat. 14° 11′ S. nth
Long. 23. 40. 30″ East.

R. Leeba

R. Loeri   Main branch of the L
              or Zambesi

R. Leena

Borotse valley known in
               North as L
               Milui & M

R. Chobe

R. Njoko

R. Leeambye

Sekeletu

R. Chobe

R. T.

Street, a chronometer watch with a stop hand made by Dent's of the Strand, an artificial horizon and a pair of compasses. From the start of this journey, and during all his subsequent ones, Livingstone would fill his journals and diaries with longitudes and latitudes, altitudes, maps and figures for rainfall. No creature, insect or plant was too small to escape his attention and he would write numerous natural descriptions every day.

During his 1,200 mile journey to Luanda Livingstone encountered the problems of African travel that he would experience time and again in the future: the heat, rains and mud; the Africans' demands for *hongo* (payment in cloth or beads for the right to pass through a particular chief's territory); the substantial payments needed for food (however inadequate); delays caused by hospitable chiefs who wished to detain him and delays caused by hostile tribesmen who wished to rob or kill him. Livingstone and his men were often in mortal danger. In such circumstances Livingstone drew strength from the Bible, making comparisons with Christ's hardships that many of his former missionary colleagues would have thought blasphemous: 'See, O Lord, how the heathen rise up against me as they did to Thy Son . . . Should such a man as I flee? Nay verily.'[39] Then there was the constant possibility that his own men might desert or mutiny, or that he would finally succumb to repeated attacks of malaria. Struggling across rivers and through tropical forests when suffering from a racing heart, agonising headaches, dizziness, shivering, vomiting and diarrhoea was not a routine for any but the exceptionally resilient. Indeed, the hardships that Livingstone endured during his years of exploration would kill many of his companions.

Even Livingstone's resilience had its limits however. When he finally arrived at Luanda on the Atlantic seaboard he was close to death. Fortunately, a British ship's surgeon, with years of experience in treating tropical diseases, was in Luanda and able to save him. Nevertheless, from 24 April to 14 June 1854 Livingstone was too weak to lift his pen and could not write a letter unaided until early August. He could have sailed back to Britain in one of the three British warships in harbour at Luanda and would undoubtedly have been welcomed as a hero if he had done so. He was made aware of his fame while still in Angola when he read an article in *The Times* in which Lord Clarendon, the Foreign Secretary, described his journey as 'one of the greatest geographical explorations of the age'.[40] Livingstone transcribed this into his diary without comment, perhaps reflecting that Silva Porto and Caetano Ferra, another Portuguese trader, had made the identical journey before him without arousing any interest in England.

It has been suggested that Livingstone decided to go ahead with his original plan of crossing the continent from coast to coast because returning to Britain would have meant abandoning his Kololo porters. As he would later leave them at Tete for four years, this argument is unconvincing. His real reason for pressing on lay in his determination to save his expedition from what he considered to be failure. Livingstone vigorously denied being an explorer pure and simple. Instead he claimed to have abandoned static missionary work solely in order to open the continent to commerce and Christianity. Since traders and missionaries would hardly rush to follow a route that had all but killed the resourceful Dr Livingstone, he knew he had failed in his most important objective. Even if his route had been safe and viable he had not located a malaria-free region within reach of the Zambezi. He had no choice but to return to Linyanti and from there to pioneer a feasible route to the east coast.

Livingstone left Luanda in September 1854 and reached Linyanti after many delays a year later. Although he brought Sekeletu less cloth and fewer guns than requested, a Portuguese colonel's uniform delighted the young chief, and when Livingstone promised to return again, bringing him in exchange for his continuing support an iron rocking-chair, spectacles containing green glass, bullets and numerous other items, the chief decided to loan Livingstone 114 men.

During the three years of his travels Livingstone had suffered twenty-seven attacks of fever, and yet at Linyanti he wrote an astonishing letter, later despatched to the LMS directors, in which he stated: 'I apprehend no great mortality [in South Central Africa] among missionaries, men of education and prudence who can, if they will, adopt proper hygienic precautions.'[41] Such disastrous false optimism would lead to tragedy.

On 3 November Livingstone left Linyanti intending to carry out his plan of following the Zambezi to its mouth at Quelimane on the Indian Ocean. He had first heard about Mosioatunya or 'the smoke that thunders' five years earlier, but so obsessed was he by now with the navigability of the river east of the falls and with finding a healthy area for settlement that he underestimated by half both the width and the height of this wonder of nature, which he would shortly name the Victoria Falls. Only when writing his book, *Missionary Travels and Researches in South Africa*, over a year later, did he honour the Falls with

**The Royal Geographical
Society Gold Medal**
Awarded to Livingstone in 1855
and presented to him
on 15 December 1856
By William Wyon, 1856
5.4 cm (diameter)
THE DAVID LIVINGSTONE CENTRE
(cat. no. 3.28)

The Royal Geographical Society's
highest honour, the gold medal,
was awarded to Livingstone in
May 1855 (while he was still
travelling in Africa) in response to
his despatches sent to the Society.
The medal itself, which bears
Queen Victoria's profile on the
obverse and Britannia on the
reverse, was presented to
Livingstone at a special meeting of
the Society held on 15 December
1856, a few days after his return
to Britain.

famous phrases such as 'scenes so lovely must have been
gazed upon by angels in their flight.'

East of the falls he soon came upon hilly country, which
instantly excited him. The Batoka Plateau was higher
and therefore cooler than the adjacent river valley; it was
fertile and well-watered but not swampy. One drawback
was the proximity of the Ndebele just to the south
('savage, cruel . . . and devoid of all moral courage')[42]
but Livingstone was still convinced that the Batoka Plateau
was exactly what he had been seeking: a healthy centre
from which commerce and Christianity could send out
cleansing waves in wider and wider circles until the slave
trade and internecine strife in south-central Africa had
been washed away. Now it only remained for him to prove
that traders could enter the mouth of the Zambezi and
sail up river for a thousand miles.

In order to investigate the Batoka Plateau Livingstone
had left the river, making a loop to the north of almost
250 miles. He consequently missed seeing the Cabora
Bassa rapids, which were impassable. He might have
discovered their existence had he taken boiling-point
measurements for height above sea level when he left the
Zambezi, just east of the Falls, at the start of his detour
and when he returned to the river, west of Zumbo, at the
end of it. But by an astonishing oversight he failed to do
so on both occasions, and so did not realise that the river
fell by 600 feet in the section that he had missed. The fall
in height that he did note as occurring between Linyanti
(3,702 feet) and Zumbo in Mozambique (1,537 feet) ought
to have been a warning, but Livingstone's determination
to prove the river navigable must have inclined him to
ignore it. If he had faced up to the truth of this journey
he would have spared himself far worse disappointment
three years later.

Livingstone arrived at Quelimane on 25 May 1856,
almost four years after leaving Cape Town bound for the
Zambezi. His 5,000 mile journey had included the first
authenticated crossing of sub-Saharan Africa by a
European and remains one of the two or three greatest
feats of land exploration in history. He embarked for
England in HMS *Frolic*, a warship that had been paying
regular calls at Quelimane for several months in the
expectation of his arrival – the British Government having
been informed of his plans by Mr Edmund Gabriel, the
consular official with whom he had stayed in Luanda.

Dr Livingstone returned to Britain in December 1856 and
received a hero's welcome. He was given medals and

prizes, including the Royal Geographical Society's gold medal; he received the freedoms of half a dozen cities; he became an honorary DCL of Oxford University; he had an interview with the Prince Consort and a private audience with the Queen. Two thousand guineas were raised for him by public subscription and he dined out 'in the best society' almost every evening, drinking champagne in spite of his teetotal principles.[43] Livingstone enjoyed being lionised and his claim to have hated publicity comes strangely from a man who insisted on wearing his distinctive peaked cap everywhere he went.

During the first eight months of 1857 Livingstone wrote his first book, *Missionary Travels and Researches in South Africa*, the title being intended to underline his contention that his travels had served an evangelical purpose. In this literary *tour de force* he exhibited impressive gifts as a descriptive writer, a sharp sense of humour and an instinctive feeling for what people who knew nothing of Africa would find interesting. The book was written under pressure and, at times, gives the impression of being a collection of scenes rather than an integrated whole, but the public was not disappointed. Thanks to John Murray's generous royalty arrangements Livingstone made a fortune from the 70,000 copies sold – in excess of £12,000 (£5,100 of which he promptly settled on his family).

Public ignorance of Portuguese discoveries made Livingstone's achievement seem all the more remarkable. In Britain few people realised that Rodrigues Graca had reached south-western Katanga from Angola in 1846. Nor was it known that while Silva Porto had failed to cross the continent in 1853, two of his African attendants had marched on and had succeeded in reaching the east coast at Kilwa. In 1856 the commonly held British view of south-central Africa, outside geographical circles, was of a dry and infertile area like the Sahara. Livingstone's descriptions of mighty forests, magnificent waterfalls and wide grasslands naturally caused amazement.

As well as praising Livingstone as an explorer, the expanding penny press conveyed to the public the unexamined assumption that he was a great missionary. As missionary societies rarely dwelled upon the obstacles to success, the public imagined Africans converting in groups after a single sermon. Neither Livingstone himself, nor the directors of the LMS, who were nursing a £13,000 overdraft, felt inclined to breathe a word about the solitary convert who had lapsed.

Much of Livingstone's initial publicity came through the efforts of Sir Roderick Murchison, President of the Royal Geographical Society (RGS). Founded in 1830 – with the

37

T. Picken, lith.   Published by John Murray, Albemarle St. May 1857.   Day & Son, Lith.rs to the Queen.

THE VICTORIA FALLS, OF THE LEEAMBYE OR ZAMBESI RIVER CALLED BY THE NATIVES MOSIOATUNYA. (SMOKE SOUNDING)

MISSIONARY TRAVELS

AND

RESEARCHES IN SOUTH AFRICA;

INCLUDING A SKETCH OF

SIXTEEN YEARS' RESIDENCE IN THE INTERIOR OF AFRICA,

AND A JOURNEY FROM THE CAPE OF GOOD HOPE TO LOANDA ON THE WEST
COAST; THENCE ACROSS THE CONTINENT, DOWN THE RIVER
ZAMBESI, TO THE EASTERN OCEAN.

BY DAVID LIVINGSTONE, LL.D., D.C.L.,

FELLOW OF THE FACULTY OF PHYSICIANS AND SURGEONS, GLASGOW; CORRESPONDING MEMBER OF THE
GEOGRAPHICAL AND STATISTICAL SOCIETY OF NEW YORK; GOLD MEDALLIST AND CORRESPONDING
MEMBER OF THE ROYAL GEOGRAPHICAL SOCIETIES OF LONDON AND PARIS,
F.S.A., ETC. ETC.

*Tsetse Fly.—Magnified.—*See p. 571.

WITH PORTRAIT; MAPS BY ARROWSMITH; AND NUMEROUS ILLUSTRATIONS.

LONDON:
JOHN MURRAY, ALBEMARLE STREET.
1857.

momentous coast-to-coast crossing of the continent, was one of the non-fiction bestsellers of the Victorian period. This fine copy of the first edition, with its coloured frontispiece of the Victoria Falls, was presented to John Arrowsmith, map maker for this and Livingstone's later books, by Livingstone and his publisher John Murray.

aim of promoting geographical exploration and publishing accounts of new discoveries for those interested – this society had been incompetently run by naval officers for many years, and was only now starting to fulfil its founders' purposes. The RGS had awarded Livingstone a cash prize for reaching Lake Ngami from Kolobeng and with this money he had bought much of his scientific equipment for his transcontinental journey. Murchison's high opinion of the explorer's achievements made him eager to help Livingstone in future, simultaneously (he hoped) boosting the RGS's membership by the association. The thought that Livingstone might return to missionary work and be lost to exploration was not an agreeable one to Murchison.

At Quelimane Livingstone had found letters awaiting him from both Murchison and Arthur Tidman, Foreign Secretary of the LMS, which confirmed for him what he had already suspected: namely that he would soon be leaving the LMS for an exploring role as yet to be defined. Murchison wrote a letter of ecstatic praise in which he made it plain that he wanted to help Livingstone to further any geographical plans he might have. Arthur Tidman also praised Livingstone, but, since he dreaded being put under public pressure to send missionaries to dangerous and inaccessible places, he warned him that the directors were 'restricted in their power of aiding plans connected only remotely with the spread of the Gospel', and would not 'be in a position, within any definite period, to venture upon untried, remote, and difficult fields of labour'.[44] Angered by this letter, Livingstone wrote to Murchison confiding that if the LMS wanted him to settle at a mission station he would 'prefer dissolving my connection with the Society and following out my plans as a private Christian', yet ending by making it clear that his poverty would make this course very hard for him.[45] This was an open invitation for Murchison to seek alternative employment for him, and Murchison recognised it as such.

Arthur Tidman probably realised that Livingstone would never again accept a post as a settled missionary, but given the LMS's financial problems Tidman needed to hang on to Livingstone until his name had attracted sufficient funds to clear the Society's overdraft. He therefore had no desire to press Livingstone to make rapid decisions about his future. This also suited Livingstone, who wanted to avoid being criticised for leaving the LMS for better pay. (As a British consul his pay would be five times higher than the £100 per annum he had received as a missionary but would be very little in comparison with his book earnings.) Meanwhile Murchison had made the initial approach to

Lord Clarendon, the Foreign Secretary, that would eventually lead to Livingstone's appointment as leader of a government-sponsored expedition to the Zambezi.

It is beyond the scope of a brief biographical study to follow the intricacies of Livingstone's negotiations with the Foreign Office and his tangled dealings with Arthur Tidman. Suffice it to say that it was irresponsible of Livingstone to embarrass the directors of the LMS into making a public appeal for funds to be used specifically for sending missionaries to the Kololo and the Ndebele tribes, without first having been certain that he and his wife would be able to reside with them (which had never been likely).

The missionaries, Helmore and Price, and their wives and children joined the Kololo in February, a month notorious for fever. They found a bitter Sekeletu; Livingstone never arrived to smooth their way; and by Christmas Price and two of Helmore's children were the sole survivors. While responsibility for the deaths of six out of the nine who went to the Barotse valley cannot be laid entirely at Livingstone's door, his failure to show regret afterwards, and his inclination to blame the missionaries themselves for the disaster, underline a fundamental weakness in his character.

On 4 December 1857 Livingstone gave a lecture in the Senate House at Cambridge that would have far-reaching consequences. Again, as in *Missionary Travels*, Livingstone minimised the harsh conditions he had faced and poured scorn on the idea that working in Central Africa involved 'sacrifice'. 'I never made a sacrifice,' he insisted before making an impassioned plea. 'I beg to direct your attention to Africa: I know that in a few years I shall be cut off in that country, which is now open; do not let it be shut again! I go back to Africa to try to make an open path for commerce and Christianity; do you carry out the work which I have begun. I leave it with you!'[46] With his sunburnt face and strangely foreign-sounding voice, Livingstone had a profound effect upon his learned audience, some members of which would, in due course, found the Universities' Mission to Central Africa.

In December 1858, some months after Lord Clarendon had offered, and Livingstone had accepted, employment as a British consul with a roving commission extending through Mozambique to the regions west of it, the House of Commons voted £5,000 to pay for 'Dr Livingstone to embark on a voyage of discovery upon the Zambezi'. Livingstone had earlier turned down the leadership of a larger expedition, preferring to return to Africa more modestly with six Europeans and a paddle-steamer

John Murray (1808–1892)
By David Octavius Hill and
Robert Adamson, 1840s
Calotype print, 20.5 x 15.2 cm
NATIONAL PORTRAIT GALLERY
LONDON
(cat. no. 2.31)

The son of the founder of the publishers John Murray, Murray published Livingstone's *Missionary Travels and Researches in South Africa* in 1857 and subsequently his *Narrative of an Expedition to the Zambesi* (1865), co-written with Charles Livingstone. In 1874 he published Livingstone's posthumous *Last Journals*. Seen here in an important early photograph by Hill and Adamson, Murray had taken charge of the family firm in 1843 and was to become one of the great publishers of the Victorian period. Murray followed the success of Livingstone's *Missionary Travels* with Smiles' bestseller, *Self-Help*, and Darwin's *Origin of Species*, both published in 1859.

Overleaf

'Elephant in the Shallows of the Shire River, the steam launch firing'
By Thomas Baines, 1859
Oil on canvas, 46 x 65.7 cm
ROYAL GEOGRAPHICAL SOCIETY
(cat. no. 4.5)

This painting by Thomas Baines, artist-storekeeper to the Zambezi expedition, shows an incident from early January 1859 when Livingstone took the steam launch, the *Ma Robert*, up the River Shire, a tributary of the Zambezi. Here he encountered and hunted large herds of elephants. It most closely relates to John Kirk's account, dated 5 January, when an elephant shot by the party 'instantly turned to us, spread out its enormous ears, curled its proboscis up like a butterfly and raised its tail in the air like a bull.' Baines had not joined the party but, according to his inscription on the back of the picture, painted it from a description given to him by George Rae, engineer on the expedition.

**Hoisting the foremost
section of the steam launch,
the _Ma Robert_**
By Thomas Baines, 16 May 1858
Pencil on paper, 19.3 x 27.4 cm
ROYAL GEOGRAPHICAL SOCIETY
(cat. no. 4.9)

This is one of a group of drawings
by Thomas Baines, which provide
a vivid record of the Zambezi
expedition's early days. This
drawing dates from two days after
the expedition ship, the _Pearl_,
arrived at the mouth of the
Zambezi. Baines shows the crew
assembling the steam launch, the
Ma Robert, on board the _Pearl_.
Named after the Kololo name for
Mary Livingstone, 'the mother of
Robert' (Livingstone's eldest son),
the vessel proved easy to assemble
but otherwise a disaster. It was
flimsily constructed and impossible
to fuel.

**Hoisting the central section
of the _Ma Robert_**
By Thomas Baines, 16 May 1858
Pencil on paper, 19.1 x 27.5 cm
ROYAL GEOGRAPHICAL SOCIETY
(cat. no. 4.10)

In a companion drawing to
cat. no. 4.9, Baines shows the
central section of the steam launch,
the _Ma Robert_, being hoisted from
the deck of the Zambezi
expedition ship, the _Pearl_.

carrying a smaller steamer and an iron house in sections.

Although Livingstone admitted in a private letter to the
Duke of Argyll that his ultimate objective was the creation
of 'an English colony in the healthy highlands of Central
Africa', he did not mention this to Lord Palmerston, the
Prime Minister, nor to his Foreign Secretary, neither of
whom wanted to cause offence to their oldest ally Portugal,
whose colony, Mozambique, extended almost to the
Batoka Plateau.[47]

The agreed aims of the expedition were to chart the
Zambezi and to find out as much as possible about the
agricultural potential and mineral wealth of the whole
region. Presuming that any rapids in the river would not
present an obstacle to reaching the Victoria Falls when the
river was high, Livingstone decreed that the expedition
should proceed to the Batoka Plateau along the river, erect
the iron house and begin agricultural experiments to
establish that enough sugar and cotton could be grown
to start a viable trade in both.

The members of the Zambezi expedition set sail in March
1858 on board _Pearl_, the Colonial Office steamship, and
almost at once Livingstone suffered a disappointment.
When everyone else had recovered from seasickness, Mary
Livingstone continued to vomit. She was pregnant again.
Her husband had intended to take her and their youngest
son, the six-year-old William, to the Zambezi, while the
older children remained with their grandparents in
Scotland. But now Mary would have to be left behind at
the Cape to spend time with her parents at Kuruman and
then return to Scotland. Livingstone had been so busy in
Britain that his wife and family had seen very little of him;
this pregnancy was a savage blow to Mary as well.

The expedition reached the mouth of the Zambezi on
14 May and almost immediately the members began to
fall out with one another. While in Luanda Livingstone
had become friendly with Commander Norman
Bedingfeld RN and had chosen him to be commander of
the paddle-steamer and chief of navigation, but a series of
misunderstandings quickly brought threats of resignation
from the naval officer. Instead of exercising diplomatic
skills, Livingstone treated Bedingfeld to his most
withering sarcasm:

> A pretty extensive acquaintance with African
> Expeditions enables me to offer a hint which, if you
> take it in the same frank and friendly spirit in which it
> is offered, you will on some future day thank me and
> smile at the puerilities which now afflict you. With the

Hoisting the foremost section of the Steam Launch Ma Robert from on board the Pearl. West Luabo River. AM 16 May 1858
T Baines

Hoisting the Central Section of the Steam Launch Ma Robert from on board the Pearl. West Luabo River. PM 16 May 1858
T Baines

change of climate there is often a peculiar condition of the bowels which makes the individual imagine all manner of things in others. Now I earnestly and most respectfully recommend you try a little aperient medicine occasionally and you will find it much more soothing than writing official letters. [48]

It is hardly surprising that Bedingfeld was soon on his way back to England. A leader needs to be able to identify with those under him and to share their experience, but from the time of his problems with his fellow missionaries Livingstone had shown that he had no understanding of others. His years alone had made him self-sufficient and disinclined to talk unless he had something to say. Only his fellow Scot, Dr John Kirk, who had been a doctor in the Crimea and was an experienced botanist, managed to get on with Livingstone.

Livingstone's younger brother Charles, a Nonconformist minister whom he had engaged as his personal assistant and photographer, would harbour grudges over trivial incidents and then influence his brother to reprove men such as the expedition's young geologist, Richard Thornton, and the gifted official artist, Thomas Baines. While both the Livingstones detested the Portuguese, Baines and Thornton enjoyed the company of the residents of the trading settlement at Tete and entertained them in response to the hospitality they had themselves received. This led Charles to accuse Baines of stealing sugar and other stores. The final consequence of Charles's interventions would be the dismissal of both the hard-working artist and the 21-year-old geologist, who had never been properly supervised or instructed by Livingstone. Eventually the two brothers would themselves argue and even come to physical blows with one another, Charles screaming at David that he was 'serving the devil' and should be called 'the cursing consul of Quillimane [sic]'. [49]

The expedition's steamer, the *Ma Robert*, also created difficulties, since it consumed too much fuel and, after frequent groundings on sandbanks, leaked like a colander. A few miles west of Tete she was holed above the waterline and Livingstone and other expedition members were forced to continue on foot, clambering over gigantic rocks for four days. The weather was hot and the going was so rough that only John Kirk went on with Livingstone for a further two days. On 2 December the two men were horrified to see the start of the Cabora Bassa rapids – the first rapid being thirty feet high. This was what Livingstone had so narrowly missed seeing in 1856. His entire plan for the Zambezi expedition had depended upon being able to reach the Batoka Plateau by river, and it now appeared

Charles Livingstone
(1821–1873)
By an unknown photographer
1860s
Albumen carte-de-visite
8.5 x 4.8 cm
THE DAVID LIVINGSTONE CENTRE
(cat. no. 4.50)

Livingstone appointed his younger brother, Charles, as his personal assistant and photographer on the Zambezi expedition. The appointment was a disaster. He had no photographic expertise and, far worse, he proved a divisive influence, turning Livingstone against other members of the party and effectively causing the dismissal of artist-storekeeper Thomas Baines and the young geologist Richard Thornton.

47

Tom Jumbo, the head Krooman of the Ma'Robert
inviting natives to come on board.
noon May 25 1858 — West Luabo River
West branch
T Baines

48

The Ma Robert aground at the head of the
Eastern branch of the West Luabo River
Monday May 24 1858. T Baines —

that 'God's highway' was as navigable as a flight of steps.

Cut off from the whole area that he had hoped to open up for traders, Livingstone made an astonishing volte-face. God's masterplan for Africa, he decided, had evidently never included the Kololo, the Batoka Plateau and the upper Zambezi. With a single-mindedness at which his companions could only marvel, Livingstone transferred his entire attention to the River Shire, which flowed into the Zambezi a hundred miles from the coast.

In 1856, at Tete, Livingstone had met another Portuguese trader, Candido José da Costa Cardosa, who had told him that the River Shire was fed by a vast lake, forty-five days' march from Tete. It occurred to Livingstone that if the lake could be claimed by the expedition as a discovery, the disaster of Cabora Bassa might yet be mitigated. And if the Shire was bordered by healthy highlands, these uplands might be an acceptable substitute for the Batoka Plateau as an area for the settlement of missionaries and traders. In due course Livingstone reached Cardosa's lake (Lake Nyasa, now Lake Malawi, the second largest lake in Africa) and claimed it as his. But Livingstone soon made a less pleasing discovery: namely that the Arab Swahili slave trade had reached the upper Shire, which, it appeared, lay directly on the slave route from Katanga to the coastal town of Kilwa. This meant that the only possible highland area suitable for European settlement and accessible from the Shire was being plundered for slaves by Arabs from Zanzibar and Kilwa. Meanwhile, the local tribes were fighting one another in their efforts either to co-operate with the Arab slavers for gain (in the case of the warlike Ajawa tribe), or to impede the Arabs (in the case of the more conciliatory Mang'anja tribe). Further south the Portuguese were also taking slaves.

The Shire Highlands were fertile, well-watered and only 200 miles inland, but while Livingstone prayed that this area would become a European trading and missionary centre, he realised that unless the slave raids could be stopped no traders would come – which, in turn would rule out future conversions. The solution, he wrote to tell the Foreign Secretary, would be the establishment of a new British colony, since colonists alone would have the resources (and firepower) to end the lawlessness. At this date, however, the British government had no interest in carving out African colonies, as Livingstone discovered when he received from the new Foreign Secretary, Lord John Russell, a very firm refusal to become involved. Earlier Lord Palmerston had returned Livingstone's proposals with a note: 'I am very unwilling to embark on new schemes of British possessions. Dr L . . . must not be

'Tom Jumbo, the head Krooman of the *Ma Robert* inviting natives to come on board'
By Thomas Baines, 25 May 1858
Watercolour over pencil on paper
19.8 x 28 cm
ROYAL GEOGRAPHICAL SOCIETY
(cat. no. 4.12)

Baines' drawing records an early encounter with local inhabitants when the Zambezi party was exploring the river's delta. John Kirk described this meeting in his journal entry for 25 May 1858, explaining how Tom Jumbo, head of the expedition's African crew, was sent out to make contact. 'He at last persuaded them to remain by shewing that his colour was the same as theirs', Kirk writes, '. . . after some palaver, neither side understanding one word of the other, they were induced to come along-side. We went on and for some time the canoe kept ahead, showing us the way'.

49

The *Ma Robert* aground
By Thomas Baines, 24 May 1858
Watercolour over pencil on paper
19.2 x 27.7 cm
ROYAL GEOGRAPHICAL SOCIETY
(cat. no. 4.11)

Baines' drawing shows an incident that took place within the first two weeks of the Zambezi expedition's arrival off the coast of the river. On a foray along one of the minor branches of the Zambezi Delta – no more than a 'ditch' according to John Kirk – the ill-fated launch ran aground.

In this moving letter to his mother, Livingstone reports the death of his wife Mary. 'Everything else that happened in my career', he writes, 'only made the mind rise to overcome it, but this takes away all my strength . . . There are regrets which will follow me to my dying day.'

allowed to tempt us to form colonies only to be reached by forcing steamers up cataracts.'[50] Unfortunately, by that time Livingstone had invited the recently formed Universities' Mission to make the Shire Highlands the base for its first mission station in Africa.

As Livingstone should have foreseen, within weeks the missionaries had become embroiled in a tribal war; for the first time in his life Livingstone was forced to fire on Africans. They were Ajawa slave traders, but it nevertheless appalled him to have become personally involved in a skirmish that ended with six 'enemy' deaths. Livingstone had not warned the missionaries about the lawlessness of the area nor about its total dependence on the expedition's steamer for supplies. When the public learnt about the dangers to which the missionaries had been exposed Livingstone was blamed for deceiving them. Criticism of Livingstone mounted when the leader of the mission, Bishop Mackenzie – the first Anglican bishop to reside in Central Africa – died of fever, as did three more of his party of seven.

At this inauspicious moment Mary Livingstone joined her husband on the Zambezi after leaving her new baby in Scotland. Having spent little time with her in London, Livingstone was horrified to discover, now that he was closeted with her in the steamer, that during their long separation she had lost her faith and become an alcoholic. She reproached him bitterly for having left their children's upbringing to her alone without providing adequate funds. Robert, their eldest son, had run away from a succession of boarding schools in England and Scotland, and in 1863 had sailed for America and enlisted in the Northern forces under a false name. He wrote his father a moving letter shortly before he died. 'I have changed my name for I am convinced that to bear your name here would lead to further dishonours to it.'[51] Livingstone had written harshly about his son's 'vagabond ways' but Robert emerges from his final letter as gentle, honourable and brave. He was wounded in a battle at Laurel Hill, Virginia, and died, aged eighteen, in a Confederate prison camp in North Carolina.

Mary Livingstone contracted malaria and died at Shupanga on the banks of the Zambezi on 27 April 1862. In spite of her drinking and her hard words, Livingstone was heartbroken. 'There are regrets which will follow me till my dying day,' he admitted.[52] One of his colleagues noticed that 'his recent loss seems to have had some effect of a softening kind on him.'[53]

The final phase of the Zambezi expedition was dominated

by Livingstone's herculean struggle to assemble and launch on Lake Nyasa an armed steamer (costing £6,000 and paid for out of his own pocket) in a hopeless last-ditch attempt to prevent slave traders gaining access to the Shire Highlands by crossing the lake or the River Shire. After a prolonged drought the River Shire was lower than it had been for many years, but this did not deter Livingstone. He decided to drag the steamer over many miles of sandbanks, bringing his men to the verge of mutiny.

A civil war was raging in the Shire Highlands and the country was gripped by famine. Corpses were thrown into the river and Livingstone often saw crocodiles tearing at bloated limbs. His ideal location for a British colony had become in his own words 'a desert strewed with human bones'.[54] On 2 July 1863 he received the Foreign Secretary's inevitable order of recall. It was not delivered in the dignified fashion he might have desired. 'Hallo you . . . chaps. No more pay for you after December,' shouted the cockney labourer from the Universities' Mission. 'I brings the letter as says it.'[55]

The surviving members of the Zambezi expedition returned to Britain in the summer of 1864. They brought back copious new information about the Zambezi, the Shire, the Ruo, the Rovuma and Lake Nyasa, and although many field notes were never written up as reports the expedition's maps and observations made a significant contribution to knowledge of south-central and south-east Africa, and exposed a new arm of the slave trade. But because Livingstone had always claimed that his purposes were practical – the establishment of trade and missions, the creation of a colony – there was a great sense of anticlimax. The editor of *The Times* listed the failures:

> We were promised cotton, sugar and indigo . . . and of course we got none. We were promised converts and not one has been made. In a word, the thousands subscribed . . . have been productive only of the most fatal results.[56]

There were no banquets, no official receptions, but Livingstone dined with Lord Palmerston, took tea with Mr Gladstone and was received by the Foreign Secretary. While still in Africa he had tried to place the blame for the anarchic conditions in the Shire Highlands on the Portuguese and had made public statements about the participation of Portuguese subjects in the slave trade. He had therefore made it most unlikely that he would ever again be permitted to enter Mozambique. This would cut him off from all the areas he had previously explored.

Livingstone's wife Mary joined the Zambezi expedition on 31 January 1862. Within three months, on 27 April 1862, she had died from fever. She was buried at Shupanga the following day under a giant baobab tree. In spite of years of being apart Livingstone was shattered by her death. Nonetheless, his pencil comments on this sketch of her grave, made in preparation for an illustration to his *Narrative of an Expedition to the Zambesi*, are disquietingly cool and matter-of-fact. His suggested adjustments, written along the top, concern the size of the baobab and the formation of the tree in the centre of the drawing.

**Anna Mary Livingstone
(1858–1939)**
By an unknown photographer
1860s
Albumen carte-de-visite
8.8 x 5.7 cm
THE DAVID LIVINGSTONE CENTRE
(cat. no. 5.29)

Born at Kuruman in November 1858, while her father was on the Zambezi expedition, Anna Mary was Livingstone's youngest child. Father and daughter did not meet until his return to Britain in the summer of 1864.

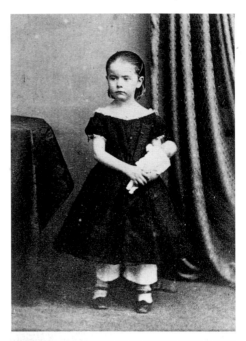

**Agnes Livingstone,
Livingstone's sister
(1823–1895), and Anna Mary,
his daughter (1858–1939)**
By an unknown photographer
c. 1870
Albumen carte-de-visite
8.8 x 5.7 cm
THE DAVID LIVINGSTONE CENTRE
(cat. no. 5.28)

Charles Livingstone advised his brother to find a rich widow and settle for a life of prosperous retirement, but at fifty-one Livingstone was not ready for that. On his way home he had written, 'I don't know whether I am to go on the shelf or not. If I do, I make Africa the shelf.'[57] But where in Africa he should go, he could not yet determine, except that it would have to be north of the Portuguese possessions.

As on his previous visit home, Livingsone was kept busy for many months writing a book, this time the cumbersomely titled *Narrative of an Expedition to the Zambesi and its Tributaries*. He admitted to friends during what would be his last visit home that he regretted having seen so little of his children over the years. 'Oh why did I not play more with my children in the Kolobeng days? Why was I so busy that I had so little time for my bairns?' He tried to get to know his youngest daugher, Anna Mary, but she disliked being kissed by this strange man with a moustache who never stopped writing. Livingstone gave her a black doll, though she would have preferred a white one.[58]

In September 1864 Livingstone broke off his writing to go to Bath for the annual meeting of the British Association, at which he had been invited to lecture on the Portuguese slave trade. The main attraction at Bath was expected to be a fierce debate between Richard Burton and John Speke on the probable location of the source of the Nile. Although Livingstone did not acknowledge it at the time, or afterwards, the Speke-versus-Burton Nile controversy marked the beginning of his own passionate interest in the source of that river.

In 1858, after travelling into the interior from Zanzibar, John Hanning Speke and Richard Burton had become the first Europeans to stand on the banks of Lake Tanganyika. On their return journey Speke had made a detour to the north on his own and had arrived at the southern shore of a vast lake, which he had named Victoria Nyanza and had declared to be the source of the Nile. Irritated beyond measure not to have gone with Speke, Burton contemptuously dismissed his companion's claim to have solved the world's greatest geographical mystery.

Travelling with James Augustus Grant in 1862, Speke had returned to his lake, though this time to its northern side, and had found an outlet, which he called the Ripon Falls and claimed was the Nile itself. In 1864 Samuel White Baker discovered an alternative source. Lake Albert, as he named it, was a large lake 150 miles north-west of Speke's, and had a river flowing out at its northern end. Nobody would know which lake was the true source until a direct connection had been established with the lower Nile. It would not be known for another thirteen years that Victoria Nyanza *was* the primary source.

The ticket-holders at Bath never heard the keenly awaited debate between Burton and Speke: Speke had died in a shooting incident the day before – whether it was suicide or an accident is still debated.

It is more than likely that Sir Roderick Murchison asked Livingstone while he was in Bath whether he would like to be sponsored by the RGS to solve the riddle of the Central African watershed once and for all, but in September 1864 Livingstone was not ready to commit himself to a purely geographical aim. Nevertheless, his desire to work beyond other men's lines must have made the prospect of outsmarting rival explorers an attractive one. He derided Speke as 'a poor misguided thing' who 'gave the best example I know of the eager pursuit of a foregone conclusion'.[59] Livingstone – himself a master of the foregone conclusion – was starting to form his own. Could the Nile, which flowed for 4,000 miles through the largest desert in the world, really issue from so small an outlet as Speke's Ripon Falls?

In Livingstone's view the Nile source could easily lie much further south: perhaps even south of Lake Tanganyika. A river rising there could flow into that lake and issue out of its northern end, ultimately draining into Speke's or Baker's lake, or maybe flowing west of both and becoming the Nile much further north, as Burton had suggested. Although his own theories had similarities with Burton's, ironically Livingstone's hatred of the well-known Arabist and traveller gave him an additional incentive for participating in the search for the source. In 1864 Burton gave evidence to a House of Commons Select Committee on West African Settlements and argued against any increase in British involvement in the area, at the same time attacking missionaries as misguided interferers. This led Livingstone to describe Burton as 'a moral idiot . . . wicked, impure and untruthful'.[60]

In January 1865 Murchison wrote to Livingstone, formally inviting him to go out to Africa 'unshackled by other avocations than those of the geographical explorer' to settle on behalf of the RGS 'a question of intense geographical interest: namely the watershed or watersheds of South Africa'.[61] Owing to previous conversations between the two men, Murchison referred to the area south of Lake Tanganyika as a possible starting point. Livingstone accepted the invitation because he knew that

Manuscript map of Speke and Grant's route from Zanzibar to the Nile
By John Hanning Speke, 1863
Ink and watercolour on ruled paper laid on to linen
38.2 x 30.5 cm
ROYAL GEOGRAPHICAL SOCIETY
(cat. no. 5.11)

This spectacular map, inscribed and dated by Speke 26 February 1863, records his route with James Augustus Grant from the coast near Zanzibar, indicated on the right, around the north-west edge of Lake Victoria and thence to the Nile. As the upper part of the map

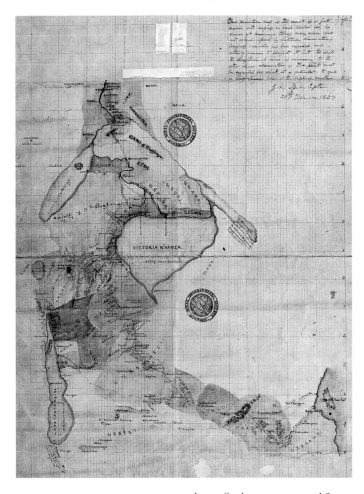

shows, Speke was prevented from charting the course of the Nile's stream from the lake and travelled instead across country. This led to doubts being cast on his claim to have settled the question of the Nile's source, still unresolved at the time of his death in September 1864. He has indicated that the colouring of the map is intended to give 'a comprehensive view of the size of the countries' traversed.

'Missionaries Buying Food at Magomero'

By Charles Meller
(after Henry Rowley), August 1863
Watercolour over pencil on paper
17.5 x 25 cm
THE UNITED SOCIETY FOR THE
PROPAGATION OF THE GOSPEL AND
RHODES HOUSE LIBRARY
(cat. no. 4.32)

This episode from the early days of the Universities' Mission to Central Africa was drawn by Charles Meller after a sketch by Henry Rowley. It is one of a group relating to the UMCA mission. Meller, a doctor by training, had travelled to the Zambezi with members of the mission in 1861 and had close liaisons with both Livingstone's Zambezi party and the UMCA missionaries. He presumably made this drawing while he and Rowley were at the Kongone estuary, awaiting evacuation from Africa in August 1863. It was used as a plate in Rowley's *Story of the Universities' Mission to Central Africa*, 1866.

David and Charles Livingstone, John Kirk and Charles Meller visiting Bishop Mackenzie's grave

By Charles Meller, 1863
Watercolour over pencil on paper
17.5 x 25 cm
THE UNITED SOCIETY FOR THE
PROPAGATION OF THE GOSPEL AND
RHODES HOUSE LIBRARY
(cat. no. 4.26)

Meller's drawing records the poignant visit of Livingstone and members of his party to Bishop Mackenzie's grave on the island of Malo in January 1863. Mackenzie had died there almost exactly a year before. Livingstone marked the occasion by erecting a cross above the grave.

'Last Visit to Chibisa'

By Charles Meller, 15 July 1863
Watercolour over pencil on paper
17.5 x 25 cm
THE UNITED SOCIETY FOR THE
PROPAGATION OF THE GOSPEL AND
RHODES HOUSE LIBRARY
(cat. no. 4.28)

Meller's drawing shows the UMCA settlement, with its tiny church, at Chief Chibisa's village, eighty feet above the River Shire. The missionaries had moved there after abandoning their original settlement at Magomero in 1862. They were to leave shortly after Meller made this drawing, having lost two further colleagues to fever.

Middle right
'Mission Station at Magomera'
From *The Story of the Universities' Mission to Central Africa*
By Henry Rowley
Published by Saunder's, Otley & Co, London, 1866
QUENTIN KEYNES
(cat. no. 4.67)

The history of the disastrous Universities' Mission to Central Africa was written by Henry Rowley, one of the surviving missionaries. This vignette shows the huts built by the missionaries at the Mang'anja village of Magomero. The fact that the huts were square, as opposed to the round dwellings of the Africans, is a poignant metaphor for the cultural dissonance that characterised much of the UMCA episode. Rowley's text below the engraving underscores this point when he writes that 'good substantial huts and houses were being built on a regular plan, and Magomera was beginning to lose its uncivilised appearance'.

Right
Charles Frederick Mackenzie (1825–1862)
By an unknown photographer
Late 1850s
Albumen print, 19.5 x 14.8 cm
THE UNITED SOCIETY FOR THE PROPAGATION OF THE GOSPEL AND RHODES HOUSE LIBRARY
(cat. no. 4.47)

Ordained Bishop of Central Africa in January 1861, Mackenzie was leader of the ill-fated Universities' Mission to Central Africa. On Livingstone's recommendation, the small mission established its base in July 1861 among the Mang'anja, in the area he had named the Shire Highlands. Mackenzie died from fever six months later, after an abortive attempt to meet up with Livingstone to collect supplies. The mission was finally abandoned in 1864 but not before the deaths of three others in Mackenzie's original party. The episode gave rise to intense criticism of Livingstone back in Britain.

Sketchbook given to Horace Waller by John Kirk, May 1863
Leatherbound sketchbook
14.5 x 26.5 cm (closed)
CURATORS OF THE BODLEIAN LIBRARY, RHODES HOUSE LIBRARY
(cat. no. 4.57)

This sketchbook is inscribed on the flysheet, 'John Kirk/Zambesi Expedition/Rovuma/1862' and below this, 'gave this to HW May 5 1863'. Earlier sheets have been cut out and most, if not all of the drawings, seem to be by Horace Waller. Most of the drawings relate to the UMCA's second settlement at Chibisa's village and the final period of the mission. This page shows a village dance.

by going to this region he would find himself in the heart of Arab slave-trading activities. 'I would not consent to go simply as a geographer,' he told a friend.[62] Practical consequences had always been vital to him and now he argued that if he was successful in his Nile search he would be better able to defeat slavery. 'The Nile sources', he wrote, 'are valuable only as a means of enabling me to open my mouth with power among men. It is this power which I hope to apply to remedy an enormous evil.'[63] Elsewhere he stated that the purpose of his new expedition would be to make 'another attempt to open Africa to civilising influences'[64]; but as he admitted to John Kirk, 'The slave trade must be suppressed as the first great step to any mission – that baffles every good effort.'[65] Livingstone therefore felt that for his exploration to have any practical effect he would have to send home sufficiently damning information about the Arabs' East African slave trade to persuade the British government to implement a naval blockade that would prevent the export of slaves to Saudi Arabia and the Persian Gulf via Kilwa and Zanzibar. In 1865 the Foreign Office view was that whereas the British people had had a special moral obligation to outlaw the West African trade because of their own former involvement, no similar obligation existed for suppressing the eastern trade, which they had already limited by treaties with the Sultan of Zanzibar – treaties which, as Livingstone knew, were not honoured by the Sultan's subjects.

Once Livingstone had convinced himself that geographical objectives could be combined with an anti-slavery crusade, he turned all his attention to fund-raising for his expedition. The Foreign Office offered £500 – a third of what he needed. It did not entitle him to a pension and was dependent on his handing over all his geographical field notes on his return. Written instructions informed him that he was not to 'make any promise to, or to enter into any arrangement with chiefs, which might form an embarrassment to Her Majesty's Government'. This document, fumed Livingstone, was 'the most exuberant impertinence that ever issued from the Foreign Office'.[66] Only James Young, the inventor of paraffin, whom Livingstone had first met as a student in Glasgow, imposed no preconditions when offering the extra £1,000 that made it possible for the explorer to set out.

Livingstone left England on 13 August and returned to Africa via Bombay, where he sold the *Lady Nyassa* and collected the Africans who had helped him sail her to Bombay early in 1864. Of these Chuma (one of the slaves freed by members of the Universities' Mission in 1861) and Susi and Amoda (who had both been engaged by

John Hanning Speke (1827–1864) and James Augustus Grant (1827–1892) with Timbo
By Henry Wyndham Phillips
c. 1864
Oil on canvas, 127 x 157.5 cm
P. G. H. SPEKE
(cat. no. 5.1)

Speke, on the right, poses with James Augustus Grant, his companion on his expedition of 1860–1863 to confirm Lake Victoria as the source of the Nile. Phillips' highly unusual portrait must have been painted between their return to Britain in the summer of 1863 and the spring of 1864, when it was shown at the Royal Academy exhibition. It is possible, though, that he had met the two explorers on a visit to Egypt in 1863. According to the RA exhibition catalogue, the African leaning over between the two men is identified as 'Timbo, a young native from the country of the Upper Nile'. Speke is shown with his hand resting on a map, holding dividers, while Grant sketches. There are natural history specimens in the foreground and, behind Speke, his hunting rifle and a prominent Union Jack.

Livingstone at Shupanga in 1863) would still be with the explorer when he died in 1873. On the advice of Sir Bartle Frere, the Governor of Bombay, Livingstone took on a dozen sepoys from the Bombay Marine Battalion and nine boys from the government-run school for freed African slaves at Nasik.

On 19 March 1866 Livingstone landed on the East African coast 600 miles north of Quelimane. He had engaged another ten men from the island of Johanna, and his party now numbered thirty-five. This was a very small expedition by usual African standards – Speke and Burton, for example, had never travelled with less than 130 men. Large parties could take more cloth and beads to pay for food and were less likely to be robbed by avaricious chiefs. In addition to his porters and attendants Livingstone took an assortment of mules, donkeys, buffaloes, cows and camels to see whether any could survive the attentions of the tsetse fly.

Alone once more, with a band of Africans who, unlike Europeans, he thought he could rely on to follow orders, Livingstone believed he could repeat the triumphs of his transcontinental journey. 'The mere animal pleasure of travelling in a wild unexplored country is very great,' he would write at the outset.

> When on lands of a couple of thousand feet elevation, brisk exercise imparts elasticity to the muscles, fresh and healthy blood circulates through the brain, the mind works well, the eye is clear, the step is firm . . . Africa is a wonderful country for appetite.[67]

Livingstone's intention was to march inland along the River Rovuma and then, after passing the southern end of Lake Nyasa, to head north towards the region south of Lake Tanganyika where he expected to find the Nile's source. Unwisely he rejected Sir Roderick Murchison's advice to go first to the north end of Lake Tanganyika to see whether the river there flowed on northwards to Baker's Lake Albert. If he had done this, Livingstone would at once have known that any river he found west of Lake Tanganyika would have to be followed north at all costs, since no alternative source for the Nile could exist in Lake Tanganyika itself. When Livingstone eventually established that there was no link between Lakes Tanganyika and Albert (in 1871) he was too weak to trace the River Lualaba north to establish whether it was the Nile.

Livingstone's followers did not prove as reliable as expected. From the outset the Nasik boys and sepoys dawdled and maltreated the animals. Although Livingstone took on twenty-four more porters in early May, by August he was down to twenty-three in total;

and within eighteen months his party numbered only nine. Five rebels soon reduced the number to four, but though Livingstone had railed at his white companions for minor failings he forgave his deserters and took them back at once when they begged him to do so. 'More enlightened people often take advantage of men in similar circumstances,' he wrote in his journal. 'I have faults myself.'[68] Not even the desertion of the man carrying his medicine chest was greeted with fury, though his treachery had endangered everyone's life.

In the light of these problems, it is clear that Livingstone's decision during his last journeys to travel with Arab slave traders was forced upon him by absolute necessity. He squared his conscience on logical grounds: if he starved he would not be able to write the reports that alone would persuade the British government to outlaw all seaborne transport of slaves. By travelling with the enemy he also learnt more about the slave trade. Nor were individual Arab slavers as bad as the generality. Muhammad Bogharib, with whom Livingstone often travelled, treated his personal servants (all of them slaves) very much better than most British factory owners treated their employees.

Illness, the rains, the slave trade and tribal disturbances denied Livingstone any success with his geographical aims until the autumn of 1867. By that year's end he had visited Lake Moero and established that Lake Bangweulu, which was linked to Moero, was probably the primary source of a colossal river, the Lualaba, which emerged from Moero and flowed north parallel to Lake Tanganyika. In the following year Livingstone mapped Lake Bangweulu and immediately wrote the first of many draft despatches to the Foreign Secretary claiming to have found the source of the Nile. In a letter to Kirk, now Acting British Consul at Zanzibar, he repeated this claim and added, almost as an afterthought, 'I have still to follow down the Lualaba, and see whether . . . it passes Tanganyika to the west, or enters it and finds an exit into Baker's lake [Albert].'[69]

A year later Livingsone had made no progress with his geographical search. He had been ill, there had been widespread disturbances caused by the slave trade and he had been forced back to Ujiji, the Arab trading town on the eastern shores of Lake Tanganyika. In July 1869 he set out with Muhammad Bogharib for Manyema – the region west of Tanganyika – hoping to reach the Lualaba and follow it north. At Ujiji he had been upset by Arab reports that the Lualaba flowed north-west and not north-east, as it would have to in order to be the Nile. He comforted himself with the thought that the Lualaba was large enough to supply both the Congo and the Nile, but anxieties on the subject would never leave him.

Mutesa, Kabaka of Buganda
By John Hanning Speke, 1862
Watercolour over pencil on paper
in a bound volume
24.8 x 16.2 cm (closed)
ROYAL GEOGRAPHICAL SOCIETY
(cat. no. 5.9)

Speke arrived at the court of Mutesa, the king of the Baganda, on 19 February 1862; he was the first European to meet him and to traverse his country. He stayed there for over four and a half months, developing a cordial relationship with the young king and eventually negotiating his passage northwards. This drawing of Mutesa is inscribed in Speke's hand 'M'tesa King of Uganda in his Throne room preparing for a blister'. Speke gave Mutesa medical treatment while he was with him and it is presumably for this reason that Mutesa is naked. On the facing page is a list of watercolours with directions for their use.

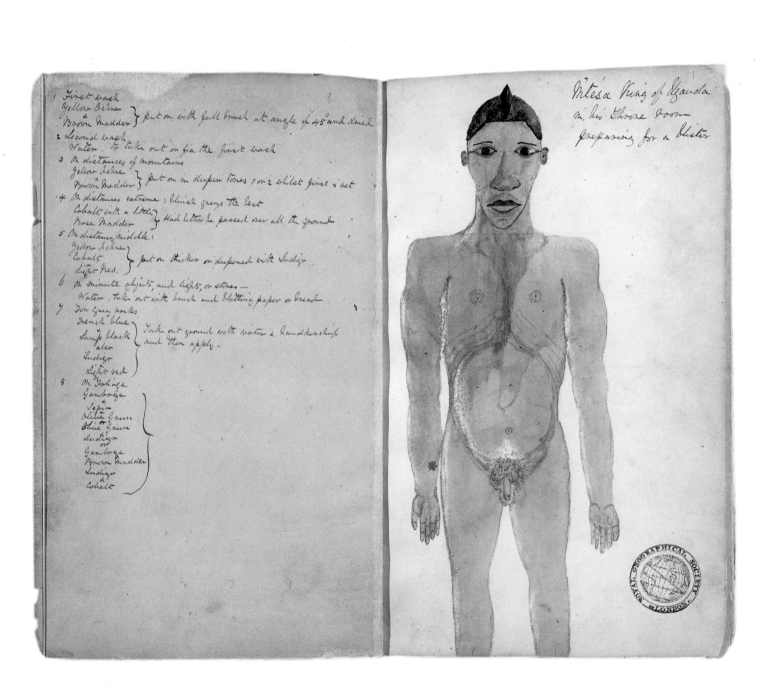

60

Grant followed Speke to the court of Mutesa, the king of the Baganda, arriving in April 1862; his drawing records the two explorers at an audience with the dowager Queen Mother. Although her authority was waning in favour of her son, both Speke and Grant were required to pay her due respect.

In Manyema Livingstone was prostrated by fever, anal bleeding, and, worst of all, by deep ulcers on his feet that made walking impossible. It was the ulcers that forced him to remain at Bambarre, a town midway between the Lualaba and Lake Tanganyika, from July 1870 to February 1871. During this time ill-health and inactivity made him introspective and prone to fantasise; he read the Bible right through four times and began toying with the ideas that Moses had visited the area south of Tanganyika and that the account of the Nile's source given in Herodotus's *History* was factual.

In August 1870 two Arabs called Josut and Moenepembé arrived in Bambarre and told Livingstone of the existence of four sources situated close together in the region west of Bangweulu. The sources of the Zambezi and Kafue can indeed be found in that locality within a hundred miles or so of two minor sources of the Lualaba. Livingstone now jumped to the conclusion that these two tributary sources probably constituted the Lualaba's most southerly point of origin and could therefore be considered that river's primary source rather than the River Chambezi and Lake Bangweulu, which he had already visited and mapped. Consequently he decided that he would have to return to the region within the next couple of years to settle the matter. So just when his health was deteriorating and he needed to preserve his strength, he was planning to undertake this awesome additional task.

In February 1871, his ulcers at last having healed, Livingstone was ready to set out for the Lualaba, which he reached before the end of March at the town of Nyangwe (550 miles north-west of Lake Bangweulu). In order to find out the direction the Lualaba took further north and also to discover where its tributary, the Lomani, rose, Livingstone needed canoes. The Lualaba was two miles wide at Nyangwe, yet because the local Arabs feared that Livingstone wanted to spy on their slaving activities they refused to help him.

He was still vainly trying to acquire canoes from the Arabs when, on 15 July, he witnessed a massacre of the African inhabitants of Nyangwe by the Arabs. The shooting began in the market and continued as terrified people fled into the Lualaba, where hundreds were drowned. The Arabs' reckoning of 400 deaths was probably a considerable underestimate. This atrocity and similar attacks in surrounding villages were evidently intended to scare the Manyema tribes into abject obedience to Arab demands. For Livingstone, there could now be no question of accepting assistance from Arabs ever again. The pain and suffering of two years had therefore been futile: without

Arab canoes and supplies he could neither trace the Lualaba north, nor the Lomani south. His only choice was to return to Ujiji where he had left supplies in 1869. He arrived there on 23 October to find that all his goods (to the value of £600) had been stolen. There was a tribal war raging east of Ujiji so he could not expect Kirk to send supplies from Zanzibar for many months.

Survival on Arab credit seemed to be the humiliating prospect ahead of him until, most unexpectedly, on what he thought was 28 October but was probably a day earlier, he heard that a large caravan was approaching. Later that day he saw an immaculately dressed white man step forward from a host of onlookers, preceded by a tall African carrying the Stars and Stripes. This stranger raised his helmet and said as formally as he could, but in a voice that nevertheless trembled with excitement, 'Dr Livingstone, I presume?'

In December 1866 some of Livingstone's deserters had arrived in Zanzibar with a concocted story about their master having been killed in the interior. When obituaries appeared in the British press they were respectful but not as extensive or as emotionally charged as might have been expected for one of the world's greatest explorers. If Livingstone had died in 1856 the coverage would have been very different, but that would have been before Burton, Speke and Baker had made their discoveries, and before serious damage had been done to Livingstone's reputation by the deaths and disappointments of the Zambezi expedition.

Nevertheless, Livingstone had not been entirely forgotten after 1866. Before Henry Morton Stanley 'found' him in 1871 the Commons had voted Livingstone a further £1,000 and the Treasury had paid £1,200 towards the cost of an expedition to Africa that successfully disproved the fabricated murder story. No letters were received from Livingstone between the autumn of 1869 and the summer of 1871, but John Kirk, the Acting British Consul at Zanzibar, had never believed him dead or even in grave danger and had recently managed to get supplies to him in Manyema. It would certainly have surprised Kirk very much had he known that Mr James Gordon Bennett, the editor of the *New York Herald*, had already decided that if one of his reporters could find Livingstone, and interview him in the heart of Africa, he would have engineered one of the century's greatest scoops. But Mr Bennett's instinct was impeccable. His reporter, Mr Stanley, would not only make world news but would also transform the British public's perception of Livingstone's character, laying the groundwork for posterity's myth of the saintly missionary.

or at least prehistoric times when Beke was a water crab — Finlay a waterwagtail and I a stickleback — Arrowsmith may have been a tadpole man to Vulcan — Now not a soul in the world knows till my Despatch goes home ~~that the~~ the watershed is 700 miles long — So Sir R. must announce a greater discovery still. These dreamers must have hit on the division of labour in dreaming and he must award them about 200 miles each — It is really foolish & presumptuous

Northern on very back to any emergency
12 December 1871 [1871]

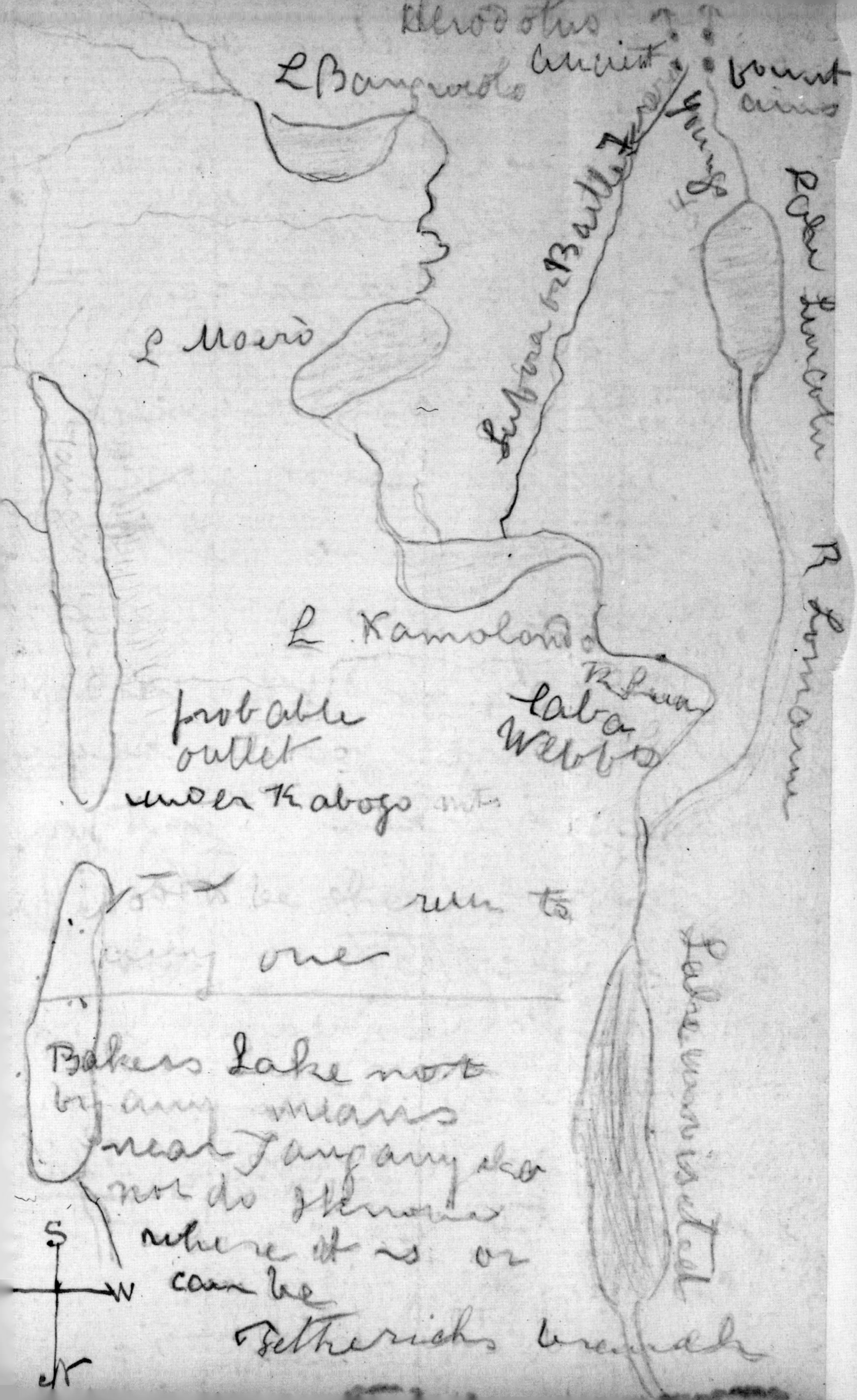

Herodotus

L Bangweolo   Ancient   mountains

young

L Moero

Lufira or Bartle R

Lake Lincoln R Lomame

L Kamolondo

R Luama

Laba Welobo

probable
outlet
under Kabogo mts

... be ... run to
... one

Bakers Lake not
by any means
near Tanganyika also
nor do I know
where it is or
can be

S
N

Fethericks branch

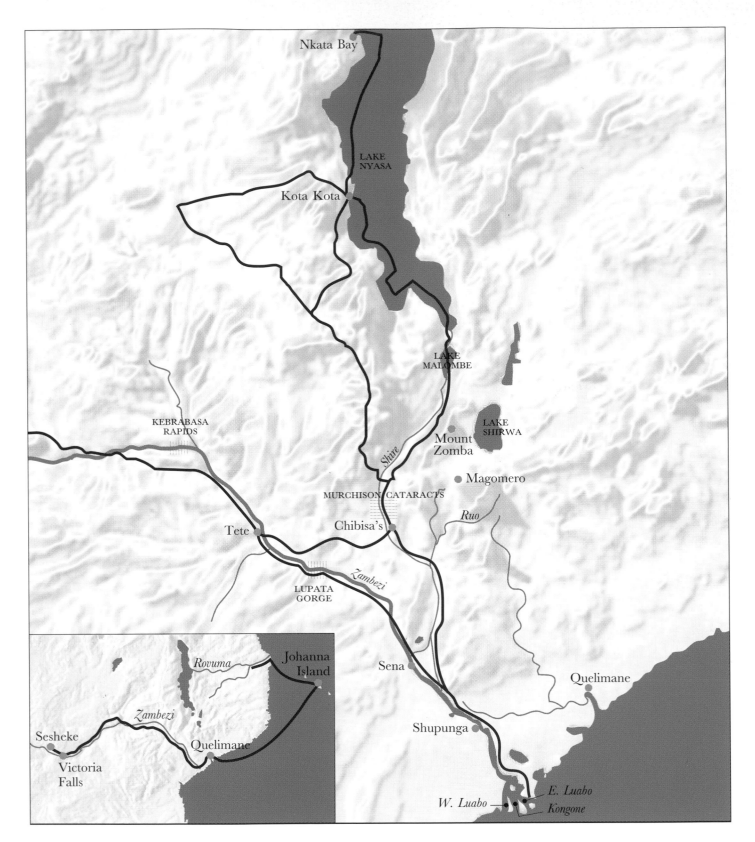

Nkata Bay

LAKE
NYASA

Kota Kota

LAKE
MALOMBE

KEBRABASA
RAPIDS

LAKE
SHIRWA

Mount
Zomba

Shire

Magomero

MURCHISON CATARACTS

Ruo

Chibisa's

Tete

Zambezi

LUPATA
GORGE

Sena

Quelimane

Shupunga

W. Luabo

E. Luabo

Kongone

Rovuma

Johanna
Island

Zambezi

Quelimane

Sesheke

Victoria
Falls

Sketch Map of the Zambezi Expedition

Towns and places

Livingstone's route

Rivers and waterways

0   25   50   75   100 miles

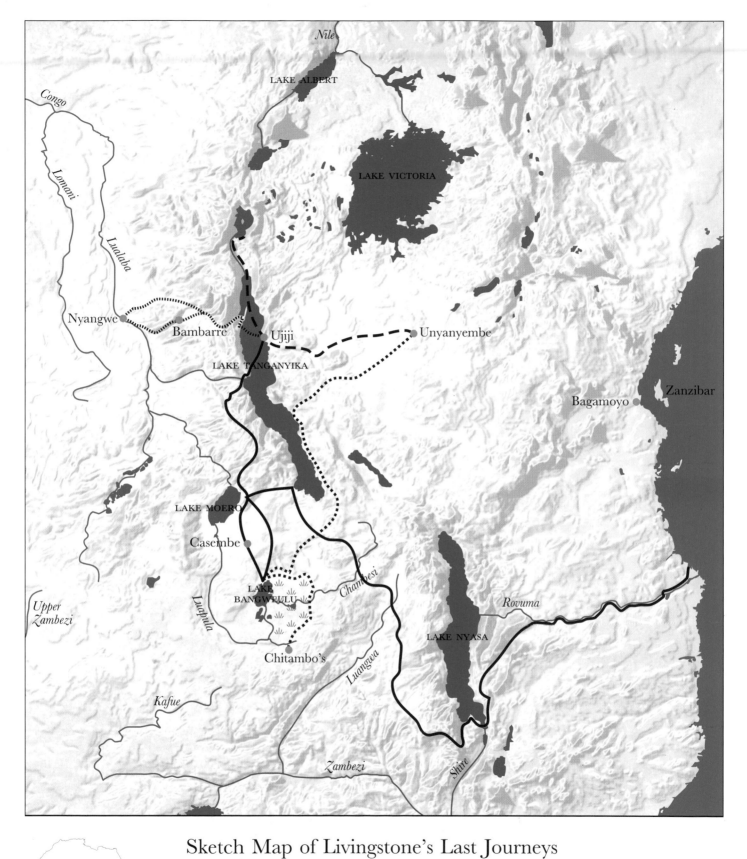

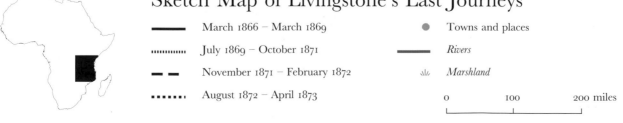

Sketch Map of Livingstone's Last Journeys

—— March 1866 – March 1869	● Towns and places
·········· July 1869 – October 1871	—— Rivers
– – – November 1871 – February 1872	⚶ Marshland
•••••• August 1872 – April 1873	

0   100   200 miles

of the RGS, and by those who knew Livingstone personally like John Kirk, would not reduce the impact of Stanley's writings in the wider public arena.

After a couple of months with Livingstone, Stanley wrote in his diary, 'I have had some intrusive suspicions, thoughts that he [Livingstone] was not of such an angelic temper as I believed him to be during my first month with him.' Stanley had been shaken by Livingstone's habit of making 'reiterated complaints against this man and the other' and had come to suspect that 'his strong nature was opposed to forgiveness'.[70] That Stanley should subsequently choose to ignore the flaws in Livingstone's character and describe him as a man 'as near an angel as the nature of living man will allow', can be attributed in part to his belief that it made a better story to have discovered a forgotten saint rather than a brave but embittered man. But the misrepresentation also had deeper origins.

Stanley had not started life as an American but was born in Wales, the illegitimate son of a Denbighshire farm-worker. When only five he had been consigned to the St Asaph workhouse by his mother. Livingstone's own harsh childhood and his extreme sensitivity to possible slights enabled him to understand Stanley's shy and prickly manner and to empathise with him. Stanley would in turn prove to be more to him than a bringer of badly needed supplies, although these could hardly have come at a more providential moment.

'That good brave fellow has acted as a son to me,' Livingstone told his daughter Agnes.[71] And it is not fanciful to suggest that Stanley, who had never known his alcoholic father, saw Livingstone in the corresponding role of an ideal father: 'His manner suits my nature better than that of any man I can remember of late years. Perhaps I should best describe it as benevolently paternal.'[72] When he suffered from fever Livingstone nursed him, Stanley later recorded, 'with tender and fatherly kindness'.[73] Of course the Livingstone whom Stanley found in 1871 was no saint, but age and an increasing sense of his own limitations had softened, though not eliminated, his irascible and vindictive traits. 'I shall not hide it from you,' Livingstone admitted to Agnes with a humorous self-deprecation rare in earlier years, 'that I am very old & shaky – my cheeks fallen . . . the mouth almost toothless . . . a smile that is of a hippopotamus – a dreadful old Fogie.'[74]

During the five months the two men spent together they travelled to the northern tip of Lake Tanganyika and

Henry Morton Stanley (1841–1904)
By C. H. Nedey of Alexandria after an earlier photograph
c. 1867–1870
Albumen carte-de-visite
9.1 x 5.2 cm
QUENTIN KEYNES
(cat. no. 5.23)

This early portrait may date from the time of Stanley's success as a special correspondent attached to the British invasion of Abyssinia in 1868. His despatches for the *New York Herald* scooped the indignant British press by a week and established his reputation as a brilliant journalist.

67

Top
Stanley's helmet
ROYAL GEOGRAPHICAL SOCIETY
(cat. no. 5.58)

On the morning he expected to meet Livingstone at Ujiji, Stanley recorded that he chalked this helmet carefully and wrapped a new *pugeree* around it. Such helmets were standard hot-weather kit for soldiers and civilian travellers.

Livingstone's cap
ROYAL GEOGRAPHICAL SOCIETY
(cat. no. 5.57)

Livingstone had such caps made at Starkey's of Bond Street, and they became a key element of his public image, appearing in a variety of photographs and featuring prominently in the engravings that illustrated *Missionary Travels and Researches in South Africa*. This is believed to be the one he doffed to Stanley.

discovered that the river there – the Lusize – flowed into the lake not out of it. Because this ruled out any possibility of there being a connection between Lake Tanganyika and Lake Albert, Livingstone knew that his entire Nile quest now depended upon his proving that the Lualaba was the Nile. Unfortunately, he was still determined to head south to find the 'four fountains [sources]' west of Bangweulu before tracing the river north.

Although Livingstone knew that his family wanted him to come home to recuperate, he flatly refused. It has been suggested that he might have returned in 1872 if Stanley had not given him the impression that John Kirk and the Foreign Office were trying to force him home by denying him supplies and funds. In truth, there were no circumstances in which he would have returned when so close (in his opinion) to solving the riddle of the African watershed. There was a financial consideration, too. Ironically, when British newspapers, thanks to Stanley, were again praising him in the extravagant terms of 1856, Livingstone himself knew nothing of it and feared that unless he could prove that the Lualaba was the Nile he would be reduced to poverty on his return. Nothing was left of his earlier literary earnings, and Stanley had brought him the painful news that the money he had received for the sale of the *Lady Nyassa* had been lost in the failure of a Bombay bank. 'To return unsuccessful', Livingstone warned Agnes, 'would mean going abroad to an unhealthy consulate to which no public sympathy would ever be drawn.'[75]

Stanley landed in England on 1 August 1872 and all through that month, and into September, it was not unusual to see in newspapers double pages devoted exclusively to his famous 'meeting'. Of greater significance for the future was the fact that Stanley had brought to England Livingstone's journals and his despatches on the slave trade, containing an account of the massacre at Nyangwe. Since 1871 a House of Commons Select Committee had been considering whether to recommend the abolition of the seaborne Arab trade. That it did so in September, a month after Stanley's return, was due in no small measure to the timely arrival of Livingstone's evidence, though John Kirk and Sir Bartle Frere also deserve credit. On 5 June 1873, under threat of a naval bombardment, the Sultan closed the slave market in Zanzibar for ever. Livingstone had longed to strike an effective blow against 'this open sore of the world', and had written one of his most moving indictments of the

This photograph shows the three principal members, including Livingstone's youngest son, of a search expedition sponsored by the Royal Geographical Society and substantially funded by public subscription. The search was launched in December 1871, after Stanley's famous meeting with the explorer but before news of it had reached Britain. They learnt of Stanley's *coup* at Bagamoyo on 28 April 1872.

slave trade while in Manyema in 1871: The strangest disease I have seen in this country seems really to be broken-heartedness, and it attacks free men who have been captured and made slaves.' He talked to many captives who were wasting away from a disease apparently without physical cause. 'They ascribed their only pain to the heart, and placed the hand correctly on the spot, though many think that organ stands high up under the breast bone.'[76]

On 25 August 1872 Livingstone set out on his final journey, accompanied by fifty-six men sent from the coast by Stanley and by his own five stalwarts who had shared every vicissitude and danger since 1866. They were James Chuma, Abdullah Susi, Edward Gardner, Hamoydah Amoda and Nathaniel Cumba, generally referred to as Mabruki. Livingstone planned to follow Lake Tanganyika to its foot and then to skirt the southern shore of Lake Bangweulu and march west to Katanga and the four sources.

By mid-October Livingstone was tired and ill with dysentery. Milk alone restored his health so it was a disastrous setback when his six cows strayed into a belt of tsetse fly and died soon afterwards. By early November the rains had begun and his anal bleeding returned. By mid-January 1873 Livingstone had reached the north-eastern shore of Bangweulu but by then his health was precarious and deteriorating. In 1868 when he had first visited the lake he had mapped it incorrectly and concluded that it was 150 miles long rather than the 25 miles it actually was. Nor had he realised that it was surrounded by swamps that, to the east of the true lake, extended for more than a hundred miles. Once Livingstone entered these swamps he would never again know where he was with any certainty.

On 24 January he wrote in his journal, 'Carrying me across one of the broad deep sedgy rivers is really a difficult task . . . the main stream came up to Susi's mouth, and wetted my seat and legs. One held up my pistol behind, then one after another took a turn, and when he sank into a deep elephant's footprint, he required two to lift him.'[77] The party often covered no more than a mile and a half in a day, wading for hour after hour through oozing mud and overflowing streams. The wonder is that so few deserted, but now all of them seemed tied to the dying man and felt unable to abandon him. Livingstone's journal contains no trace of self-pity at this time and his appreciation of nature continued almost to the end.

Caught in a drenching rain, which made me fain to sit, exhausted as I was under an umbrella for an hour . . .

As I sat in the rain a little tree frog about half an inch long, leaped onto a grassy leaf and began a tune as loud as that of many birds, and very sweet; it was surprising to hear so much music out of so small a musician. I drank some rainwater as I felt faint – in the paths it is now calf deep.[78]

In late March, still wet and cold and suffering the agonies of internal haemorrhage, Livingstone wrote defiantly, 'Nothing earthly will make me give up my work in despair. I encourage myself in the Lord my God and go forward.'[79] On 19 April, two weeks before his death, Livingstone wrote the greatest of his many understatements: 'It is not all pleasure, this exploration.'

By mid April they were finally clear of Bangweulu but Livingstone, though determined to press on, had to be carried on a litter. On 27 April he made the last entry in his journal: 'Knocked up quite and remain – recover – sent to buy milch goats. We are on the banks of R. Molilamo.' Only a week earlier he had been making detailed observations about temperature, cloud cover, the speed of the flow of rivers and their precise direction.

When he could no longer walk his men carried him for a further three days, as carefully as they could since the slightest jolt was anguish to him. (After his death it was found that a blood clot the size of a man's fist had been obstructing his lower intestine.) At Chitambo's village, near the River Luapula (which connected Bangweulu with Lake Moero) Livingstone could go no further. His followers built a hut and in it, in the early hours of 1 May 1873, David Livingstone died. He was found kneeling by his bed, as if in prayer, shortly after 4 a.m. He was sixty years old.

The decision made by Livingstone's followers, on the morning after their master's death, to preserve his body and carry it to the coast was a remarkable one since it would certainly have been safer for them to have buried it where he had died. At best they might have been forced to pay a heavy fine if discovered by any chief to be carrying a body; at worst they could have been accused of witchcraft and attacked. It can be argued that they took the body to the coast to avoid punishment or to claim a reward, but this is unconvincing. The reason for the devotion of Chuma and Susi and the other longest-serving followers had been Livingstone's gentleness with them and with all Africans. Far from being flogged or chained to stop them deserting – as regularly happened on other explorers' expeditions – they had always been treated with affection. They may not have understood Livingstone's

Verney Lovett Cameron (1844–1894)
By Maull & Fox, c. 1876
Albumen cabinet print
16.3 x 10.4 cm
ROYAL GEOGRAPHICAL SOCIETY
(cat. no. 6.9)

73

Cameron led the last of the expeditions sent out by the Royal Geographical Society to give support to Livingstone. The expedition set out from Bagamoyo at the end of March 1873 but, dogged by illness, became stranded at Unyanyembe. It was there, in October, that Cameron heard news of Livingstone's death. The body, carried by Livingstone's followers, arrived a few days later.

aims but they knew what these had cost him in health and effort, and without doubt they respected him as a great man. To honour him they wished to take his body back to his own people and to return to them the records he had kept with so much care.

In analysing the life of a great man there is always a fundamental problem: to be great is to be different, so ordinary criteria of judgement fall short. The point at which determination becomes obsession, and self-sacrifice self-destruction is very hard to estimate. Yet even if Livingstone's determination is called obsessive – and it was – it must be acknowledged that without inflexibility he would never have left the mill, never have qualified as a doctor and never have ended his life near the swamps of Lake Bangweulu; without it he might have made a better husband and father, and a more likeable man. In the same way, had Livingstone been a precise and rational thinker, rather than an idealist, he would never have attempted to cross Africa without backing or his own supplies. Optimism enabled him to take on tasks that rational men would never have attempted; optimism also led to most of his failures.

Livingstone's dogged refusal to give in when facing overwhelming odds, his uncomplaining acceptance of agonising pain and his lonely death still conjure up powerful images. That any man should willingly have undergone such hardship seemed to his contemporaries, and still seems, so remarkable that to ask whether he achieved his aims or deceived himself appears in the end churlish and beside the point. Those who wept in the streets on the day of his funeral did not know that the Lualaba was not the Nile. Had they done so, knowledge of Livingstone's misconception would probably have deepened the pathos of his death.

The whole span of Livingstone's achievement was apparent then as something unique and so it still seems today: it is not simply a matter of the vast distance he tramped over, nor of the geographical discoveries he made, for his contributions to enthnology, natural history, tropical medicine and linguistics were also substantial, as were his roles as a crusader against the slave trade, a colonial theoretician and a prophet. Livingstone had always claimed that he was opening the way into Africa for others, and there, at last, his optimism was to prove well founded, since the events of the thirty years following his death would show that he had done exactly that – with consequences he would sometimes have applauded but more often deplored.

74

Lake Nyasa Left-handed
Apple Snail
'Lanistes sp.' Lanistes nyassanus
(Dohrn, 1865) collected by
John Kirk, 1861
BY PERMISSION OF THE TRUSTEES
OF THE NATURAL HISTORY
MUSEUM
(cat. no. 4.105)

78

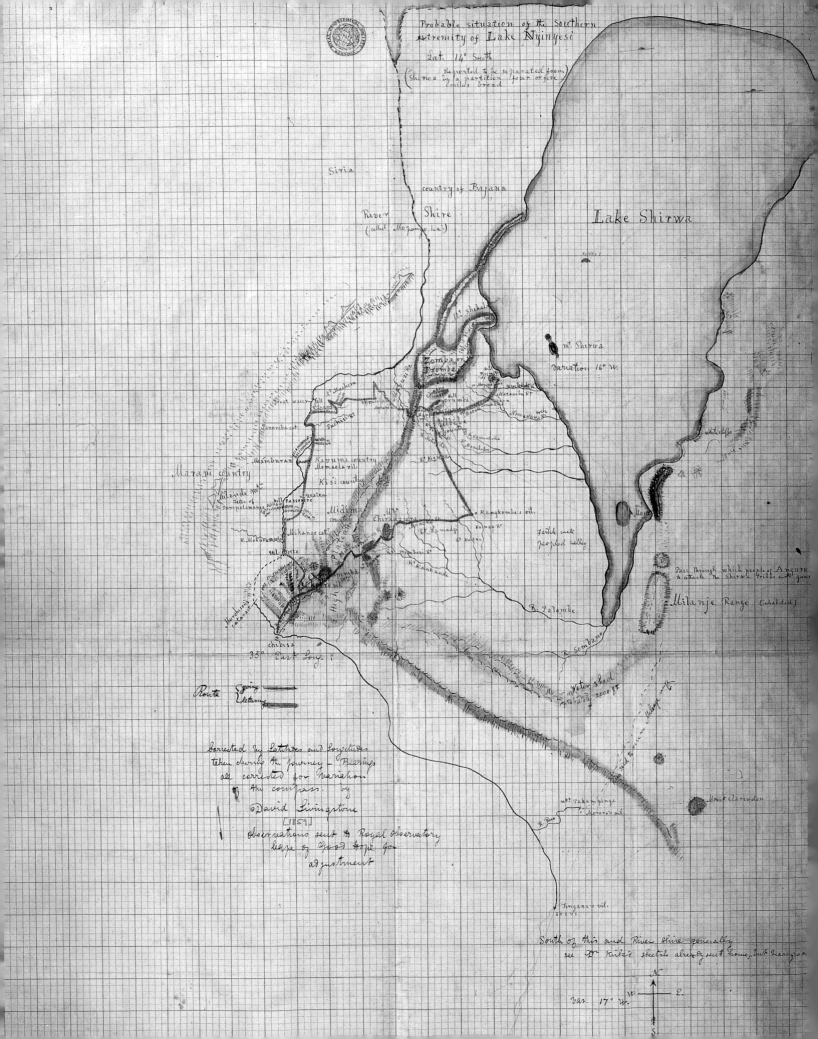

Probable situation of the Southern
extremity of Lake Nyinyesi
Lat. 14° South
Reported to be separated from
Shirwa by a partition four or five
miles broad

Siria

country of Bajana

River
Shire
(called Mojenyo Lui)

Lake Shirwa

Mt. Shirwa
Variation 16° W.

Zomba or
Dzombe

Maravi country

Kapuma country

Kisi country

Midima
country

Chiradzura

o Kangkombas vil.

Fertile well
peopled valley

Pass through which people of Angura
to attack the Shirwa tribes with guns

Milanje Range (inhabited)

R. Palombe

R. Sombane

35° East Long.?

Chibisa

Route { going
        { returning

Water shed
2000 ft.

Corrected by Latitudes and longitudes
taken during the journey — Bearings
all corrected for variation
of the compass. by

David Livingstone
[1859]
Observations sent to Royal Observatory
Cape of Good Hope for
adjustment

Mount Clarenden

Tingane's vil.

South of this and River shire generally
see Dr Kirk's sketch already sent home, but bearings

N
W E
Var. 17° W.
S

Manuscript map of Lake Shirwa (now Chilwa) and the River Shire (detail)
By David Livingstone, c. 1859
Ink and watercolour on squared paper laid on to linen
100 x 67.2 cm
ROYAL GEOGRAPHICAL SOCIETY
(cat. no. 1.2)

This extraordinary map records Livingstone and John Kirk's route in April 1859, when they explored the upper reaches of the River Shire on foot, visiting Lake Shirwa (now Chilwa) on 18 April 1859. Livingstone has also indicated at the top of the map the 'Probable situation of the Southern extremity of Lake Nyinyesi', a much larger lake than Chilwa, which he and Kirk had heard reports about from local people. This proved to be Lake Nyasa (now Lake Malawi), Livingstone claiming its discovery on 17 September 1859.

In April 1859 Livingstone was making his way to Lake Shirwa, in what is now Malawi. His companion was Dr John Kirk, and the two men got on well despite Kirk's reservations about Livingstone's leadership of the ill-fated Zambezi expedition. Kirk was less sympathetic than Livingstone towards Africans, whom he called 'niggers', and even allowing for the fact that those they met in a nearby village were middlemen in the slave trade and accosted them rudely, the language Kirk used in his diary ('blackguard', 'beast') can only be described as racist:

> . . . We were rather wild at our reception by such a set of low rascals and they soon saw that we were rather up for fun and shooting or not shooting them was altogether indifferent to us and that if we had a good chance we would not lose it. Little did they know that it was our respectability in England and our wish to pass without getting a bad name that kept us back.[1]

Kirk was from Forfarshire, like Livingstone a Scot, but his reference to 'England' as if it were their homeland is typical of Scots during this period. Livingstone himself would commonly conflate Scotland with an overall political entity called 'England' rather than 'Britain' and wrote from Quelimane to Edmund Gabriel in Luanda in 1856 about the Royal Navy's operations against slavers:

> If our cruisers have done nothing else, they have conferred a good name on the English . . . They [the natives] say, 'These English love the black people much.' This is so far in our favour in endeavouring to propagate our blessed Christianity.

The word 'our' seems to refer to 'the English', and he writes elsewhere of 'We English'. Livingstone continues:

> I feel convinced that God has gracious designs towards the Africans. They are an imperishable race . . . Then as our Burns has it: 'Then let us pray that come it may/For come it will for a' that/When man and man the world o'er/Shall brothers be for a' that.[2]

In 1859 Livingstone would write in his journal, 'There is room to spare for English emigrants to settle and work the virgin soil of the still untilled land of Ham.' But sharing his thoughts not long before with a fellow Scot, Sir Roderick Murchison (the distinguished geologist who presided over the Royal Geographical Society), he had been thinking of 'Scotch' settlers. 'The interior of this country ought to be colonised by our own countrymen . . . I think twenty or thirty good Christian Scotch families with their ministers and elders would produce an impression in ten years that would rejoice the hearts of all

81

John Kirk (1832–1922)
Albumen cabinet print after an
earlier photograph
(photographer unknown, *c.* 1857)
12.3 x 8.7 cm (oval)
ROYAL BOTANIC GARDENS, KEW
(cat. no. 4.46)

Educated in medicine at the
University of Edinburgh, Kirk
was appointed by Livingstone as
Medical Officer and Economic
Botanist to the Zambezi
expedition in 1858. He proved an
outstanding member of the
party. It was Kirk who collected
many of the ethnographic and
natural history specimens
dispatched from the Zambezi to
museums in Britain and who
recorded the expedition in
journals, watercolours and the
earliest photographs to be taken
in that region of Africa. As
British Vice-Consul, and later
Consul-General, to Zanzibar
from 1866 to 1887, Kirk was of
vital support to Livingstone's
later journeys.

George Rae (?1831–1865)
By an unknown photographer
Early 1860s
Albumen carte-de-visite
7.5 x 5.7 cm
THE DAVID LIVINGSTONE CENTRE
(cat. no. 4.49)

Livingstone appointed Rae
engineer to the Zambezi
expedition in February 1858.
Almost certainly a native of
Blantyre like Livingstone, and an
experienced seaman, Rae
managed to stay the course of the
expedition until its end in 1864.

lovers of our race.[3] And asking Sir Roderick to find a job for Kirk after the Zambezi expedition foundered in 1864 he wrote: 'Being a Scotchman and really a very able and amiable fellow . . . I am quite sure he would be a credit to any appointment either at home or abroad.'[4]

After failure in the 1690s to establish a colony in Central America the Scottish political and commercial classes had accepted Union with England in 1707 partly as an entrée to empire, for by that date the English had already begun to carve out a vast overseas empire. 'Clannishness' was not confined to Highlanders, and partiality for fellow Scots (which would later bind Livingstone, Kirk and Murchison) ensured that Scots became dominant in some parts of the empire, in others, merely influential. Within a few years of the Union, Scots were rampant on rich Caribbean sugar islands. Within fifty they owned about a quarter of all taxable land on the largest and richest of them all, Jamaica.[5] After Wolfe's capture of Quebec, Scots moved in to dominate the Canadian fur trade, and by Livingstone's day a Highland Scot, Sir George Simpson (head of the Hudson's Bay Company), ruled an area comparable to the domain of the Russian Tsar, while a black Scot, Sir James Douglas (son of a Scottish planter by a Creole Guyanese woman) was the first Governor of British Columbia. Dunedin, so named after Edinburgh, marks the Scottish impact on New Zealand. Scots were big in Australian wool and in the lucrative tea and opium trades with China.

From the Union onwards Scots sucked in a disproportionate share of the rich patronage flowing from the East India Company. In the developing Indian Raj they came to form the 'core of the civil service'.[6] Others grew rich as soldiers and traders. Even when Company rule was abolished after the Indian Mutiny of 1857 Scottish influence on the sub-continent did not abate. In 1865 Livingstone wrote drily to Kirk from Bombay that James Augustus Grant, another famous traveller in Africa, had been 'toasted in Calcutta' at a St Andrew's Day dinner. 'Scotchmen predominate there as well as here and all are pretty clannish.'[7] Livingstone himself might be seen as yet another clannish 'Scotchman on the make', using England as a battering ram to smash open doors to opportunity. But in fact few career or commercial opportunities existed in Africa. Scots had to discover new opportunities for themselves, and Livingstone did not hope for a fortune and an estate back home in Scotland. He wanted to be God's instrument in saving the continent.

It seems apt that four Scots – Livingstone, his brother Charles, John Kirk and George Rae – were the first white

men known to have seen the glories of Lake Malawi, for Scots had played a disproportionate role in the opening up of Africa to European understanding. James Bruce (1730–1794) was famous for his travels in Ethiopia, Mungo Park (1771–1806) for locating the River Niger; while Hugh Clapperton (1788–1827) and W. B. Baikie (1825–1865) increased knowledge of West Africa. In the missionary field, where Scots were extremely prominent, even Robert Moffat, Livingstone's remarkable father-in-law, was dwarfed by the mighty John Philip – a byword for malice among Afrikaners until the fall of apartheid and perhaps beyond because of his championship of native Africans.

Philip is an excellent example of 'self-help', a doctrine that was very important in nineteenth-century Britain but is easily misunderstood today. At a time when working men contended against the novel and often horrific conditions of life established by the new industrialism and the effects of great slumps in trade, self-help emphasised the virtues of hard work, thrift and sobriety as safeguards against destitution and as the means of rising to respectability and retaining it. But according to Samuel Smiles (1812–1904), the Scot who became the most famous exponent of the creed, the objective was not *nouveau riche* wealth. It was 'independence': the capacity to function freely and with dignity, without need to defer to aristocrats or unfair employers. Smiles, a doctor from the small Lothian town of Haddington, encountered self-help first, not as ideal but as reality, during the era of Chartism in Leeds, where he observed the passion for 'self-improvement' among working men who were defying conditions far worse than those Livingstone endured as a child in Blantyre. Self-improvement entailed self-education. And the purpose of that education was not merely to improve marketable skills but also to permit appreciation of the arts (the poetry of Robert Burns was much loved in the North of England) and, above all, understanding of God's universe through science. Smiles's book *Self-Help*, published in 1859, drew all these elements together and gave them literary shape, using examples from the lives, real or mythologised, of many well-known men and some quite obscure ones.[8]

Though self-help had been a spontaneous response (throughout Britain) to industrialism, it was particularly congenial to the Lowland Scottish temperament. Philip was an early and awesome example. Born in Fife in 1775, the son of a handloom weaver with a serious library, Philip left school at eleven to become a weaver himself, but rose through self-education to become a mill manager. He resigned in disgust at his employer's attitude to child and female labour and trained for the ministry. Like

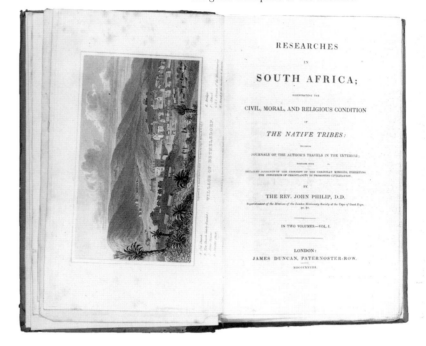

Like Livingstone's large manuscript
map (cat. no. 1.2), Kirk's sketch
map records his and Livingstone's
exploration on foot of the River
Shire and Lake Shirwa (now
Chilwa) in April 1859.

Top
'Mongazi Village'
By John Kirk, April 1859
Watercolour over pencil on paper
7.2 x 12 cm
BY PERMISSION OF THE TRUSTEES
OF THE NATIONAL LIBRARY OF
SCOTLAND (cat. no. 4.21)

Kirk's drawing shows village
dwellings seen on his exploration
of the River Shire and Lake
Shirwa (Chilwa) with Livingstone
in April 1859.

Above
'Dzomba from the East'
By John Kirk, April 1859
Watercolour over pencil on paper
7.2 x 12 cm
BY PERMISSION OF THE TRUSTEES
OF THE NATIONAL LIBRARY OF
SCOTLAND (cat. no. 4.20)

Dated 19 April by Kirk, the day
after he and Livingstone arrived
at the shore of Lake Shirwa
(Chilwa) on their exploration of
the Shire region, this watercolour
shows a distant view of Mount
Dzomba (now Zomba), which lay
to the north of their route.

Livingstone he was a Congregationalist, and like
Livingstone, he was drawn to the London Missionary
Society (LMS), whose projects he zealously extolled in his
Aberdeen church. His captivated congregation were,
however, incensed when the LMS asked him to go to South
Africa to reform their missions, at that time racked by
scandal. He arrived at the Cape in 1818 and at once entered
political and social controversy, which surrounded him for
the next quarter century as he crusaded on behalf of the
Khoikhoi ('Hottentots') whom the Boers had enslaved.[9]

Livingstone should be seen primarily as momentously a
self-improving Lowland Scot. It was commonplace at the
time to compare the militant Xhosa of the Eastern Cape
with Scottish Highlanders before Culloden – clans of
cattle keepers who stole cattle but had martial virtues –
and it is conventional now to attribute Livingstone's
respect and affinity for African chiefs and native healers
('witch doctors') to his grandfather's birth on the Gaelic-
speaking isle of Ulva. Livingstone boasted of his family's
Highland origins and was delighted that he was cheered
'as a man and a brother' when he visited the Duke of Argyll
in 1864.[10] But he had been equally pleased six years earlier
by acclaim from Lowland cotton workers. His reply to their
address reveals the kind of Scot he was: self-improving,
puritanical and dogged, with no yen to swagger about in
a plaid or kilt.

> In Africa I have had hard work. I don't know that
> anyone in Africa despises a man who works hard.
> Eminent geologists, mineralogists, men of science
> in every department, if they attain eminence, work
> hard and that both early and late. That is just what
> we did . . .[11]

Burns's phrase 'the man of independent mind', from his
great anthem *For A' That and A' That*, which Livingstone
remembered at Quelimane, defines a major part of the
self-help ethos. Smiles, indeed, quoted Burns approvingly
in his book, at the head of a chapter on 'Money – Its Uses
and Abuses':

> Not for to hide it in a hedge
>   Nor for a train attendant,
> But for the glorious privilege
>   Of being independent.

However, Smiles felt constrained to add that 'unhappily'
Burns's 'strain of song was higher than his practice: his
ideal better than his habit'.[12] This was grossly unfair, since
Burns had worked very hard, farming, reading and
writing, endeavouring to provide for his bairns. But he had
celebrated the joys of tavern life and had been an open

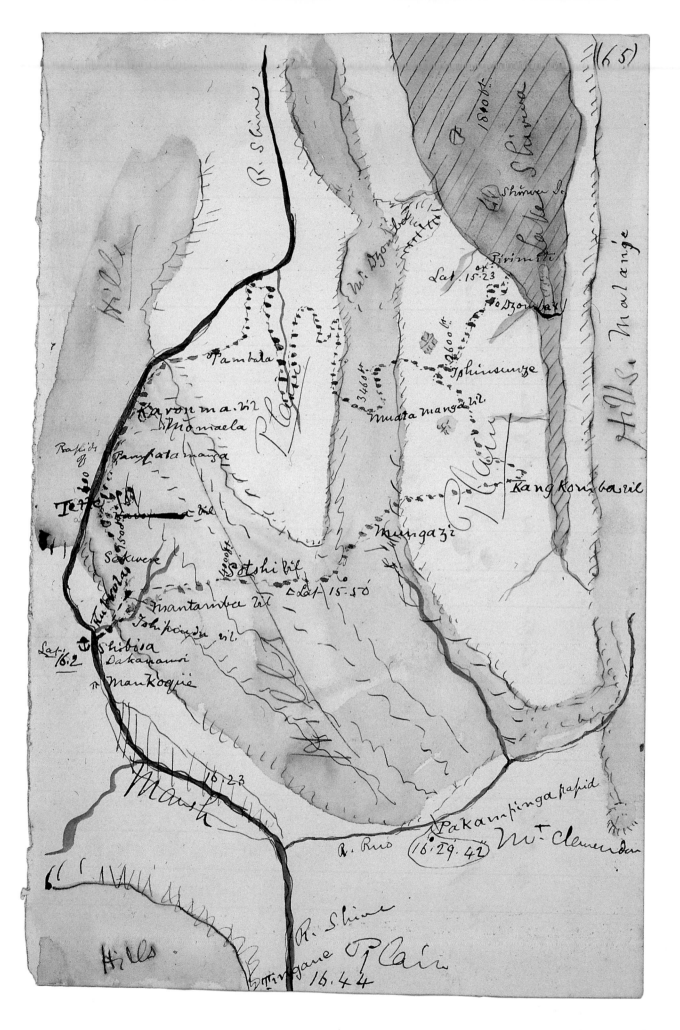

R. Shire

18.00 ft

Shirwa

Mt Dzomba

Shirwa I.

Pirimiti

Lat. 15.23

Hills Malanje

Dzomba

2600 ft

Tshinsunze

Pambala

3460 ft

Muata manga vil.

Plain

Kavouma. vil.

Momaela

Kangombavil

Pampatamanga

Rapids of

Tette

Mungazi

Plain

Sakwere

4100 ft

Sotshibil

Lat. 15.50

Tshikolas

Mantamba vil.

Tshikonde vil.

Lat. 16.2

Tshibisa

Dakanamoi

Mankoquie

Marsh

16.23

Pakampinga rapid

R. Ruo

16.29.42

Mt Clarendon

Hills

R. Shire

Tingane Plain

16.44

87

womaniser. Such 'habits' did not conform to the ethos. Livingstone, by contrast, seemed a perfect model of Smilesian self-help. To understand why, it is worth considering Smiles himself and some of his Scottish heroes.

According to a standard misreading Smiles was a zesty, blatant exponent of the idea that one should work hard, rise in life and make money. This falsification of his views, still prevalent today, was a source of some disappointment to the author. As a writer his speciality was biography, and he believed that the lives of worthy men would show others the true path, which was certainly not that of Mammon. In the 1870s he published three biographies. One, which he agreed to write only under pressure and with great reluctance, was of George Moore, a very successful warehouseman. In his autobiography Smiles mused:

> With this exception, I have always selected my own subjects. It has been said that I wrote the lives only of successful men. This is, of course, a mistake. Robert Dick was not a successful man, for he died not worth a farthing. Thomas Edward was not a successful man, for he rarely made ten shillings a week by his cobbling.[13]

Dick (1811–1866), a Thurso baker, was fascinated by local fossils and became an indefatigable and quite significant geologist. He attracted the approving attention of the great Murchison himself but failed in his trade. As Smiles put it:

> He was content to be poor, so long as he was independent, and free to indulge his profound yearnings after more knowledge. Though he attended carefully to his business . . . he was ruined by competition.[14]

Smiles's lives of Moore and Dick appeared almost simultaneously in 1878. As Smiles ruefully noted, that of Moore went through many editions but the one edition of Dick's did not even sell out.[15]

The Life of a Scottish Naturalist: Thomas Edward (1876) fared better – a second edition was called for. Edward, from Banff, born in 1814, was a cobbler who studied 'beasties', as he called them, 'simply that I might learn all I could concerning the beautiful and wonderful works of God'. He was honoured in the naming of two tiny marine creatures, which he had found in the Moray Firth: *Conchia Edwardii* and *Anceus Edwardii*. Despite his low income he brought up eleven children 'respectably and virtuously'. He was highly regarded by Charles Darwin, who backed

his successful claim to a Civil List pension, and was elected to several learned societies.[16] The story is inspiring even now.

The great Hugh Miller was a model for such men and personally encouraged Dick. The son of a Cromarty seaman, Miller (1802–1856) developed a passion for geology while exploring his local beaches and rocks, and worked as a stonemason after he left school. He began to publish bad verse but good prose, and his fiery pen was put to use when controversy erupted in the 1830s over patronage in the Church of Scotland. A law passed at Westminster in 1712 permitted landlords to appoint ministers disliked by their parishioners. Leaders of opposition to such unPresbyterian goings on summoned Miller to Edinburgh, and he was put to work editing *The Witness*. A successful twice-weekly newspaper, it was a powerful influence contributing to the Disruption of 1843 when Thomas Chalmers led 400-or-so ministers and elders out of the annual General Assembly of the Established Church to set up a new Free Church. Afterwards, with spreading fame as a geologist, Miller became Edinburgh's leading literary and scientific light. Smiles acknowledged his achievement in *Self-Help*. Formed by his labours as a stonemason, Miller 'simply kept his eyes and his mind open; was sober, diligent and persevering; and this was the secret of his intellectual growth'.[17] Unfortunately this great exemplar of self-help had blown his brains out on Christmas Eve not long before Smiles's tract was published . . .[18]

Granted that Miller wasn't ideal, how would Thomas Carlyle, son of a stonemason, serve as an example in Smiles's catalogue? Smiles praised him for reconstructing the manuscript of his history of the French Revolution after his maid had used it to light the fire – 'an instance of determination of purpose which has seldom been surpassed'.[19] But Carlyle, brilliant, sneering, hectoring (and virulently racist), was a controversial polemicist, about whom industrious folk might have doubts.

Livingstone, however, was to prove a completely edifying hero, not least because he persevered after the failure of his great Zambezi expedition and ended his days without European companions, chasing a geographical chimera through foul country and dangerous beasts despite his piles and fevers. He was Will personified.

When Thomas Edward addressed the boys of a school near Liverpool (in about 1880) he exemplified and extolled a virtue central to self-help: 'the will, the will to do and to win . . . Whenever I wished to do anything, I did it . . .

The day never dawned, nor the night lowered, however stormy, that kept me back.' One wonders if his admirer Smiles had ghosted the script for this man who spoke in the 'broadest of Aberdeen Scotch'.[20]

Though Livingstone's tongue was also thick – 'it seemed almost foreign', one English friend wrote – no one would have been allowed to ghost for him.[21] Men who worked, or tried to work, with him criticised Livingstone for many things, but never for lack of will. How could they, when he drove a small ship over 2,500 miles of ocean, from Africa to Bombay, in forty-five days, with no engineer, a crew of only twelve – of whom nine were Africans, even more inexperienced than he was – and only fourteen tons of coal for when the wind failed? Even when Kirk was bitter about Livingstone's apparent lack of 'kindly feelings', he wrote privately that he still respected the man's 'energy and force of mind'.[22]

Livingstone's love of 'independence' was extreme. Unlike Philip's, it led him away from confrontation with 'bad' men of his own colour towards a lonely martyr-like end. He raged, privately, with extraordinary arrogance, against his colleagues on the Zambezi expedition, writing of himself in the third person:

> The whole of the exploration would have been more easily accomplished by the commander alone than when burdened by the baggage of his European underlings, and the unflinching energy with which he surmounted every obstacle and rendered the expedition so far successful would have received the approbation of his countrymen had he been alone.[23]

A colleague at Kuruman, the Reverend Walter Inglis, while noting Livingstone's 'dry Scotch humour', remembered that 'His face wore at all times the strongly marked lines of potent will.' A religious journalist who saw him address a public meeting said that this face was 'typically that of a countryman from the North', meaning Scotland.[24] And indeed, in Lowland Scotland there were ingrained traditions of dour stubbornness and wilful self-sacrifice. Livingstone by his own account resisted his father's efforts to make him read about the grim and gentry-hating lives of the seventeenth-century Covenanters who had resisted unto death by martyrdom the attempts of Charles II and James VII to destroy their Presbyterian faith. But in habits, if not in theology, Livingstone represented the Covenanting tradition.

Livingstone was brought up in the tradition of 'Independent' Puritanism. The 'Old Scots Independents',

David Livingstone
By Maull & Polyblank, 1857
Albumen print
19.8 x 14.7 cm (arched top)
NATIONAL PORTRAIT GALLERY
LONDON
(cat. no. 3.16)

Livingstone mentions that he sat for the photographers Maull & Polyblank in a letter to his publisher John Murray, dated 18 November 1857.

89

Overleaf
Thomas Guthrie (1803–1873)
By James Edgar, 1862
Oil on millboard, 54.7 x 45.7 cm
SCOTTISH NATIONAL PORTRAIT
GALLERY
(cat. no. 3.5)

The urban poor of Britain were sometimes thought to be in as much need of 'a civilising mission' as the peoples of Africa, Asia and North America. Here the Reverend Thomas Guthrie – Scottish preacher, philanthropist and the 'apostle' of the ragged school movement – administers to city children.

members of a little sect founded in 1768, were the originators of the Scottish Congregationalist tradition that Livingstone's father joined when he broke from the Established Kirk to attend a chapel in Hamilton. David Dale, the philanthropic Congregationalist who opened the New Lanark mills (made so famous by his son-in-law Robert Owen) was a prominent neighbour, just a few miles away, of the Blantyre Livingstones, and George Shepperson is surely right to argue that this may have been 'more than a coincidence' in the formation of Livingstone's social conscience.[25]

But the sect was galvanised and made prominent by the revivalism of Robert and James Haldane, of a prominent Perthshire lairdly family. While the Haldanes were moved by the French Revolution to reassert the democratic principles of Independency, once the creed of Cromwell's troopers, they coupled this with the evangelical and missionary spirit of the potent new anti-slavery movement, led by William Wilberforce. Though laymen, their preaching during a tour of the North of Scotland inspired a Society for Propagating the Gospel at Home, founded in 1797. Robert sold his estate to fund the Society and within a year this had germinated a Congregationalist body, with James as its pastor, and a Tabernacle in Leith Walk, Edinburgh.

90

The basic Congregational principle was defined as complete self-government by church members. By 1807 there were eighty-five more churches practising it. But the principle guaranteed splits, and when the Haldanes adopted Baptist views there was a rupture that left the fifty-five churches that had formed the Congregational Union in 1812 'independent' of the brothers, but stripped of funds. The Union persevered and grew.

This was the contumacious but relatively liberal minded and ecumenically inclined body to which Livingstone's father, Neil Livingstone, turned. Its strong connections with the LMS made it natural for David to seek employment from that Society. The Hamilton Congregational Church, which Livingstone attended, had been founded by James Haldane in 1807. Its meeting house was known locally as the 'Wee Kirk', being very small. However, its members, we are told, 'invariably' gave more than much larger congregations to collections for LMS missions abroad.[26]

The Independent tradition was such that Livingstone cannot be described as heretical, though he eventually became so thoroughly ecumenical and so little concerned with formal group worship that he might be said to have

moved away even from Protestantism itself. (Privately he suspected that his notion that the monastery of medieval Catholicism, in its original purity, was superior to the LMS mission would appal his 'stiff' Hamilton brethren.) On his return to Scotland as hero, in 1858, he stood before the members of the Hamilton Congregational Chapel – now a much larger building, erected in 1841 – and called for the 'sinking of sectarian differences in the proclamation of the same gospel which all the churches share'. Referring to the 1843 Disruption he said, 'I believe that every Scotch Christian abroad rejoiced in his heart when he saw the Free Church come out boldly on principle . . . I am sure that I look on all the different denominations in Hamilton and in Britain with feelings of affection. I cannot say which I love most. I am quite certain I ought not to dislike any of them.'[27]

In one of his last letters, written in 1872, Livingstone wrote:

> The religion of Christ is unquestionably the best for man. I refer to it not as the Protestant, the Catholic, the Greek or any other, but to the comprehensive faith which has spread more widely over the world than most people imagine, and whose votaries of whatever name are better than any outside the pale . . .[28]

He was not ready to slip into the liberal twentieth-century habit of seeing equal good in all faiths. Though he noted in 1863 that in Africa 'The belief in one Supreme Being who made and upholds all things is universal,' he was not reverting to eighteenth-century Deism either. He added that what Africans lacked was a 'correct notion of the controul [sic] he exercises over the affairs of the world'.[29] He retained a strong sense of God's Providence, though he was not inclined to use the term. God intervened in the world, and he could personally act for God. He was driven like a Puritan, but a non-Calvinist 'independent' one.

We must not fall into the error of seeing Livingstone as 'really', or merely, an imperialist seeking economic opportunity under the hypocritical mask of missionary evangelism. Gary Clendennen pertinently notes that 'One can easily detect the "hidden hand" of Adam Smith and the Scottish Enlightenment in . . . Livingstone's economic philosophy.'[30] The political economist Smith, author of *The Wealth of Nations* (1776), had objected to slavery. It was not only inhumane but also economically, as we would say today, counter-productive. Smith's vision, however, was coolly secular. His 'hidden hand' was at most the non-interventionist God of the Deists, the Divine Watchmaker who had made and wound up the world and

James Young (1811–1883)
Attributed to Sir John Watson
Gordon, 1850s
Oil on canvas 76.3 x 63.2 cm
PRIVATE COLLECTION
(cat. no. 2.3)

Livingstone first met the chemist
and industrialist James Young
while he was studying at the
Andersonian University, Glasgow,
from 1836 to 1838. The two
became lifelong friends. Young,
who made a fortune from the
distillation of paraffin, acted as
one of Livingstone's trustees,
administering the financial affairs
of his family while he was on the
Zambezi expedition and giving
him support from his own pocket
after 1857.

would now let it run its own way, which was the way of economic self-interest. Legitimate 'free' trade, Smithites argued, would quickly drive out the slave trade. And Livingstone did argue this. But he attached to this idea the notion of godly communities of missionaries and settlers led to Africa by him. God desired such colonies in order that people freed from dependence on Portuguese or Arab slave traders could be connected, as producers, with the world market.

Livingstone's obsessive quest for cotton, or at least the potential for cotton production, in the highlands of Central Africa, should not be seen as crudely 'imperialist'. Free trade did not imply unfair dominance, but the opposite – mutual benefit. The cotton manufacturers of Lancashire to whose interests he appealed had been led politically by 'free traders' – Richard Cobden and John Bright – who were vehement opponents of empire. After the Indian Mutiny, Cobden expressed to Bright his horror at the supposed atrocities of the sepoys but blamed them on the absurdity of British rule in India – 'based upon the assumption that the natives will be the willing instruments of their own humiliation' – and deplored the unjustified contempt of 'niggers' shown by servants of the Raj.[31] Even though these men lost to Palmerstonian Whiggery in the General Election of 1857, there was still no appetite for empire in the British parliament. Garrisons overseas were seen as a waste of money. The heyday of territorial imperialism had not dawned at the time of Livingstone's death in 1873 and the 'Scramble for Africa' had not yet begun. Livingstone's own logic was simply that cotton was the great commodity of world trade – comparable to oil today – and that demand for it would assist the great cause he shared with the Haldane brothers, with Philip, and with the Congregationalists of Hamilton: the ending of slavery.

In the first edition of *Self-Help* Smiles merely praised Livingstone briefly among other low-born missionaries. In later editions he gave him pages. Beside the hard work in Blantyre, the devoted reading and botanising, the manual work at the mission stations, Smiles extolled Livingstone's attitude to money. He needed a new steamship for African work at a cost of £2,000. 'This sum', Smiles noted, 'he proposed to defray out of the means which he had set aside for his children arising from the profits of his books of travels. "The children must make it up themselves," was in effect his expression . . .'[32] Livingstone was happy that his old friend James 'Paraffin' Young, who was the first oil mogul (through his exploitation of the West Lothian shale seams), should profit from his own observation of the potential of the coalfields of the Zambezi region in the dawning era of steam navigation. But, to quote Clendennen again:

> [his] analysis of Africa's economic potential contained precious few provisions for his own personal gain . . . As far as he was concerned, the economic development of Africa should benefit all Africans . . . as well as whomever among the Scottish poor migrated thither to work for the common cause.[33]

God had made him His instrument. If his book *Missionary Travels* attracted attention to the author, it also drew interest towards Africa, and Livingstone could use his reputation as 'explorer' and scientist (he was appointed Fellow of the Royal Society in 1857) to further humanitarian aims far more extensive than David Dale's.

Though passionate interest in science was far from being a Scottish monopoly, the Scottish universities had put Scotland in the forefront of scientific enquiry and it excited interest at most levels of society. Another misconception about Livingstone, which must be dispelled, is that he had to struggle to reconcile science with belief in God. On the contrary: in his day, to study the natural world was to affirm and consolidate faith in Him. Those Scots who led the movement to set up mechanics institutes and philosophical societies throughout Britain believed that natural science 'elevated the mind, and quickened the sense of wonder at the Creator's work'.[34] Livingstone was a Christian. He was also a genuine scientist, as his day understood the term. There was no contradiction.

It is true that Livingstone's insatiable observations of geology, fauna and flora were sometimes vitiated by his obsession with his programme for helping God to save Africa. He was particularly interested in the tsetse fly and the way it barred the use of animals it attacked in certain parts of Africa, but he completely failed – refused – to grasp the similar role of mosquitoes bearing the malaria that could decimate the missionaries and settlers he wished to bring. This does not make him any less of a scientist than do errors deriving from prejudice in the work of such men as Murchison. (Indeed, in our own day political programmes and ethical considerations manifestly affect the work even of the most brilliant scientists.) When Murchison praised Livingstone above all for the 'astronomical observation' by which he had 'determined the longitude as well as the latitude of so many sites' he was not, as some have supposed, condescending to him as mere surveyor. He was associating him with Newton's astronomy and with the most prestigious and godly of sciences: physics.[35]

93

Before Livingstone's death, Darwin's *Origin of Species* (1859), together with the professionalisation of science and its withdrawal into laboratories, was beginning to rupture the perfect union established between religion and the observation of nature. But Tennyson, who in famous passages of *In Memoriam* (1850) foreboded a rupture between science and faith was, like most very good poets, ahead of his time. And poets a generation earlier had not foreseen the divorce between science and poetry itself, considered axiomatic after Darwin. When Livingstone was growing up scientific knowledge, religious truth and poetic appreciation of nature marched together.

Reading his accounts of what he saw in Africa one is constantly struck by Livingstone's alternation, from paragraph to paragraph, of precise observation with aesthetic rapture. His accounts of his early life explain this if we reread them with the understanding that science, religion and poetry were not then at odds. Thus he praises his father for providing at home 'a continuously consistent pious example such as that the ideal of which is so beautifully and truthfully portrayed in Burns's "Cottar's Saturday Night"'. Although his father wanted him to read stiff religious works, Livingstone preferred books about science and travel. Though the Congregationalist church deacon did beat his son for this preference, there is no reason to suppose that he opposed David's discovery, through 'the works of Dr Thomas Dick, "The Philosophy of Religion" and "The Philosophy of the Future State" that my own ideas that science and religion are not hostile but friendly to each other [were] fully proved and enforced'.[36]

A brilliant young Dundonian of today, W. N. Herbert, has fun at the expense of a fellow townsman in his verse sequence 'The Testament of the Reverend Thomas Dick':

> No irony could touch the telescopic length
> of your desire to explicate space.
> You sent theoretic steam engines to the stars
> at twenty miles per hour, taking nearly
> four thousand years to make your point and reach
>   Uranus. You
> were our McGonagall of science, who inspired David
>   Livingstone to
> plunge through Africa's dark galaxy
> spreading news of your Future State:
> a Heaven of astronomers . . . [37]

Herbert grasps at, yet misses the point. Yes, astronomy was the heavenly science. But for post-Newtonian, pre-Darwinian thinkers, the observations of physicists did actually display God.

Herbarium specimen of
Barringtonia racemosa (L.)
Spreng., collected by John
Kirk, October 1862
ROYAL BOTANIC GARDENS, KEW
(cat. no. 4.92)

Kirk's specimen of the *Barringtonia* has been preserved with his original field drawings.

Four botanical drawings of
Barringtonia racemosa
(L.) Spreng.
By John Kirk
May 1859–March 1860
Pencil, watercolour and ink on paper, each 18.1 x 12.4 cm (maximum)
ROYAL BOTANIC GARDENS, KEW
(cat. no. 4.24)

A number of Kirk's field drawings of botanical specimens, often accompanied by the specimen itself, are preserved in the Herbarium at the Royal Botanic Gardens, Kew. Here he has drawn the stem and fruit of the *Barringtonia*. He recorded further details of the plant, which he had found growing around the mouth of the Zambezi, in his journal of 3 August 1859. 'It has the habit of the mangrove', he writes, 'where the tide leaves the roots. They consist of a series of pillars supporting the stem in the mud.'

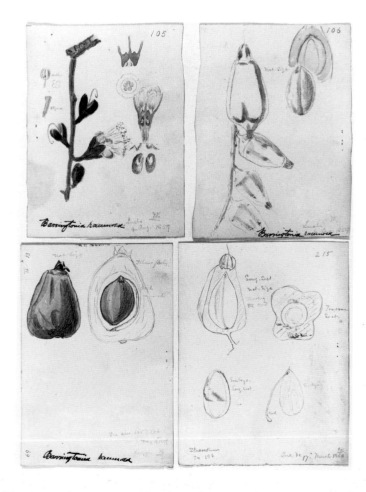

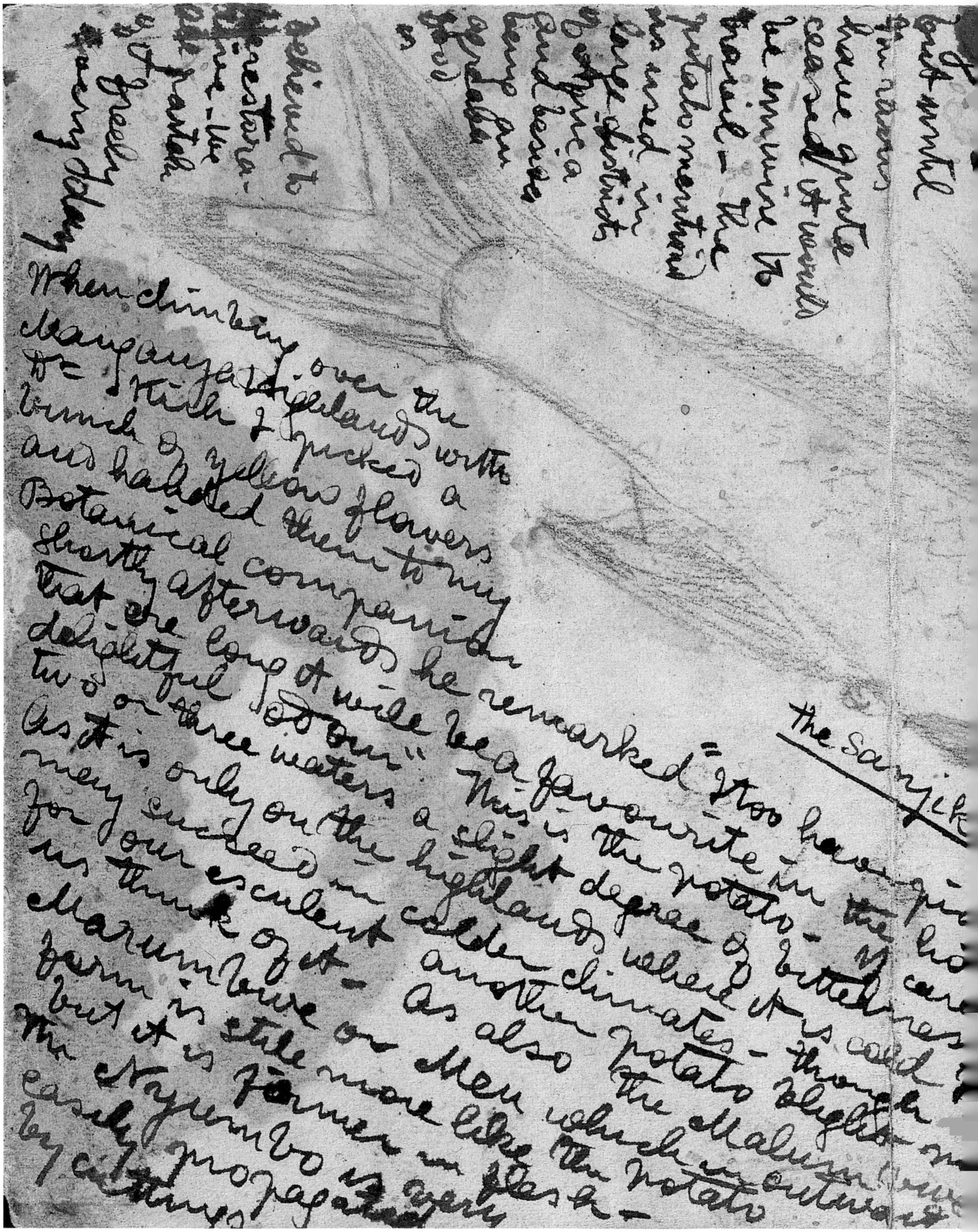

96

...but until ...an ...have quite ceased it would be immune to travel — the (potato mentioned) is used in large districts of Africa and besides ...

... believed to ... restore ... ... partial ... ... greatly ...

the Sanjik

... too having in the ... ... favourite in the ... ... the potato ... bitterness ... ... degree of ... cold ... ... highlands where it is ... ... another climates — though the Malvin ... ... colder another potato slightly ... ... also the the Malvin wint... ... when which the potato ... ... still more likes the ... ...

When climbing over the mangau... island with Stück & picked a bunch of yellow flowers and handed them to my Botanical companion. Shortly afterwards he remarked that one would be a long while ... delightful ... two or three waters ... as it is only on the ... may succeed in ... for our think of it — Marum live or ... form is still more ... but it is former ... the Nayumbo it very easily propagated by cuttings ...

Manuscript sheet with a sketch of a fish from Lake Nyasa (now Lake Malawi)
By David Livingstone
c. 1868–1870
Pencil and ink on paper
19.2 x 27.5 cm
PRIVATE COLLECTION
(cat. no. 4.62)

97

Livingstone first visited Lake Nyasa on 17 September 1859, claiming its discovery. It is likely, however, that this drawing of a fish specimen, inscribed by him 'Sanjika', dates from his last journeys when he skirted the southern edge of the lake on his way to Lake Tanganyika.

**Medicine chest used by
Livingstone on his last
journeys**
1860s
Leather case with glass bottles
containing drugs and medical
implements
12 x 17.5 x 32 cm
COURTESY OF THE TRUSTEES OF
THE SCIENCE MUSEUM
(cat. no. 5.53)

The drugs include concentrated
liquid ammonia, used in treating
snake bites. Some bottles in the
chest bear the label of 'Treacher
of Bombay and Poona', suggesting
that Livingstone may have
obtained them when he sailed to
India in 1864 after the collapse of
the Zambezi expedition.

**Letter from David
Livingstone to Sir Richard
Owen, 29 December 1860**
Manuscript letter, 21.3 x 36.5 cm
BY PERMISSION OF THE TRUSTEES
OF THE NATURAL HISTORY MUSEUM
(cat. no. 3.21)

Writing from the Zambezi to his
friend and teacher Sir Richard
Owen, Livingstone speculates on
Darwin's theory of natural
selection. He admits that he only
knows Darwin's *Origin of Species*
from reviews – 'the book itself has
not yet come this length' – but
asserts that 'there does not seem to
be any great struggle for existence
going on in this wide continent'.
Owen was the most fervent scientific
opponent of Darwin's ideas.

Livingstone wrote about the 'intense love of nature'
awakened and gratified in his youth by scouring the
countryside for 'herbal simples'. He became a scientist
with two aims. As a doctor he would try to cure those
diseases that God had his own reasons for inflicting. He
would never see any contradiction between tsetse fly and
leprosy on the one hand and the idea of a Benevolent
Creator on the other. 'Herbal simples', also sent by God,
could cure diseases – the 'wise women' who practised in
the Scottish countryside (like 'witch doctors' in Africa)
could have assured Livingstone of this. Secondly, by
observing the natural world he would obtain better
understanding and love of his Creator, and bring these,
through publication, to other people.

In his youth he came upon a limestone quarry where,
like Hugh Miller, he was rapt. 'It is impossible to describe
the delight and wonder with which I began to collect the
shells of the carboniferous limestone which crops out in
High Blantyre and Cambuslang.' Geology could be seen
as the Scottish science *par excellence*. Though the claim
that James Hutton of Edinburgh (1726–1797) was the
founder of modern geological science is inflated, it is
true that his *Theory of the Earth* (1795) was immensely
influential. This Newtonian 'paean to the beneficent
intentions of the Creator', as it has been described,
'elevated geology, among believers, to a prestige second
only to that of physics.' Just as Newton had shown that
the mathematical integrity of the solar system and stars
proved the existence of a powerful creating mind, so
Hutton presented geological phenomena as evidence that
such a balanced and purposeful earth must be the result
of intelligent design.[38]

The notion of Livingstone as mere traveller upon the face
of God's earth – not a real scientist, only a 'field worker'–
is diametrically opposite to the thinking of the early and
middle nineteenth century. He was, if you like, Thomas
Edward in motion. Susan Faye Cannon argues that the
great model for advanced scientists was Alexander
Humboldt (1769–1859), the German who went about with
a large collection of scientific instruments attempting to
cope with 'everything from the revolutions of the satellites
of Jupiter to the carelessness of clumsy donkeys'. Such a
scientist would discover endless miracles of perfect natural
adaptation. Only a very intelligent, and essentially kind,
Creator could be the 'great organiser' of such an amazing
system of interrelations. The effect of Darwin's book
and its reception was to destroy such confidence, since it
seemed to show that natural selection was 'not intelligent,
not good, and not even necessarily progressive'.[39]

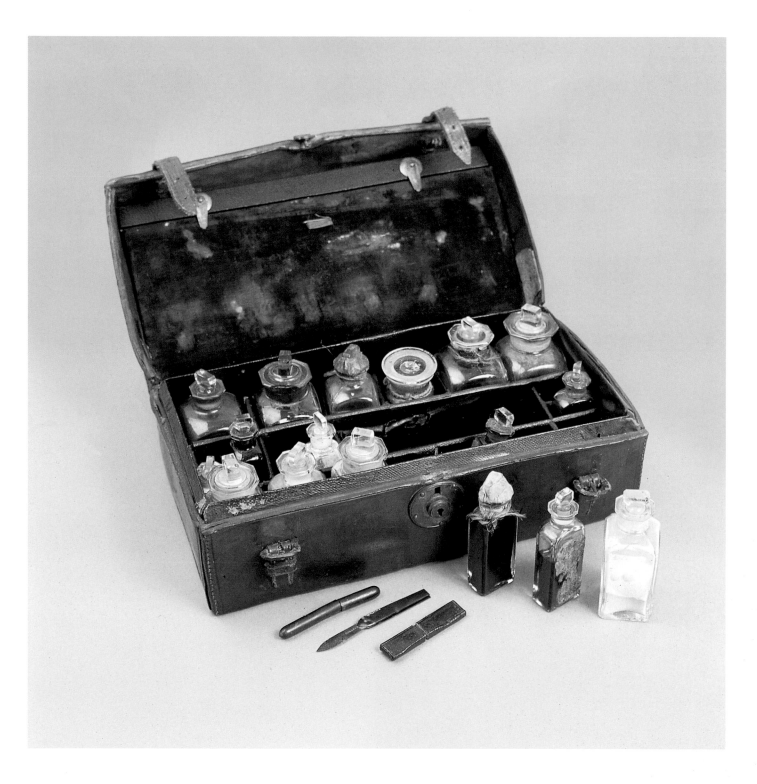

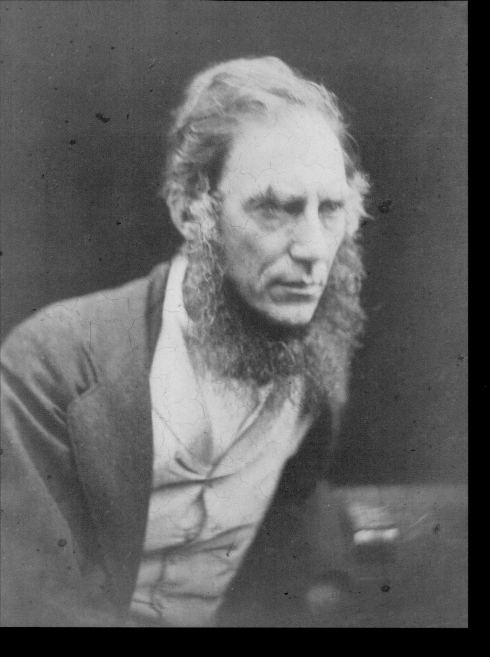

Sir Joseph Dalton Hooker (1817–1911)
By Julia Margaret Cameron
c. 1868
Albumen print, 31.8 x 25.4 cm
THE ROYAL PHOTOGRAPHIC
SOCIETY, BATH
(cat. no. 3.15)

Joseph Dalton Hooker was
assistant to his father, Sir William
Jackson Hooker, at the Royal
Botanic Gardens, Kew, from 1855
to 1865 when he succeeded him as
Director. Like his father he was an
important source of information
on botanical matters for
Livingstone and advised him on
the selection of John Kirk as
Economic Botanist to the Zambezi
expedition. Both Livingstone and
Kirk directed consignments of
natural history specimens from
the Zambezi to Kew via the
younger Hooker.

Letter from David Livingstone to Sir Joseph Dalton Hooker, 28 July 1857
Manuscript letter, 17.9 x 22.2 cm
ROYAL BOTANIC GARDENS, KEW
(cat. no. 3.20)

In his letter Livingstone describes,
and crudely illustrates, a type of
plant that he had observed floating
on the River Shire. The circle on
the drawing, he explains, indicates
'a nut which Sebituane the chief
liked so much he made it a part of
the tribute from the tribes he
subjected'. He goes on to say that
he, too, had enjoyed eating it and
inquires as to the identity of
the plant.

during the explorer's stay in Britain (1856–1858) and while he was conducting the Zambezi expedition. This marble bust by the Pre-Raphaelite sculptor Thomas Woolner was commissioned in April 1859 by Hooker's son. The nose was damaged when it was being positioned at the Royal Academy exhibition in 1860.

Letter from David Livingstone to Sir William Jackson Hooker, 5 February 1857

Manuscript letter, 17.9 x 22.2 cm
ROYAL BOTANIC GARDENS, KEW
(cat. no. 3.19)

In this letter, written two months after his return to Britain from his first period of exploration, Livingstone reports that he is preparing some seed specimens to send on to the botanist.

Spirally curved elephant's tusk, presented by Livingstone to Sir Richard Owen
Approximately 87 x 18.2 cm
THE DAVID LIVINGSTONE CENTRE
(cat. no. 2.59)

This abnormally formed tusk is said to have been collected by Livingstone on his coast-to-coast journey of 1853 to 1856 and given to Sir Richard Owen as a natural curiosity.

Sir Richard Owen (1804–1892)
By Maull & Polyblank, 1856
Albumen print
19.8 x 14.6 cm (arched top)
NATIONAL PORTRAIT GALLERY
LONDON
(cat. no. 3.17)

One of the leading naturalists of his period, and a dominant figure in the Victorian scientific establishment, Owen taught Livingstone in 1840. The two remained on friendly terms, Livingstone sending Owen natural history specimens from Africa and corresponding with him about his observations on African wildlife.

Livingstone's passion for detail in nature was such that he could write off the cuff to a correspondent who unexpectedly wanted his help in collecting examples of parasites:

> I never observed any parasitical insects on the elephant or rhinoceros, except a kind of worm between the eyeball and lid in the latter. I have observed the different kinds of intestinal worms in the bowels of the rhinoceros and zebra . . . On the wild pig a small kind of flea abounds.[40]

He took a friendly interest in Darwin.[41] But the man who had first described the Victoria Falls had been formed in an epoch when there seemed to be no conflict between aesthetic delight, religious awe and scientific discovery. In his account of his approach to the Falls he is in raptures over the beauty of the Zambezi:

> The whole scene was extremely beautiful; the banks and islands dotted over the river are adorned with sylvan vegetation of great variety of colour and form. At the period of our visit, several trees were spangled over with blossoms . . . The silvery mohonono, which in the tropics is in form like the cedar of Lebanon, stands in pleasing contrast with the dark colour of the motsouri . . . Some trees resemble the great spreading oak, others assume the character of our own elms and chestnuts; but no one can imagine the beauty of the view from anything witnessed in England . . . scenes so lovely must have been gazed upon by angels in their flight.

But when he reaches the Falls themselves his description becomes as matter of fact as possible:

> As [the mass of water] broke into (if I may use the term) pieces of water all rushing on in the same direction, each gave off several rays of foam, exactly as bits of steel, when burnt in oxygen gas, give off rays of sparks . . . Of the five columns, two on the right and one on the left of the island were the largest, and the streams which formed them seemed each to exceed in size the falls of the Clyde at Stonebyres, when that river is in flood.[42]

'England' is positioned in relation to the Falls aesthetically: Scotland is the homeland where Livingstone learnt to think in terms of mensuration, 'scientifically'. But he is also the countryman of Walter Scott, whose techniques of description he imitates (they derive from conventions of the 'picturesque' in landscape gardening and landscape painting). And one is reminded also of Scott's twentieth-century successor as the dominant figure in Scottish arts and letters, C. M. Grieve (Hugh MacDiarmid), a Marxist

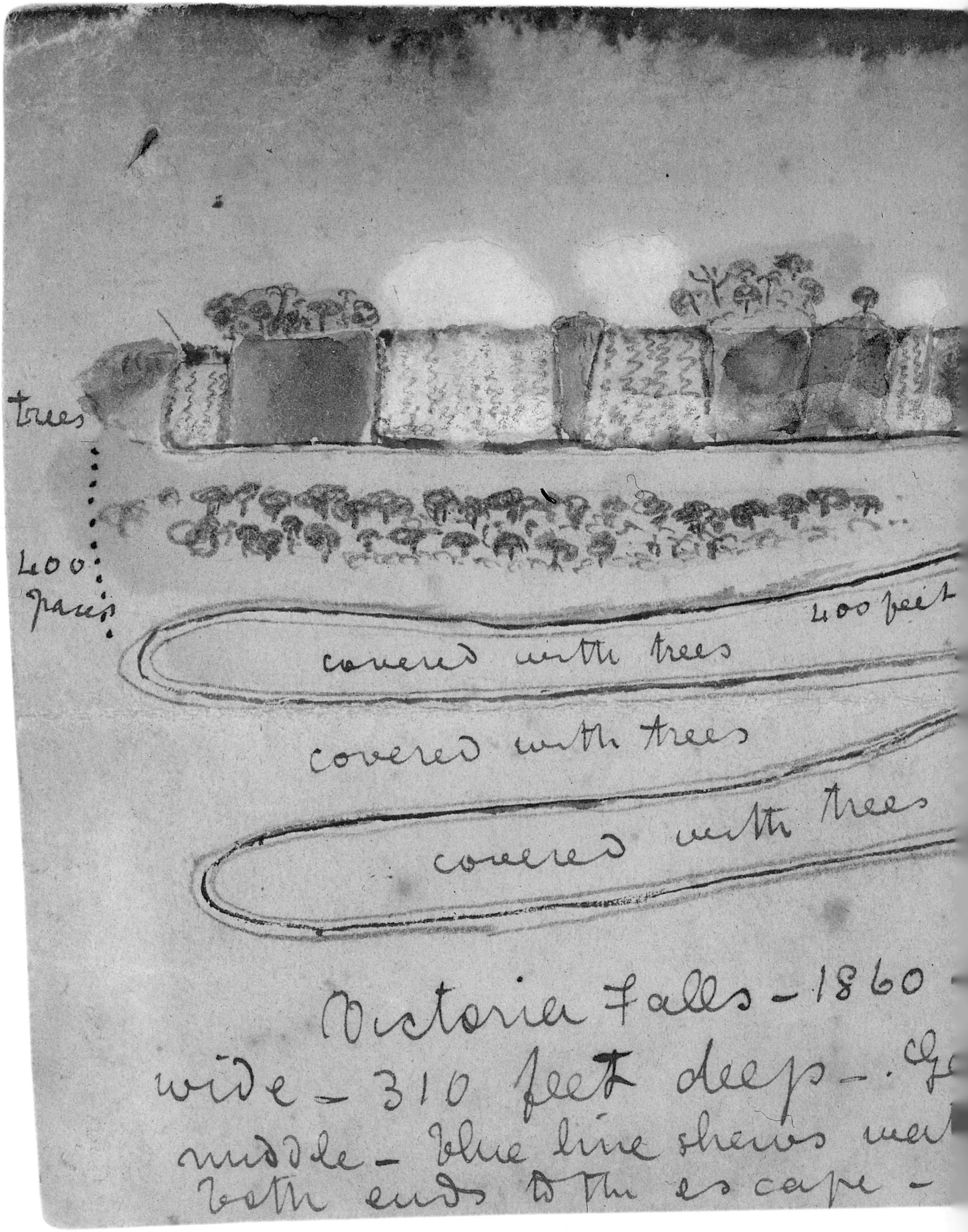

trees

400
paces

400 feet

covered with trees

covered with trees

covered with trees

Victoria Falls – 1860
wide – 310 feet deep – the
middle – blue line shews wen
both ends to the escape –

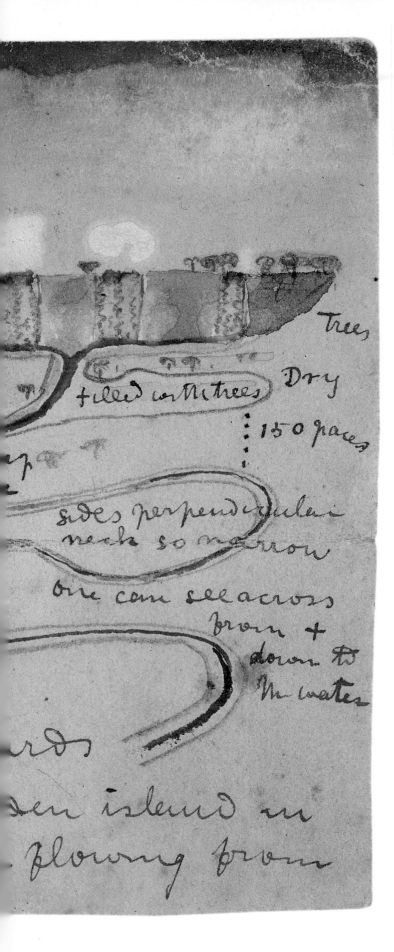

Trees

filled with trees) Dry

⋮ 150 paces

sides perpendicular
neck so narrow

one can see across
from +
down to
the water

rds

en island in

flowing from

and materialist who attempted in his later verse to put poetry and science together again after their rupture in the late nineteenth century.

In his combination of inspiration and matter-of-factness Livingstone prefigures characteristics of twentieth-century Scottish intellectual life. This is not surprising, for he was formed in, and extended, Scottish intellectual and social traditions. The image of steel burning in oxygen would have appealed to MacDiarmid.

Sketch of the Victoria Falls
By David Livingstone
(?)August 1860
Watercolour over pencil, inscribed in ink, on card, 12.6 x 15.3 cm
ROYAL GEOGRAPHICAL SOCIETY
(cat. no. 2.20)

This sketch is thought to date from Livingstone's second visit to the Victoria Falls in August 1860. He had first seen them in November 1855. Its purpose is almost entirely one of recording, giving details of their width and height and the configuration of the massive gorges cut by the River Zambezi.

Overleaf
Herd of buffalo opposite Garden Island, Victoria Falls
(detail)
By Thomas Baines, *c.* 1862–1865
Oil on canvas, 46 x 65.7 cm
ROYAL GEOGRAPHICAL SOCIETY
(cat. no. 2.1)

This self-consciously artistic depiction of the Falls is by Thomas Baines, artist-storekeeper on Livingstone's Zambezi expedition. Baines' views of the Victoria Falls, the first ever to be painted, were worked up from drawings done in 1862, after his dismissal from Livingstone's party, when he travelled in the company of James Chapman across South West Africa to the Zambezi. They formed the basis of a lavish folio edition of lithographs, *The Victoria Falls, Zambesi River*, published in 1865.

4.81
Fly whisk used by Livingstone on
the Zambezi expedition
Shredded plant fibre, 38 x 15
THE DAVID LIVINGSTONE CENTRE
(358)

Felix Driver

David Livingstone and the Culture of Exploration in Mid-Victorian Britain

The meeting of the British
Association for the
Advancement of Science,
Bath, September 1864
By an unknown photographer
1864
Albumen print, 10.8 x 7.2 cm
BATH ROYAL LITERARY AND
SCIENTIFIC INSTITUTION
(cat. no. 5.25)

Livingstone, wearing his familiar
peaked cap, stands on the mound to
the left of centre while his friend
and great supporter Sir Roderick
Murchison, the President of the
Royal Geographical Society, is
prominent in light-coloured coat,
trousers and hat. The photograph
records a key occasion in the
history of Victorian exploration of
Africa. Murchison had invited
Livingstone to attend the Bath
meeting of the British Association
for the Advancement of Science in
order to adjudicate at a dramatic
confrontation between Richard
Burton and John Hanning Speke
over the source of the Nile.
Famously, Speke died on the
eve of the debate.

David Livingstone and the Culture of Exploration in Mid-Victorian Britain

For two days before his funeral in Westminster Abbey on 18 April 1874 David Livingstone's remains lay in state at the offices of the Royal Geographical Society in Savile Row, surrounded by palms and lilies. It was from there that the coffin made its way to Westminster, borne into the Abbey by some of his closest associates, including Henry Morton Stanley, whose 'discovery' of Livingstone had so astonished the geographical establishment in 1872; John Kirk, recently appointed Consul-General at Zanzibar, who had been botanist and medical officer to Livingstone's Zambezi expedition; Horace Waller, the Anglican clergyman who was soon to edit Livingstone's *Last Journals*; and the hunter-travellers William Oswell and William Webb. In life Livingstone had been an unreliable and frequently disappointing hero; in death he had become a saint. Each of the pall-bearers on that day in April 1874 was staking a claim upon his memory; and though they came together to lay him to rest, each one had a distinct version of the Livingstone myth. The effort to memorialise him was subsequently to take many forms, celebrating Livingstone the missionary, the explorer and the pioneer of empire.

The purpose of this essay is to sketch a context in which to understand the promotion and reception within Britain of Livingstone's African travels. The Victorian struggle to keep the Livingstone myth alive was to prove remarkably successful. Yet it was a struggle that brought out the differences as well as the similarities between those who claimed to represent him. And just as Livingstone's followers disagreed over the best way to continue his work, so too historians have continued to argue right up to the present day over whether Livingstone was really a missionary, really an explorer or really an imperial pioneer. The enduring power of the Livingstone myth lies precisely in its simultaneous appeal to a number of different interest groups. If we are to understand what Livingstone's life and work meant to mid-Victorians, therefore, we have to consider the various contexts in which his African projects took shape. In what follows I outline a cultural and political map of the major networks that helped sustain Livingstone both in his life and after his death: the missionary and anti-slavery organisations; the scientific communities (principally the RGS); and the political institutions of government. But it is necessary first to ask a more fundamental question: why did African exploration attract so much public attention in mid Victorian Britain?

Fig. 2

A Map of African Literature
Illustration from *An African Sketch-Book* by William Winwood Reade
1873
ROYAL GEOGRAPHICAL SOCIETY

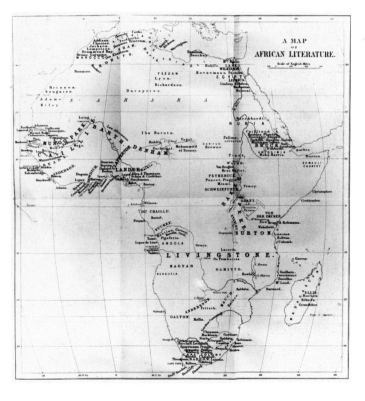

The Culture of Exploration

The idea of exploration captured the imagination of the reading public during the nineteenth century. They were consumed by tales of adventure in faraway places, they marvelled at the exploits of lone travellers like Mungo Park or David Livingstone in Africa, and they were enthralled by the tragic heroism of figures such as Sir John Franklin, who perished in his search for the North-West Passage. Even for – perhaps especially for – such a subversive writer as Joseph Conrad, such heroic efforts to extend the dominion of science over the globe embodied the militant idealism of British exploration. In an essay first published in 1924 he describes explorers as 'adventurous and devoted men . . . conquering a bit of truth here and a bit of truth there, and sometimes swallowed up by the mystery their hearts were so persistently set on unveiling'.[1] For Conrad, however, the romance of exploration led inexorably to disenchantment. Subsequent explorers were, he said, 'condemned to make [their] discoveries on beaten tracks';[2] or, worse, to find their romantic dreams shattered by mere opportunists and fortune hunters. Conrad's description of his own journey on the River Congo in 1890 provides an instance of this overwhelming sense of disenchantment: 'there was no shadowy friend to stand by my side in the night of enormous wilderness', he recalled, 'no great haunting memory, but only the unholy recollection of a prosaic newspaper "stunt" and the distasteful knowledge of the vilest scramble for loot that ever disfigured the history of human conscience and geographical exploration.'[3] In alluding to the celebrated encounter between Stanley and Livingstone in 1871, and the subsequent 'Scramble for Africa', Conrad was registering a profound sense of loss. For him, it seems, Livingstone was the last of the heroic explorers, and Stanley the first of a new breed: men of the modern world, hell-bent on worldly gain.

For most of the Victorian reading public, however, it was the romance rather than the disenchantment that held sway. Acres of print space – in books, tracts, periodicals and newspapers – were devoted to celebrating distant feats of exploration beyond the known horizon. The figure of the explorer seemed to draw together the most cherished national ideals in an age of supreme confidence about the virtues of the British: a fearless sense of adventure, selfless dedication, heroic valour and technological mastery. It was David Livingstone's sheer energy, the power of his will, that won him a place in Samuel Smiles's paean to the virtues of self-help, published in 1859. The image of Livingstone as a 'pathfinder', a maker of ways through the

Fig. 3
**Reception for Speke and
Grant at the Royal
Geographical Society,
22 June 1863**
From the *Illustrated London News,*
4 July 1863
ROYAL GEOGRAPHICAL SOCIETY

African Kit.

12	Blankets (Grey), & 2 pr scarlet do. from Grindlay [Wright & Co]	73
4	Bags, leather for shooting	do
1	Bits, set of, in box handle	do
1	Balance, spring, to 60 lbs.	do
2	Beds, iron by Brown & Co. Price - 28 lbs each	
2	Belts for revolvers.	Grindlay
2	Bridles, watering, for donkeys	do
4	Cards, playing, packs	do
2	Chairs, iron by Brown & Co.	each 12½
1	Digester for soup.	Grindlay 15
4	Eye preservers, glass & wire	do
24	Flannel shirts	do
12	do. trousers	do
1	Horseknife, large	do
4	Hats, wide awake & glazed.	do
12	Ink powder, black & red, packets	do
-	Indian rubber - & I.R. rings	do
6	Japanned tin trunks, weights 13, 14 & 17 lbs.	do
-	Knives table 8, do sailors 6 pen for skinning apr 24 do	
8	Leggings leather, short & long pairs.	do
2	Mugs pewter without glass...	
1	Medicine chest... Citric acid (30 lbs)	26
2	Mosquito netting	Grindlay 4
2	Pillows, hair	do 2
12	Pocket hkchfs	do
2	Penholders	do
6	Pencils, of sorts, doz., W. Newton &	do
1	Rule 2ft	do
2	Sheets, white serge.	do 2
12	Shoes, by Simnett, pairs	
6	Socks, brown, half woollen doz.	Grindlay
2	Stirrup leathers, pairs	do
4	Stools iron (Brown's) 2 do sketching W. Newton 2	each iron 8
7	Sauce pans or pots, nest of tin.	Grindlay 26
16	Spoons, table 8, do tea 8.	do
12	Sail needles, large & small.	do
2	Seed, mustard & cress. lbs.	do
2	Tents 7x7 & 7 high	do both 31
-	Tools, 2 hammers, 2 saws, pincers, chisels, files &c	do
8	Trousers, drill, unbleached.	do
2	Tea pots, oval, tin.	do
40	Tea, lbs. from Striker's.	
2	Umbrellas, gingham & carriage size & white covers.	Grindlay each 3
4	Waistcoats of scotch tweed	do
2	Veils, green	do
4	Water proof sheets, white, abt 10f sq	do 30
1	Phot. Inst. (stereoscopic) for Coll. groups & chem. for Blondel..	27/6

Total weight 1450 lbs

Instruments for Observing.

3	Sextants of 8½ inch radius J. & Simms.	[Wright & Scien Inst No 228]
2	Stands for do.	do
2	art. Horizons	do
1	Chron. (gold) Barraud & Lund	
1	do (silver) Parkinson & Frodsham	
1	Lever, silver B & L. x double detaching second hands	
1	do do (Dent) x common split second hand.	
1	do do (Jones)	
3	Prismatic compasses, card less x platinum rings J. & Simms	
2	Magnetic do (pocket) Elliot.	
1	Telescope, 1 Rain Gauge (traveller's) & 1 R.G. Livingstone's	
6	Boiling Therms. 1 max & 1 min. Therm. casella.	
1	Massey's Patent log.	10 lbs
2	Bulls eye lanterns x vessels to fit for Boiling therms. casella.	

Mapping and drawing instruments.

2	Reams mapping paper - Malby & Sons.
-	Tracing paper, blk & wh. for above, W. Newton.
1	Circular brass Protractor. Elliott, 1 parallel rule on rollers. Elliott
1	Case Math. instruments Elliot.
1	Pocket compass Elliot, 150ft measuring tape, drawing board
½	Ream open foolscap graduated in sqrs.
2	Paint boxes W. Newton - brushes.
4	Block sketch books.

Books.

1	Raper's Navigation - Lost on H.M.S. "Brisk".
1	Coleman's Lunar & Naut. tables.
4	Log books, 12 Field do & 5 Long do too (Galton's)
4	Naut. almanacks for 60, 1, 2, & 3.
-	Tables for meas. breadths of rivers (Galton)
-	Maps of africa - all the recent foreign & English.

Rifles - Arms and ammunition. - Revolvers.

2	Single rifles, Lancaster's Elliptical - 40 bore	
1	Single Blisset	4 do
1	do do	16 do
1	Double do	20 do
1	do smooth Blisset	12 do
1	do Rifle do	10!!
1	Six barrelled revolving rifle, Colt	
1	Whitworth sporting rifle	
1	double smooth by ——	12 do
2	Tranters revolvers	16 lbs
500	Rounds for each rifle barrel + belts	
50	carbines x pouches, sword bayonets Royal art. pat. 1860 each 13 lbs	
200	Rounds per carbine. caps in compl.	

Presents.

Sword belt x belt by Macabe for Zanz. Sultan & G. In. Jones... G Macabe

J. Grant

African landscape, has been an enduring one.[4] Horace Waller was later to describe him as a kind of human plough, a 'hard unflinching instrument, who had gone through lands and tribes and tough problems, and had cut furrows in a wilderness of human life which no one had heard of or dreamed of'.[5]

There was no more effective symbol of British missionary, scientific and imperial endeavour during the nineteenth century than the map of Africa. No meeting concerning Africa – whether to promote missionary activity, to debate the location of rivers or lakes, or to contemplate imperial schemes – was complete without a large map of the continent. It provided the backdrop for some of the most famous geographical gatherings at the British Association's annual meetings or at the Royal Geographical Society itself (see fig. 3). Popular exhibitions designed to celebrate British achievements in Africa were festooned with maps of all kinds, showing the progress of European knowledge of the continent and the extent of British influence. At the same time, paradoxically, the rhetoric of 'darkest Africa' – of Central Africa as a region of disease, superstition and timelessness – was becoming ever more firmly established in the popular mind. Indeed, it has been said by one historian that 'Africa grew "dark" as Victorian explorers, missionaries and scientists flooded it with light'.[6]

The names of British explorers and their sponsors were inscribed on these maps, marking the lakes, mountains and settlements they had located. Livingstone's baptism of the Victoria Falls, which he first saw in November 1855, is perhaps the most obvious example. Sir Roderick Murchison, the President of the RGS at this time, had five geographical features in Africa named after him, and no less than twenty-three worldwide).[7] Each explorer into the African interior colonised a new piece of territory, opening it up for others to follow. The process was graphically illustrated in a *Map of African Literature* published in 1873 (see fig. 2), the year of Livingstone's death, which showed the white spaces of the continent being gradually colonised by the names of innumerable European explorers, Livingstone's being the most prominent of all.[8]

Missionaries and Philanthropists

David Livingstone's name was and still is closely associated with missionary enterprise in Africa. His portrait took pride of place in the London Missionary Society's board room in Westminster; according to its President (speaking in 1953) 'every Director of the Society on entering the room finds his eyes focused upon that portrait'.[9] Although Livingstone's formal relationship with the LMS came to an

Grant's journal is shown open at a page listing the substantial quantities of equipment and supplies required for the type of large-scale expedition that he and John Hanning Speke conducted. It forms a contrast to Livingstone's preferred approach of travelling light and with only a modest group of bearers.

Fig. 4

Murchison chairing the geographical section of the British Association
Punch, 1864
REPRODUCED BY PERMISSION OF *PUNCH*

David Livingstone
By Monson of Cambridge
December 1857
Oil on board, 16.5 x 12.5 cm
ROYAL GEOGRAPHICAL SOCIETY
(cat. no. 3.7)

116

Based on a photograph taken of Livingstone while he was in Cambridge delivering his celebrated lectures to the University, this portrait was previously owned by the Reverend William Monk, who published the lectures the following year. Monk records that Livingstone's lecture given on 4 December 1857 was 'crowded to excess' and that 'literally there were volley after volley of cheers'. The lectures, with their message of 'commerce and Christianity', led to the establishment of the ill-fated Universities' Mission to Central Africa.

end in 1857, his name was subsequently associated with other missionary organisations, notably the Universities' Mission to Central Africa (UMCA), whose foundation owed much to his inspiration. If Livingstone provided a symbol for pioneering missionary endeavour in Africa, this owed less to his success in converting Africans than to his energy in promoting the idea of a moral mission for the British. His assaults on the institution of slavery found ready support among the liberal intelligentsia.

Livingstone sometimes described geographical exploration as a means rather than an end in itself. As he famously remarked in the closing pages of his *Missionary Travels* (1857), 'I view the end of the geographical feat as the beginning of the missionary enterprise.' However, it is easy to misinterpret such pronouncements, as is clear from the sentence that follows: 'I take the latter term in its most extended signification, and include every effort made for the amelioration of our race; the promotion of all those means by which God in His providence is working, and bringing all His dealings with man to a glorious consummation.'[10] In this sense, Livingstone argued, scientists, soldiers and merchants were active missionaries, working for the same ends: the moral and spiritual elevation of mankind. It was precisely the plasticity of Livingstone's religious affiliations, then, that enabled his work to be taken up by such a wide range of missionary and philanthropic organisations.

It is impossible to understand the significance of Livingstone's reputation without recognising the wider cultural role of these institutions and the networks of influence that they established in mid-Victorian Britain. The largely Congregationalist London Missionary Society (LMS), for example, had been founded in 1795, and by the time Livingstone joined (in 1838) it had a worldwide network of missions in every continent, including South Africa. The UMCA was by contrast an Anglican organisation, established in response to Livingstone's 1857 appeal to the young men of Cambridge.[11] Although its first attempt at founding a mission at Magomero proved disastrous, it was later to establish a network of mission stations in East Africa from a base in Zanzibar. Its house journal *Central Africa*, distributed to all its supporters, carried a map of East Central Africa on its covers showing the 'field' of the organisation's mission, as if it were an imperial possession. Similar journals were published by the much larger Church Missionary Society, which had long-established missions in other parts of Africa.

Alongside the missionary societies, a number of other philanthropic organisations gave Livingstone their vocal

Microscope given to Livingstone by Baroness Burdett-Coutts
45 x 31.8 cm
THE DAVID LIVINGSTONE CENTRE
(cat. no. 3.27)

Baroness Burdett-Coutts (1814–1906)
By an unknown artist, c. 1840
Oil on panel, 33 x 27.1 cm
NATIONAL PORTRAIT GALLERY
LONDON
(cat. no. 3.11)

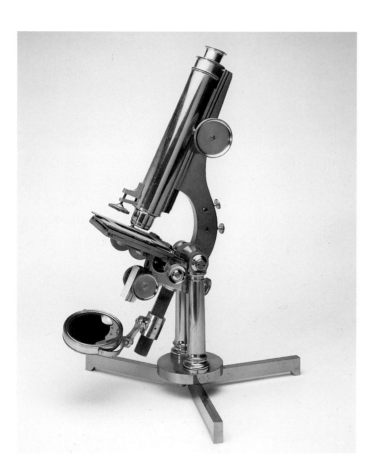

This microscope was given to Livingstone by Baroness Burdett-Coutts prior to his departure to the Zambezi in 1858. Livingstone wrote in thanks on 14 February 1858 that this and other gifts would become family heirlooms.

Livingstone's fame was such during his stay in Britain from 1856 to 1858 that he was able to establish contacts in the most influential circles. With her wide-ranging philanthropic interests, the banking heiress Angela Burdett-Coutts was an obvious sympathiser with Livingstone's plans to eradicate the slave trade in Africa. She presented him with a microscope prior to his departure to the Zambezi in 1858 and he, in turn, sent her regular accounts of the progress of the expedition.

support. In 1840 Livingstone attended a particularly momentous anti-slavery meeting at Exeter Hall, in the Strand, to hear Thomas Fowell Buxton preach the gospel of commerce and Christianity as the only remedy for the extinction of the African slave trade. Exeter Hall was a regular venue for some of the most influential philanthropic societies of the day, and their concerns made even those of the imperial government seem parochial. As one visitor put it, the voice of Exeter Hall was heard all over the earth:

> Exeter Hall has a fame. Since its erection, in about 1831, no other place in the world has attracted such crowds of social renovators, moral philosophers, philanthropists and Christians. Of late years, almost every great measure for the amelioration of the condition of the human family has had there its inception, its progress and its triumph.[12]

One of the most influential of all the organisations associated with Exeter Hall was the British and Foreign Anti-Slavery Society, founded in 1839. Building on the labours of a generation of campaigners against the slave trade, it co-ordinated a worldwide network of correspondents, its journal (the *Anti-Slavery Reporter*) regularly detailing the latest developments in every continent. (Not everyone took such telescopic philanthropy seriously, as readers of Dickens's *Bleak House* will know. A writer for *Punch* caustically noted that 'with many of the worthy people of Exeter Hall, distance is essential to love'.)[13]

Like Livingstone, the Anti-Slavery Society portrayed the values of liberty, humanity and justice as sacred gifts, to be bestowed by the British on the world at large. Although they could be remarkably critical of some aspects of European expansion, mid-Victorian anti-slavery campaigners shared many of the convictions of the day. Insisting on the indivisibility of the 'human family' (in opposition to the increasingly virulent strains of racial theory), they nevertheless drew on an established stock of racial stereotypes, drawing unfavourable contrasts between the innate 'character' of the Negro, the Arab and the European. Moreover, the quest for the abolition of slavery was not entirely disinterested; indeed, it was to offer one of the most important moral justifications for the 'Scramble for Africa' in the late nineteenth century. The slogan of 'legitimate commerce' popularised by Exeter Hall in the 1830s was plagiarised by the advocates of the new imperialism in the 1880s. There were some, even at the time, who were willing to expose this as sham philanthropy. The Scottish explorer Joseph Thomson once dismissed 'legitimate commerce' as 'magic words which give such an

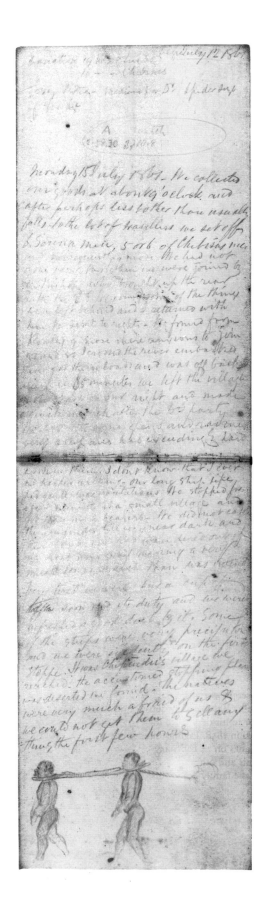

118

attractive glamour to whatever can creep under their shelter, [obscuring] the most shameful and criminal transactions'.[14] What had begun as a catch-all solution to the problem of the slave trade ended as a justification for colonial exploitation: free trade, but on European terms.

One personality who was particularly influential within African missionary and anti-slavery circles was Horace Waller, a lay missionary for the UMCA who first met Livingstone at the mouth of the Zambezi in 1861. Through his role in a number of organisations – notably the Anti-Slavery Society (whose committee he joined in 1870) and the RGS – Waller became a key figure in debates over British involvement in East and Central Africa during the second half of the nineteenth century. In his capacity as the editor of Livingstone's *Last Journals*, Waller carefully composed a potent image of Livingstone as a saintly figure, a worthy emblem of British imperial enterprise in Africa.[15] His close relationship with the Zanzibar Consul John Kirk, moreover, gave him a crucial entrée into the heart of the political establishment. Waller's extensive network of contacts, as well as his remarkable enthusiasm for both writing and intrigue, tells us much about the wider context in which African exploration was promoted during the period. Where African affairs were concerned, geographical issues melted into philanthropic ones; anti-slavery campaigns found their way into the very heart of Whitehall. A glance at Waller's personal diaries for the mid-1870s, when he was installed as Rector at Twywell, Northamptonshire, gives us a glimpse of the close relations between scientific, philanthropic and political interests in Africa.[16] January 1875 finds Waller (in addition to the normal round of his pastoral duties) attending an anti-slavery meeting in the City of London; dining with Edmund Sturge, John Kirk and Sir Bartle Frere; attending meetings at the RGS; corresponding with General Gordon; visiting the Zoological Gardens; shooting pheasant with William Webb at Newstead Abbey; addressing the prestigious Society of Arts on progress in East Africa; and mulling over the first reviews of his edition of Livingstone's *Last Journals*. Such sources provide telling evidence of the constant interchange between missionaries, philanthropists, geographers and politicians. African affairs, it seemed, were ubiquitous.

Geographers

'Of all the sciences', Conrad once famously observed, 'Geography finds its origin in action.'[17] At no time did this claim appear more apposite than in the nineteenth century, when geographers were actively involved in the exploration,

Left
Horace Waller's field journal showing his entry for 15 July 1861
Bound manuscript
15.8 x 9.5 cm (closed)
CURATORS OF THE BODLEIAN LIBRARY, RHODES HOUSE LIBRARY
(cat. no. 4.63)

This early journal by Horace Waller documents the journey undertaken by the Universities' Mission to Central Africa to their first settlement at Magomero, on the advice of Livingstone. The drawing at the foot of the page, and the following entry for 16 July 1861, records their momentous encounter with a slave convoy and their freeing of the slaves. Abolition of slavery was a primary motivation for the UMCA; reported by Livingstone, Waller and others, this particular episode became the stuff of myth.

119

Henry Rowley (died *c.* 1907) and Horace Waller (1833–1896)
By an unknown photographer
1860s
Albumen carte-de-visite
9.4 x 5.9 cm
NATIONAL PORTAIT GALLERY LONDON
(cat. no. 4.48)

This photograph shows two of the surviving members of the Universities' Mission to Central Africa, which, on Livingstone's recommendation, had formed a settlement in the Shire Highlands in 1861. The seated figure, Rowley, wrote the history of the ill-fated mission while Waller, standing, went on to become the editor of Livingstone's *Last Journals* and a powerful figure within African missionary and anti-slavery circles.

conquest and colonisation of the non-European world. Livingstone dedicated his bestselling *Missionary Travels* (1857) to Sir Roderick Murchison, in recognition of the powerful influence commanded by the so-called 'King of Siluria' in London's scientific and political communities. Murchison was an empire builder *par excellence*; in addition to his influential positions in the Geological Society, the Geological Survey and the British Association (which he helped to establish in 1831), he acted as President of the RGS for much of the mid-nineteenth century, establishing its role as a centre for learning and debate over the geography of empire.

Founded in 1830, the RGS served as a kind of information exchange for explorers, soldiers, administrators and natural scientists. It provided intelligence and maps for a range of government departments, especially the Admiralty and the Foreign Office, a service that was rewarded with the gift of an official subsidy (1854) and a royal charter (1859). Its map room was a frequent source of information for the military. In the words of one observer of scientific London (writing in 1874), 'No sooner does a squabble occur – in Ashanti, Abysinnia or Atchin – than Government departments make a rush to Savile Row, and lay hands on all matter relating to that portion of the world which happens to be interesting for the moment.' During Murchison's presidency the RGS developed into one of the most popular and fashionable scientific societies in London, known especially for its 'African nights' when (we are told) an immense audience thundered at the gate.[18] The leading Fellows exercised considerable influence in the corridors of Whitehall, largely through informal channels and networks; it was Murchison, for example, who secured David Livingstone's consular appointments in Central Africa, as well as Kirk's in Zanzibar. 'By the late 1850s', a recent biographer of Murchison concludes, 'the Royal Geographical Society more perfectly represented British expansionism in all its facets than any other institution in the nation.'[19]

In the public mind the RGS was, above all else, closely associated with exploration and travel. It published a guide on how to conduct expeditions, entitled *Hints to Travellers*, which was regularly updated after its first appearance in 1854. It loaned surveying and photographic equipment to explorers, and sometimes trained them in its use. It sponsored expeditions, including Livingstone's and several of the expeditions sent after him. The boundary-making era that was inaugurated with the 'Scramble for Africa' was to place yet further demands on geographers throughout Europe; their knowledge enabled territories

Sir Roderick Impey Murchison (1784–1871)
By Stephen Pearce, 1856
Oil on canvas, 38.7 x 32.4 cm
NATIONAL PORTRAIT GALLERY
LONDON
(cat. no. 3.8)

President of the Royal Geographical Society from 1843, Murchison was a key promoter of Livingstone's later expeditions. Murchison used his considerable influence with government to secure funding for the Zambezi expedition and, in spite of its failures, remained loyal to the explorer. He also prompted Livingstone's last journeys in search of the source of the Nile, again procuring government aid for the venture.

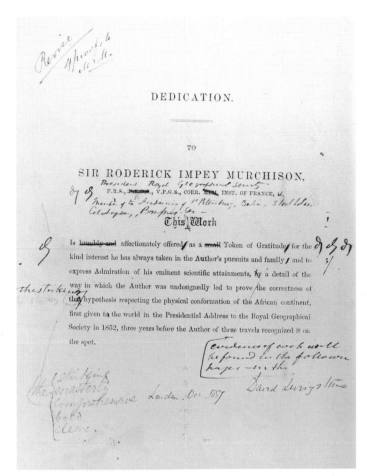

Proof dedication page to *Missionary Travels and Researches in South Africa*
By David Livingstone
Published by John Murray, London, 1857
Printed sheet with John Murray's manuscript corrections
22 x 14 cm
PRIVATE COLLECTION
(cat. no. 3.24)

Livingstone dedicated *Missionary Travels* to Sir Roderick Murchison. On this proof Murray has added Murchison's numerous honours and run through the lexicon to find the right word to praise Murchison's 'hypothesis respecting the physical confirmation of the African continent'. Rejecting 'masterly', 'comprehensive', 'bold' and 'clear', he inserts 'striking' on the proof.

121

to be evaluated, frontiers to be drawn up, wars to be fought, peoples to be conquered.

Most, if not quite all, of the famous explorers of the second half of the nineteenth century portrayed geography as a manly science, dedicated to the mastery of the earth; its books and maps were to them as much weapons of conquest as objects of contemplation. 'The study of Geography', proclaimed Henry Morton Stanley in 1885, 'ought to lead to something higher than collecting maps and books of travel and afterwards shelving them as of no further use.'[20] Such a view would have found support from Livingstone, although he may have found a more diplomatic way of saying it. Stanley's vision of geographical science as the handmaiden of colonial expansion was to be put into practice during the 1880s, when he worked for King Leopold of Belgium on the Congo and at the same time actively promoted the extension of British influence in East Africa. Stanley, like many African explorers of his generation, portrayed his work as putting into effect what Livingstone had only dreamed of; on his death in 1904 it was claimed that 'the map of Africa is a monument to Stanley'.[21] While Livingstone himself did not live to see the rapid territorial expansion of the British empire in Africa, he did bequeath it a sense of mission that was subsequently to be exploited for imperial ends.

An enthusiastic big-game hunter and adventurer, Baker turned to Africa and the problem of the Nile's source in 1861. Travelling with his wife up the Nile and across country, Baker reached a large lake in March 1864, which he named the Albert N'yanza and claimed as the true source of the Nile. Now called Lake Albert, it was later established as only a secondary source. Baker was fêted for his achievements on his return to Britain, and his highly entertaining account of his travels, *The Albert N'yanza*, published in 1866, proved immensely popular.

The mid-Victorian explorers of Africa can thus be seen as the pioneers and (in Livingstone's case) the spiritual forefathers of the new imperialism, for it was they who helped to establish new ways of seeing the world beyond Europe. The fact that explorers like David Livingstone, Richard Burton and Samuel Baker received financial support and official authority (albeit rather meagre) from the British government or its surrogates provides one measure of their significance in the history of empire making; another is their role in the creation of new myths and fantasies about the exploration of farflung corners of the world. In this sense geographical exploration did not merely overcome distance; it created imaginative geographies. If the explorers were 'conquerors of truth' (to adapt Conrad's telling phrase), it was not primarily because they revealed the truth about the regions in which they travelled (as they habitually claimed) but rather because they established particular ways of reading these landscapes and the people who inhabited them. For Livingstone, Central and East Africa was above all a landscape to be cultivated. His successors were quick to follow him into the field.

**'The Last Charge, Latooka,
17 April 1863'**
By Sir Samuel White Baker
c. 1863–1866
Watercolour over pencil on paper
22.5 x 31.3 cm
ROYAL GEOGRAPHICAL SOCIETY
(cat. no. 5.2)

**'The Start from M'rooli for
the Lake, February 1864'**
By Sir Samuel White Baker
c. 1864–1866
Watercolour over pencil on paper
22.5 x 31.3 cm
ROYAL GEOGRAPHICAL SOCIETY
(cat. no. 5.3)

One of a group of drawings by Baker, used as the basis for engravings in *The Albert N'yanza*, this records a hunting incident on 17 April 1863. Although mortally wounded, the elephant charged Baker twice, the second time pursuing him for nearly half a mile and getting 'within ten or twelve yards of the horse's tail, with his trunk stretched out to catch him'. The elephant eventually 'relinquished the chase', Baker goes on to relate, 'when another hundred yards' run would have bagged me'.

123

The drawing shows Baker and his African escort setting off to the shores of Lake Albert. 'The entire crowd was most grotesquely got up', Baker recorded in *The Albert N'yanza*, 'being dressed in either leopard or white monkey skins, with cows' tails strapped on behind, and antelope horns fitted upon their heads, while their chins were ornamented with false beards, made of the bushy ends of cows' tails sewed together'. The drawing served as the basis for an engraving in *The Albert N'yanza*, while the figure of Baker himself, riding on an ox, was embossed on the book's spine.

**'The Albert N'yanza,
March 1864'**
By Sir Samuel White Baker
c. 1864–1866
Watercolour over pencil on paper
22.5 x 31.3 cm
ROYAL GEOGRAPHICAL SOCIETY
(cat. no. 5.4)

Baker's drawing, used as the basis
for the frontispiece to volume 2 of
The Albert N'yanza, shows him and
his party setting out on Lake
Albert in two locally made canoes.
Baker records how the canoes
were merely hollowed out trees,
but that with the aid of 'an
English screw augur' he had
erected the canopy seen on the
canoe on the right. 'The
arrangements completed', he
writes, 'afforded a cabin, perhaps
not as luxurious as those of the
Peninsular and Oriental
Company's vessels, but both rain-
and sun-proof, which was a great
desideratum'.

124

**'The Welcome on our Return
to Shooa, 21 November 1864'**
By Sir Samuel White Baker
c. 1864–1866
Watercolour over pencil on paper
22.5 x 31.3 cm
ROYAL GEOGRAPHICAL SOCIETY
(cat. no. 5.5)

Baker shows himself and his wife
on their return to their base in
November 1864 after their journey
to Lake Albert. 'That evening',
Baker recounts in *The Albert
N'yanza*, 'the native women
crowded to our camp to welcome
my wife home, and to dance in
honour of our return, for which
exhibition they expected a present
of a cow'.

Lord Palmerston (1784–1865)
By Francis Cruikshank, *c.* 1855
Oil on canvas, 49.2 x 39.7 cm
NATIONAL PORTRAIT GALLERY
LONDON
(cat. no. 3.4)

Livingstone had the greatest admiration for Palmerston, whose anti-slavery policy was consonant with his own vision of Central Africa. The two men discussed the issue during Livingstone's stay in England from 1856–1858, and Livingstone's *Narrative of an Expedition to the Zambesi* carries a fulsome dedication to the statesman. As Prime Minister,

Palmerston's sanction for the Zambezi expedition had been crucial, but the expedition's failures, and the burden of Britain's existing overseas commitments, made him wary of Livingstone's schemes for colonising the region. 'Dr. L's information is valuable', he wrote in 1860, 'but he must not be allowed to tempt us to form colonies by forcing steamers up cataracts'.

126

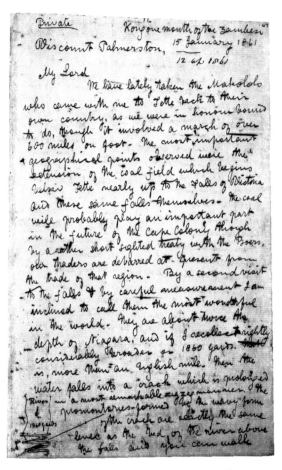

Letter from David Livingstone to Lord Palmerston, 15 January 1861
Manuscript letter, 32.2 x 20 cm
BY PERMISSION OF THE TRUSTEES
OF THE NATIONAL LIBRARY OF
SCOTLAND
(cat. no. 3.22)

Livingstone sent Palmerston detailed accounts of the progress of the Zambezi expedition. In the opening page of this letter he reports his journey back to Kololo country in 1860 and writes optimistically of coal reserves on the Zambezi, which, he ventures, 'will probably play an important part in the future of the Cape Colony'. He also describes his second visit to the Victoria Falls. He is inclined, he says, 'to call them the most wonderful in the world' and he includes a little sketch diagram of the Falls.

Politicians

On the face of George Gilbert Scott's new buildings for the Colonial Office in Whitehall, completed in 1875, there are a number of small busts and figures, the work of the sculptors Armstead and Philip. On the ground floor are five allegorical figures representing the continents of Europe, Asia, Africa, America and Australasia. On the first floor, in the window soffits, barely visible from the street, there are several small busts, late additions to the building, including those of Captain Cook, Sir John Franklin, William Wilberforce and David Livingstone.[22] That images of these men were deemed suitable adornments for such an august office of state tells us something about Victorian efforts to promote the humanitarian face of empire building. Livingstone in many ways embodied the virtues of the other figures, the scientific explorer, heroic adventurer and anti-slavery campaigner combined. As his biographers have shown, Livingstone's relationship with government departments was never particularly close; he relied heavily on intermediaries, such as Sir Roderick Murchison or John Kirk, to make his case in the corridors of power. Yet his name and what it represented came to be closely linked with British imperial designs in Africa.

The history of government policy on British involvement in Africa – and the character of the 'official mind' that directed it – has long been the subject of debate amongst historians. For the purposes of this essay it is sufficient to note that the formal acquisition of territory was only one way through which British interests in Africa could be secured; indeed it was frequently a last resort, designed to thwart the ambitions of other European powers or avert some immediate military or political threat. As long as Palmerstonian gunboat diplomacy was sufficient to secure British interests abroad, a policy summed up in a famous phrase as 'the imperialism of free trade', the formal establishment of colonies was frequently deemed unnecessary. The power of the mid-Victorian empire cannot therefore be judged merely by the amount of land placed under formal colonial rule; this would be, in another famous phrase, 'rather like judging the size and character of icebergs solely from the parts above the water-line'.[23]

It was gentlemanly capitalism that set the dominant tone of British expansionism during the nineteenth century. The Victorian reinvention of the culture of the gentleman was visible in the changing character of its leading institutions – Parliament, the City of London and the public schools – as well as in popular texts such as Samuel

This view of the British consulate
in Zanzibar is from an album of
photographs by John Kirk,
formerly of the Zambezi
expedition and Vice-Consul (later
Consul-General) in Zanzibar from
1866. Under Kirk's consulship the
island became an important centre
for British interests in East Africa.

Smiles's *Self-Help*. Imperial expansion, it has recently been suggested, was 'the export version of the gentlemanly order'.[24] The huge expansion of international trade and the vital contribution of the City of London to British wealth provided direction to British policy abroad, leading to selective expansion where conditions for trade were promising. While Livingstone's dreams for Central and East Africa found comparatively little commercial support during his lifetime, the Foreign Office was quick to identify commercial and strategic advantages in having a political presence in Zanzibar, imposing an anti-slave-trade treaty in 1845 and using military force to shore up its regime in 1859. The appointment of John Kirk as Vice-Consul there in 1866, and Consul-General in 1873, marked a new phase in the extension of British interests in the region. Kirk's close relationship with Livingstone dated from his appointment as 'economic botanist' to the Zambezi expedition in 1858. He was subsequently to be a key point of contact for all those missionaries, explorers, traders and administrators who saw themselves as following in Livingstone's footsteps in East Africa.

It was through his connections at the Royal Geographical Society that Livingstone first came to the attention of the Foreign Office. He was awarded a prize by the RGS for his discovery of Lake Ngami in 1849, and in 1854 his journey to Luanda was described by Sir Roderick Murchison as 'the greatest triumph in geographical research which has been effected in our times'.[25] Murchison was to remain a staunch ally, publicising his expeditions, securing a publisher for his *Missionary Travels* (John Murray, also responsible for the RGS *Journal*) and promoting his cause in Whitehall. (At the same time Murchison was busy using his influence at the Foreign Office to promote the extension of British scientific and commercial interests on the River Niger).[26] Even before his triumphal return to Britain in December 1856 Livingstone had entered into negotiations with Murchison concerning his future. Murchison, ever ready to exploit the publicity that had already been generated by Livingstone's discoveries, is said to have interrupted his Christmas holiday with Palmerston in order to promote Livingstone's cause. Soon afterwards he approached Lord Clarendon, the Foreign Secretary, pressing Livingstone's case for official support, waxing lyrical about the 'paradise of wealth' (both mineral and agricultural) waiting to be exploited on the upper Zambezi, and going so far as to suggest that the British might seek to acquire the territory from the Portuguese. Livingstone himself encouraged these clandestine moves in the hope that a government appointment would free him from financial dependence on the LMS. (There were recent precedents for such official

4th Earl of Clarendon (1800–1870)
By Sir Francis Grant, 1843
Oil on canvas, 61 x 50.7 cm
EARL OF CLARENDON
(cat. no. 3.6)

129

As Foreign Secretary from 1853 to 1858, Clarendon was a key figure at the time Livingstone was seeking government funding for the Zambezi expedition. Sir Roderick Murchison brokered the deal with Clarendon, securing the role of 'roving consul' for Livingstone at a salary of £500. Livingstone also pressed his own case to Clarendon by arguing for the potential economic benefits that might result from further exploration of the Zambezi. Foreign Secretary again from 1865 to 1866 and 1868 to 1870, Clarendon was also important to Livingstone during his final expedition.

130

The great traveller and linguist,
Richard Burton, turned his
attention to Africa in 1854. After
volunteering for the Crimean War
he returned there in 1856 to
conduct an expedition into the
interior of Central Africa
sponsored by the Royal
Geographical Society. With John
Hanning Speke he reached Lake
Tanganyika in February 1858,
but, to his intense irritation, failed
to join Speke on his first visit to
Lake Victoria several months later.
Livingstone despised Burton for
his low opinion of Africa and
Africans and for his
unconventional morals. Burton
'seems to be a moral idiot',
Livingstone wrote in 1865, 'his
conduct in Africa was so bad that
it cannot be spoken of without
disgust – systematically wicked,
impure and untruthful'.

support; in 1856, sponsored by both the RGS and the
Foreign Office, Burton and Speke had begun their famous
expedition to the Lakes of East Africa.) By May 1857 the
deal brokered by Murchison had taken shape: Livingstone
was to be appointed (at an annual salary of £500) as a
'roving consul' in an area that included Mozambique and
a large swathe of territory to the west. On 11 December
the House of Commons was told of Livingstone's plans to
lead a government-sponsored expedition to the Zambezi;
on the following day Livingstone was Palmerston's guest of
honour at 10 Downing Street.

Murchison's lobbying secured the full co-operation of the
Foreign Office and the Admiralty in preparations for the
Zambezi expedition, which set sail from Birkenhead in
March 1858. Livingstone's instructions to his officers give
a clear indication of his hopes for the future role of the
British in the whole of Central and East Africa. The
opening paragraph is worth quoting at length, for it
encapsulates (in uncharacteristically sober terms) the spirit
of so many contemporary expeditions to Africa.

> The main object of the Expedition . . . is to extend
> the knowledge already attained of the geography and
> mineral and agricultural resources of Eastern and
> Central Africa, to improve our acquaintance with the
> inhabitants, and to engage them to apply their energies
> to industrial pursuits and to the cultivation of their
> lands with a view to the production of raw material to
> be exported to England in return for British
> manufactures; and it may be hoped that by encouraging
> the natives to occupy themselves in the development of
> the resources of their country a considerable advance
> may be made towards the extinction of the slave trade,
> and the natives will not be long in discovering that the
> former will eventually become a more certain source of
> profit than the latter.[27]

Information, resources, cultivation and commerce: these
were the watchwords of Livingstone's mission, and they
won official sanction at the highest level. While the Foreign
Office remained wary of more ambitious schemes
involving the colonisation of land by British settlers, much
to Livingstone's disgust,[28] it found nothing exceptionable in
his moralising language. Habits of industry were to be
cultivated, free labour was to replace slavery, the idea of
private property was to be promoted and the 'moral
influence' of 'a well regulated and orderly household of
Europeans' was to be encouraged. 'We come among
them', Livingstone told his colleagues, 'as members of a
superior race and servants of a Government that desires to
elevate the more degraded portions of the human family.'

Manuscript map of Burton and Speke's route, 1857–1858
By John Hanning Speke
c. 1858–1859
Ink and watercolour on paper,
squared in pencil and laid on to
linen, 44.5 x 35.5 cm
ROYAL GEOGRAPHICAL SOCIETY
(cat. no. 5.10)

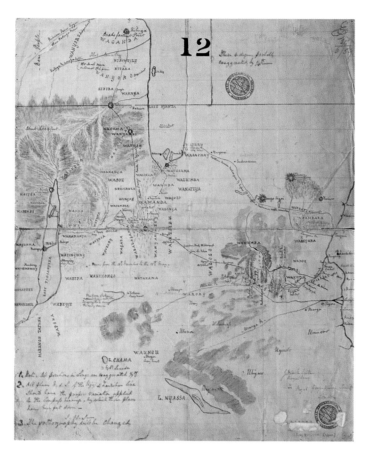

Speke's map, received from him
by the Royal Geographical
Society on 24 June 1859, records
his expedition under the
command of Richard Burton in
1857–1858. It is the earliest map to
show Lake Tanganyika, which can
be seen on the left-hand side.
Returning from Lake Tanganyika,
Speke struck out on his own and
reached the great lake that he
christened the Victoria Nyanza
(Lake Victoria) on 30 July 1858,
securing a full view of it on
3 August. The bottom end of
Lake Victoria is indicated at the
top of Speke's map. To Burton's
intense irritation, Speke claimed
Victoria as the source of the Nile.

Such a formula, symptomatic of the mid-Victorian
accommodation between racism and humanitarianism,
speaks volumes about the confidence and ambition of
the civilising mission. It was not (yet) a strictly imperial
mission; but the time for empire building was not far off.

Stanley and Livingstone

Few of Livingstone's biographers have resisted the
temptation to present Livingstone as a martyr, though they
have differed over the cause he died for, some opting for
the civilising mission, others for 'commerce and
Christianity', and still others for 'that form of religion
which we call science'.[29] The image we are given of
Livingstone in his last years is overwhelmingly that of
a lone wanderer seeking after truth and justice, his
ambitious plans for the colonisation of Central Africa
officially spurned and his relentless search for the sources
of the Nile constantly frustrated. In the course of the next
three decades, however, British colonisation of large parts
of Africa was to become a reality. In this respect the huge
publicity generated by Livingstone's meeting with Stanley
at Ujiji in 1871 might be said to have inaugurated a new
relationship between sensational journalism and sensational
imperialism, a partnership that reached its climax some
twenty years later. For his many critics (Waller and Kirk
among them), Stanley was to become a symbol of a brash
new approach to African expedition-making, amounting to
nothing less than 'exploration by warfare'.[30] For them, in
fact, Stanley was everything that Livingstone was not.
While Livingstone's tactful dealings with Africans were
said to have left behind him 'a track of light where the
white man who follows . . . is in perfect safety', as the
Anti-Slavery Reporter put it in 1878, Stanley surrounded
himself with 'an atmosphere of terror created by the free
use of fire and the sword'. Where Livingstone was said to
have brought light, Stanley brought corruption; 'he will
act as a dark shadow to throw up the brightness of
Livingstone's fame.'[31] Stanley himself acknowledged the
distinction, while placing a characteristically self-serving
interpretation on it: 'Each man has his own way. His, I
think, had its defects, though the old man, personally,
has been almost Christ-like for goodness, patience, and
self-sacrifice. The selfish and wooden-headed world
requires mastering, as well as loving charity; for man
is a composite of the spiritual and earthly.'[32]

It is tempting to paint this contrast on a broader canvas, as
the difference between two styles of cultural imperialism.
Stanley's famous encounter with Livingstone at Ujiji might
thus be said to symbolise a moment of transition; the old

131

**Henry Morton Stanley
(1841–1904) and Kalulu
(c. 1864–1877)** (detail)
By London Stereoscopic Company
c. 1872
Albumen carte-de-visite
9 x 6.2 cm
NATIONAL PORTRAIT GALLERY
LONDON
(cat. no. 5.18)

Kalulu (Ndugu M'hali) was given
to Stanley as an eight-year-old by
a slave trader and became his
close companion and personal
servant until his death. He
drowned crossing the Congo river
on Stanley's 1874–1877 expedition.
Here, in the simulated Africa of a
London studio, master and
servant re-enact their roles.

**Snuff box presented to
Stanley by Queen Victoria**
Gold, enamel and precious stones
3.7 x 8 x 6 cm
NATIONAL MUSEUM AND GALLERY
CARDIFF
(cat. no. 5.59)

Queen Victoria gave this to
Stanley on 27 August 1872 in
token of her admiration for his
finding Livingstone. He was
invited to meet her at Dunrobin
Castle on 10 September and
found, to his relief, that she was
even smaller than him but with a
'quiet but unmistakable kindly
condescension and an inimitable
calmness of self-possession.' She
thought he was 'a determined ugly
little man – with a strong
American twang.'

imperialism giving way to the new. To put it this way is
not to deny that explorers before Stanley (including
Livingstone) had argued for imperial expansion. It is
rather to emphasise the wider significance of a new
approach to exploration, both its conduct and its
representation. Stanley's methods seem to blur the
distinction between exploration and warfare so profoundly
that it becomes almost unrecognisable; as has been well
observed, all of his expeditions were 'invasions . . .
designed to overcome resistance, whether from the terrain
or from its inhabitants, and to come back with a trophy'.[33]
Following reports of brutality on Stanley's trans-African
expedition of 1874–1877, even the most ardent advocates
of African enterprise were smarting. 'Exploration under
these conditions is, in fact, exploration plus buccaneering,'
warned the *Pall Mall Gazette,* 'and though the map may
be improved and enlarged by the process, the cause of
civilisation is not a gainer thereby, but a loser.'[34]

Recognising Livingstone's significance as a symbol need
not blind us to the sordid reality of much that was done
in his name. Horace Waller's verdict on the duplicity of
some of his contemporaries speaks more forcefully to us
than he would have intended:

> You may say that by our commercial relations with
> African tribes we must surely have let in light. I reply,
> if it is to be so, it is the blaze of the burning village, or
> the flash of the Winchester rifle – at best it is the glare
> from the smoke-stack of the Congo steamer bearing
> away tons upon tons of ivory.[35]

133

MR. STANLEY,

IN THE DRESS HE WORE WHEN HE MET LIVINGSTONE IN AFRICA

Stereoscopic Co.

Copyright.

Memorialising Livingstone

On 23 October 1953, a hundred years after the commencement of Livingstone's most celebrated African journey, a small group of dignitaries gathered in London to unveil a statue dedicated to his memory in London. The site was, perhaps inevitably, the Royal Geographical Society's modern headquarters at 1 Kensington Gore, a few yards from the Royal Albert Hall. The guest of honour was Oliver Lyttelton, Churchill's controversial Colonial Secretary; he was joined by Livingstone's grandson (representing the Livingstone Memorial Trust at Blantyre), the General Secretary of the London Missionary Society and the President of the RGS. Reading the report of this event published in the *Geographical Journal*, one gets a distinct sense of *déjà vu*.[36] It is as though fifty years of Livingstone memorials – marking his birth, his first missionary journey, his writings and his death – have been sculpted into one moment, incorporating all the various aspects of Livingstone's heroic reputation as explorer, missionary and imperial pioneer. In some ways it was a singularly ill-chosen moment to memorialise the man who, in the words of the Colonial Secretary, had 'unlocked the door of the African continent and opened a new page in its history'. For, just as Lyttelton was recalling Lord Curzon's rousing tribute to Livingstone's heroism forty years earlier, Britain's African empire was beginning to crumble. On 16 December 1953 Lyttelton found himself the subject of an unprecedented censure motion from the Labour Party front bench for his handling of African affairs, including the proposed federation in Central Africa and the Mau Mau rebellion in Kenya.[37] (Lyttelton's views about Africans were not really so distant from Curzon's: as he remarked in the course of the debate, 'So far, the continent of Africa has made little contribution to the civilisation, art, letters or enlightenment of mankind.')[38] The wind of change was gathering momentum; and in only a matter of years it was to sweep across the continent with a force that no Colonial Secretary could contain. By 1966 the African empire was history; but Livingstone's statue remained, obstinate and aloof, seemingly untouched by the turbulence of the world it still inhabits.

Left
David Livingstone
By an unknown photographer
1856–1858
Ambrotype, 14.4 x 10 cm
SCOTTISH NATIONAL PORTRAIT
GALLERY
(cat. no. 3.18)

This recently discovered photograph of Livingstone was taken during his stay in Britain between 1856 and 1858. As an ambrotype (a positive collodion) it is a unique image.

135

Right
Fig. 5
Unveiling of the Livingstone Memorial at the Royal Geographical Society, 23 October 1953
ROYAL GEOGRAPHICAL SOCIETY

Overleaf
Fig. 6
'Funeral of Dr Livingstone in Westminster Abbey'
From the *Illustrated London News*,
25 April 1874
NATIONAL PORTRAIT GALLERY
LONDON

Wooden yoke removed by Livingstone from the neck of a slave
158 x 15.5 cm
THE DAVID LIVINGSTONE CENTRE
(cat. no. 3.31)

138

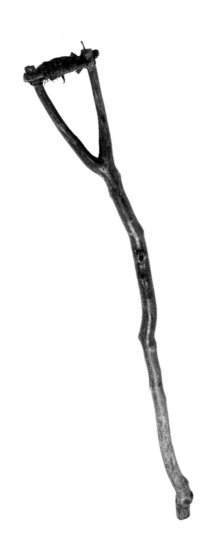

4

Wrought iron slave chains and shackles brought from Africa by Livingstone (detail)
ROYAL GEOGRAPHICAL SOCIETY
(cat. no. 3.32)

These shackles and chains were collected by Livingstone. They had been used to restrain 'human commodities' on their journey from the interior to the coast.

David Livingstone gathered together a small but important collection of African artefacts, which reflect his missionary activities, his 'explorations' and his efforts to record and promote the commercial potential of the regions he visited. Its unique appeal lies not only in its association with this particular man but also in the intriguing glimpses it offers of the Victorian encounter with Africa, for there are strong patterns discernible in what Livingstone chose to preserve and despatch to Britain. These patterns suggest that his collection, like all collections, reveals the ideological assumptions that influenced its creation.

Livingstone's encounters with Africans, and the objects and natural history specimens he collected, can be viewed within the framework in which Europe and Africa were perceived by the colonial powers for much of the nineteenth century. This framework has been described by many scholars as an unequal, if complementary, relationship based on the opposition between 'civilised' and 'savage', 'saviour' and 'saved', 'healer' and 'patient', 'actor' and 'subject'.[1] Livingstone reminded the other Europeans on the Zambezi expedition that 'We come among them as members of a superior race and servants of a Government that desires to elevate the more degraded portions of the human family.'[2] However, he also continually warned against what he called 'the stupid prejudice against colour'.[3]

His collections were grounded in an emergent colonial structure in which the myriad differences found in African societies often went unobserved by Europeans or were subsumed in a general picture of the 'colonised'. Yet Livingstone's collections do not present an undifferentiated mass of African artefacts. There are important and revealing variations within the assemblage of objects he gathered together. If collections are forms of visual ideology, then it comes as no surprise that Livingstone sent back physical evidence of the horrors of slavery. Equally unsurprising is the absence of objects associated with the other Europeans, particularly the Portuguese, with whom Livingstone had contact, as such material would lack the 'exotic' elements adhering, in the European view, to African artefacts. Objects owned or used by Zanzibar or Swahili traders, whose involvment in the slave trade he detested but with whom he sometimes travelled, are also under-represented.

Livingstone was not a collector by nature or particularly drawn to material culture. Indeed, taken as a whole, his collection reveals no significant historical depth,

142

geographical representation or ethnographic detail. By exhibiting and researching these objects together, a sense of assemblage has been created where little may have originally existed or been intended. This process is perhaps not so different from that which transformed Livingstone's field notes into a report, then a draft manuscript and finally a published book.[4]

Certainly Livingstone himself seemed little interested in material comfort and the accumulation of commodities. He expressed disapproval, for example, when Robert Moffat, whose preaching had inspired him to go to Africa, returned from a furlough in Britain with fifty tons of baggage destined for his mission. Compared to later expeditions such as Stanley's, Livingstone's were not overly encumbered. It is likely that he wished to avoid slowing down travel by adding to porters' loads with large numbers of artefacts or specimens. And in *Missionary Travels*, he offers another reason: 'Many more interesting birds were met; but I could make no collection, as I was proceeding on the plan of having as little luggage as possible, so as not to excite the cupidity of those through whose country we intended to pass.'[5]

By the time of his Zambezi expedition, and not unusually for the period and certainly in accordance with the scientific aims of the expedition, natural history specimens as well as cultural artefacts were sent home to illustrate the travel narratives or to promote the commercial potential of the regions described by Livingstone or his party. Any reader of the Zambezi expedition accounts cannot fail to spot the continual references to the difficulties of keeping the steamers fuelled. Although unusual items such as elephant bones were occasionally fed into the boiler, the most common wood used was what Livingstone mistakenly called 'lignum vitae'.[6] Writing to the Earl of Malmesbury on 26 July 1859, Livingstone complains about his underpowered steamship and suggests the tremendous volume of wood needed. 'We have in the course of one year cut up into small pieces upwards of one hundred and fifty tons of lignum vitae alone, which, according to the average prices in London during 1858, was worth about £700. This wood, when dry, was, in the absence of coal, the only fuel with which we could get up steam . . . '.[7] The Royal Museum of Scotland acquired a sample of this vital ingredient, which was described in the catalogue entry of 1863 as being from the tree used for fuel on board the steamer in the Livingstone expedition.

In the same collection, but catalogued in 1858, there is a 'sample of coal from Rivulet Natole above Tete, the first indication of true coal Dr Livingstone found in coming

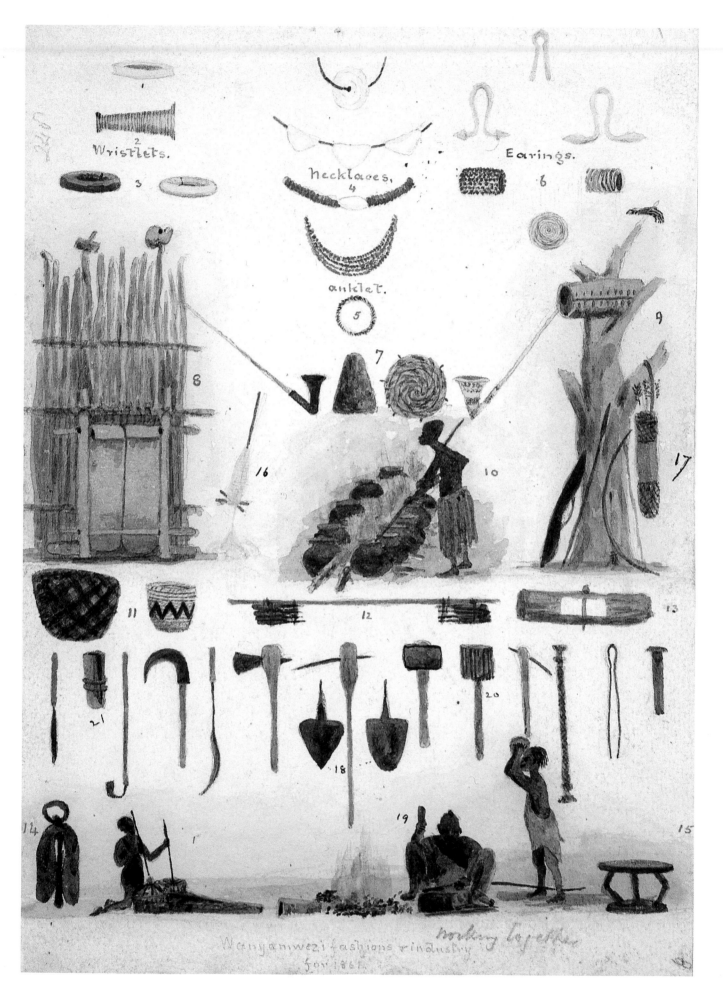

Wristlets.

necklaces.

Earings.

anklet.

Wanyamwezi fashions & industry. Nov 1861.

east'. He hoped that these coalfields would eventually provide fuel for the Cape and wrote to many of his correspondents about their potential. It was certainly good enough for use in the steamer. He records that local people did not burn coal and were surprised to see them using it to top up a wood fire.

Livingstone also sent to Scotland two 'India rubber balls' and noted that they were used in a game resembling 'fives'. The expedition used 'sheets' of this rubber against slow leaks in the steamer hull. John Kirk, the expedition's botanist, also commented on its use in games, on drum heads and as an adhesive, and described the extraction of rubber in his journal entry for 12 August 1858.

> The rough outer bark is pared off where the gum under the bark is exposed. A few punctures are made from which a thick tenacious milky juice exudes in drops, which by the finger are applied to the skin of the body. It dries immediately and by repetition of the same process, a thin coat is produced which being rolled into a ball, receives successive additions. No drying process is needed at this season. The juice is so thick that it dries on exposure for a few minutes.[8]

Kirk believed that commercial gathering of such rubber might have been possible.

Kirk sent back several artefacts to the Royal Botanical Gardens at Kew, to demonstrate the transformation of plant material into objects. This collection was probably made to fulfil his initial instructions from Livingstone and in accordance with government interest in the commercial potential of the territories through which the expedition was travelling. It may be these that Kirk refers to in his Zambezi journal for 25 June 1858, although he deposited items at other times as well.

> I am hard at work packing up, which is no joke, when all my personal baggage has to be arranged, and also when I have to pack up the specimens for home. One box of government specimens of the Doum Palm fruit and other products and manufactures of the country, I have to send off in rather an unsatisfactory state but it is better to send them home at once, even without many than to risk keeping them and taking up country.[9]

Still in the collections at Kew is a fishing net sent back by Kirk, which may be the one he describes in his journal for 31 March 1859: 'I bought a beautiful net for fish, made of Buaze fastened together with the reef knot, also two baskets for catching small fish, made of split bamboo and

Female waist beads, probably of Toka design, collected by Livingstone
Glass beads, clam shell, cowries and wood
Approximately 22 x 20 cm
THE DAVID LIVINGSTONE CENTRE
(cat. no. 4.91)

This object is illustrated in Livingstone's account of his Zambezi journey, in which he wrote: 'The younger girls wear the waist-belt exhibited in the woodcut, ornamented with shells, and have the fringes only in front'.

316   NATIVE DRESS.   CHAP. XV.

now saw many good-looking young men and women. The dresses of the ladies are identical with those of Nubian women in Upper Egypt. To a belt on the waist a great number of strings are attached to hang all round the person. These fringes are about six or eight inches long. The matrons wear in addition a skin cut like the tails of the coatee formerly worn by our dragoons. The younger girls wear the waist-belt exhibited in the woodcut, ornamented with shells, and have the fringes only in front. Marauding parties of Batoka, calling themselves Makololo, have for some time had a wholesome dread of Sinamane's "long spears." Before going to Tette our Batoka friend, Masakasa, was one of a party that came to steal some of the young women; but Sinamane, to their utter astonishment, attacked them so furiously that the survivors barely escaped with their lives. Masakasa had to flee so fast that he threw away his shield, his spear, and his clothes, and returned home a wiser and a sadder man.

Waist-belt.

145

'Waist-belt'
From *Narrative of an Expedition to the Zambesi and its Tributaries*
By David and Charles Livingstone
Published by John Murray,
London, 1865
QUENTIN KEYNES
(cat. no. 4.65)

From left to right
Section of an antelope net collected by Livingstone during the Zambezi expedition
Bark from the baobab tree
Approximately 488 x 183 cm
COURTESY OF THE TRUSTEES OF THE NATIONAL MUSEUMS OF SCOTLAND
(cat. no. 4.79)

Nets such as this one were probably strung across ravines or gorges, and game then driven into them.

Wooden headrest from the Zambezi Delta
15.5 x 18.5 cm
COURTESY OF THE TRUSTEES OF THE NATIONAL MUSEUMS OF SCOTLAND
(cat. no. 4.76)

This was presented to the Royal Museum of Scotland in 1860 by John Kirk.

Rope of African manufacture brought back from Lake Ngami by Livingstone
Plant fibre, 82 cm (length)
THE DAVID LIVINGSTONE CENTRE
(cat. no. 2.60)

According to an early museum label from Blantyre this rope was 'used by the native boatmen on Lake Ngami before their contact with Europeans'.

Below right
Two baskets collected by John Kirk on the Zambezi expedition
Palm leaf
48.3 x 28 cm; 24.2 x 39.4 cm
LENT BY KIND PERMISSION OF THE TRUSTEES OF THE BRITISH MUSEUM
(cat. no. 4.84)

No function or originating culture was specified by Kirk but his labels carefully note that these baskets are of palm (*Hyphaene*) leaf. He sent a number of artefacts back to Britain to demonstrate the transformation of plant material into useful objects.

very nicely platted together.'[10] Livingstone hoped that the plant fibre buaze might eventually be used in the commercial manufacture of rope or cloth. He submitted some of it for analysis to a London firm and reproduced its letter of cautious assessment in *Missionary Travels*, along with an illustration of the plant itself. A portion of an antelope net, collected on the Zambezi expedition, is also still held at Kew; what is probably the other half is in the Royal Museum of Scotland. Both pieces entered their respective collections in 1860, and in both cases the accompanying notes offer very little ethnographic data but state that they are made from the baobab tree. However, Livingstone may be describing the use of this net when he writes of the method by which the people he called the Badema caught game: 'Zebras, antelopes, and other animals are taken by drawing them into ravines, strong nets of baobab-bark being stretched across the narrow outlets.'[11]

Kirk also made many flora contributions, over several years, to the herbarium and living plant collections at Kew, including specimens of such things as the herbal poison used in hunting arrows on the Zambezi, accompanied with full notes on its physical effects on the prey. He discovered by 'accidental experiment', as Livingstone put it, that it was sufficiently strong to lower his pulse. Livingstone described the manufacture of poisoned arrows in his expedition account and sent several examples to Britain.

The Zambezi expedition also resulted in the formation of large faunal collections, now in the Natural History Museum in London. While this essay is primarily concerned with artefacts, the numbers are revealing for fauna specimens far outnumber objects. Considering birds alone, 193 specimens obtained and preserved by Kirk were presented to the museum in 1860 by the Foreign Office. A further forty-four birds from the Zambezi and the Shire rivers were collected by Charles Livingstone, and another thirty-nine, gathered by Kirk from the same area, were added in 1863.

Livingstone himself notes on 7 June 1859 that he has secured for the British Museum, as requested by Richard Owen, the renowned biologist, a set of elephant molars. A donation from Livingstone of elephants' skulls and teeth entered that collection in the same year, although it is difficult to prove that it is the same set to which he referred. Such specimens were also found in the private collections of Livingstone's family and friends.

Earthenware pots for catching palm sap
By Thomas Baines
(?)28 November 1859
Watercolour over pencil on paper
26.6 x 37.9 cm
ROYAL GEOGRAPHICAL SOCIETY
(cat. no. 4.17)

Like Livingstone and John Kirk, Baines was keen to record the cultural practices of the peoples of the Zambezi region. This drawing shows the collecting of sap for palm wine using earthenware pots; one such pot was sent back to Britain and is now in the British Museum. As Baines notes in his detailed inscription, the pots were slung to the stumps of palms and, as in the left-hand example, 'covered with a basket of palm leaf to protect the sap from evaporation'.

Earthenware pot for catching palm sap, collected by John Kirk on the Zambezi expedition
11.5 x 11.5 cm
LENT BY KIND PERMISSION OF THE TRUSTEES OF THE BRITISH MUSEUM
(cat. no. 4.75)

Livingstone thought that fresh palm wine was similar to champagne and observed that it aged over the course of a day and became quite intoxicating. He also made notes on its gathering: 'The top of the fruit-shoot is cut off, and the sap, pouring out at the fresh wound, is caught in an earthen pot, which is hung at the point'.

Title-page from *Narrative of an Expedition to the Zambesi and its Tributaries*
By David and Charles Livingstone
Published by John Murray,
London, 1865
QUENTIN KEYNES
(cat. no. 4.65)

NARRATIVE

OF AN

EXPEDITION TO THE ZAMBESI

AND ITS TRIBUTARIES;

AND OF THE DISCOVERY OF THE LAKES SHIRWA
AND NYASSA.

1858—1864.

BY DAVID AND CHARLES LIVINGSTONE.

WITH MAP AND ILLUSTRATIONS.

LONDON:
JOHN MURRAY, ALBEMARLE STREET.
1865.

The right of Translation is reserved.

149

Hand mill for grinding corn, collected by Livingstone
c. 1861
Stone bowl and maul
10 cm (height) x 43 cm (diameter)
COURTESY OF THE TRUSTEES OF
THE NATIONAL MUSEUMS OF
SCOTLAND
(cat. no. 4.74)

This mill was described in the Royal Museum of Scotland's catalogue as having been 'obtained from a chief up the Shire River' and is probably the one illustrated on the title-page of *Narrative of an Expedition to the Zambesi*. Later in the same book a fuller description of its use appears, describing how 'the weight of the person is brought to bear on the moveable stone and while it is pressed and pushed forwards and backwards, one hand supplies every now and then a little grain to be thus at first bruised and then ground on the lower stone, which is placed on the slope, so that the meal, when ground, falls on to a skin or mat spread for the purpose.'

Moselekatse. King of the Matabili.   Kapain 25th October 1836.

There was no one specifically assigned to the collection of objects for ethnographic analysis in the same spirit of 'scientific enquiry' that prompted the gathering of natural history specimens. However, there were instructions for furthering the aims of ethnology, as they were then defined. Charles Livingstone was to photograph the indigenous peoples he encountered: 'You will endeavour to secure characteristic specimens of the different tribes residing in, or visiting Tete, for the purposes of Ethnology.'[12] If any such photographs were taken, few seem to have survived. The artist Thomas Baines was given similar instructions for drawing the indigenous peoples he encountered, with the additional note that 'should it be possible to give the dimensions of the heads of the individuals you may select, the measurements will be highly prized. The comelier countenances should be selected rather than the uglier, as the former are always taken as the types of the European race.'[13]

Despite the fact that Charles Livingstone does not seem to have fulfilled that particular brief, there are dozens of African objects collected, preserved and sent back by David Livingstone that can be analysed for what they reveal of their originating cultures as well as the European sensibilities and lived experience of the collector.

Livingstone and the African peoples with whom he interacted often had intensely material transactions and exchanges. In speaking of southern Africa in general, and the Tswana in particular, the anthropologists Jean and John Comaroff make an observation about a process that took place elsewhere in Africa.

> With the colonial state ever more visible at their back, the Churchmen had a considerable impact upon African modes of production, dress, and architecture. The Tswana in turn strove to gain some control over the evident potency of the Europeans – potency residing in diverse objects and practices, from guns and mirrors to irrigation and literacy.[14]

That potency Livingstone demonstrated on many occasions with his magic lantern, which he used to illustrate stories from the Bible. It was not only an evangelical tool but also what he called 'the oxyhydrogen light of modern civilization'. In 1854 Livingstone was received at the court of the powerful ruler Shinte, whose viewing of the magic-lantern show is a story worth telling in some detail. Meant for home consumption to impress British audiences with the success of evangelical efforts, it exhibits the somewhat sensationalised style that Livingstone used when relating the effect of European

Mzilikazi, King of the Ndebele
By William Cornwallis Harris
25 October 1836
Watercolour over pencil on paper
38 x 28.6 cm
QUENTIN KEYNES
(cat. no. 2.13)

Harris visited the Ndebele leader, Mzilikazi, in October 1836.

151

Livingstone's magic lantern
55 x 40.7 x 15 cm
THE DAVID LIVINGSTONE CENTRE
(cat. no. 2.57)

Livingstone used his magic lantern to show Africans illustrated stories from the Bible. It served not only as an evangelical tool but also as a demonstration of European technology: 'the oxyhydrogen light of civilisation', as Livingstone called it.

Livingstone's prismatic compass
Manufactured by Cary, London
Approximately 7.5 cm (diameter)
ROYAL GEOGRAPHICAL SOCIETY
(cat. no. 5.49)

Basin given to Sechele by Livingstone, *c*. 1852
40 cm (diameter)
THE DAVID LIVINGSTONE CENTRE
(cat. no. 2.55)

A brass tray and basin, along with a copper jug, were displayed in a 1913 exhibition celebrating the 100th anniversary of Livingstone's birth. In the accompanying catalogue they were described as being 'probably used for camping when the [missionary] family travelled. These were given to the chief Sechele when the [Livingstone] household scattered'.

technology on those unfamiliar with it.

He had his principal men and the same crowd of court beauties near him as at the reception. The first picture exhibited was Abraham about to slaughter his son Isaac; it was shown as large as life, and the uplifted knife was in the act of striking the lad; the Balonda men remarked that the picture was much more like a god than the things of wood or clay they worshipped. I explained that this man was the first of a race to whom God had given the Bible we now held, and that among his children our Saviour appeared. The ladies listened with silent awe; but when I moved the slide, the uplifted dagger moving towards them, they thought it was to be sheathed in their bodies instead of Isaac's. 'Mother! mother!' all shouted at once, and off they rushed helter-skelter, tumbling pell-mell over each other, and over the little idol-huts and tobacco-bushes: we could not get one of them back again. Shinte, however, sat bravely through the whole, and afterwards examined the instrument with interest.[15]

Although at least one chief flatly refused to see the show, Livingstone often remarked on the attraction that the display of European manufactured goods had. It is important to remember, however, that 'Western commodities cannot be seen to embody some irresistible attraction that is given the status of an inexorable historical force. Indigenous peoples' interests in goods, strangers, and contact were variable and in some cases were extremely constrained.'[16]

Livingstone himself records such restraint on another occasion: 'I then showed him my watch, and wished to win my way into his confidence by conversation; but when about to exhibit my pocket compass he desired me to desist, as he was afraid of my wonderful things . . . .'.[17]

Some of those things were given by Livingstone to African leaders in a pattern not unfamiliar in southern Africa, where missionaries sought to influence chiefs through the presentation of personal gifts meant to flatter, adorn and generate consumer demand for European goods.[18] Looking at the list of presents for Sekeletu (chief of the Kololo people) that Livingstone noted in his Zambezi journal for 21 August 1860, it is clear how such commodities would eventually act as agents of incorporation into a colonial economy. 'Took to Sekeletu 4 fine rugs, 1 piece of Mohair, 2 country cloths, 2 moleskin's jackets, 2 pr moleskin trousers, 2 Scotch tweed do., 2 Alpaca jackets – exchanged one for but cloth do. – 1 Uniform scarlet coatee and band, shirts, 1 Accordion, 1 snuff-box, 3 felt hats, and one hat

and in order
to understand
their force we
must place
ourselves in
their position
+ believe as they
and homoeopathists
do that all
medicines act
by a mysterious
charm. The
term for one
may be trans
lated "Charm"
Alafa.

people along with them and not
without reason. With the following arguments
they were all acquainted:-

Medical Doctor. Hail friend!
How very many medicines you have
about you this morning. Why
you have every medicine in the country
about you

Rain doctor. Very true my friend
and I ought for the whole country
needs the rain which I am making

M.D. So you really believe that
you can command the clouds
I think that can be done by God
alone

R.D. We both believe the very
same thing. It is God that makes
the rain but I pray to him
by means of these medicines
and of course the rain is mine.
It was I who made it for the
Bakwains for many years
when they were at Shokuane,
through my wisdom their
women became fat and shining
Ask them they will tell you the
same as I do.

M.D. But we are distinctly
told in the parting words of our
saviour that we can pray to
God acceptably in his name
alone and not by means
of medicines

R.D. Truly, but God told us
differently. He made black

with gold band, 1 pair scizzors, 6 clasp knives, 2 superior knives, 1 penknife.'[19]

However, for someone who frequently wrote about the lives and personalities of individual Africans, Livingstone seems to have retained few souvenirs or markers of his relationships with them. The interaction between Livingstone and his only convert, the Kwena chief Sechele, reveals some of the complexities and ambiguities of his relationships with African peoples as well as the insights and limitations of his anthropological understanding. His accounts of this Tswana group benefited from his ability to work without an interpreter, although it has been suggested that while he read the language easily he 'had difficulty in grasping what was spoken to him'.[20]

Sechele was baptised in September 1848. As part of his conversion he gave up all but one of his wives. However, when Livingstone discovered in March the following year that one of these women was pregnant he forbade Sechele to take communion for two years. Many Europeans seemed to view polygyny as a primarily sexual arrangement rather than as an economic institution that often reflects and contributes to the wealth of the man (who has acquired the labour of more than one wife). Livingstone, however, recognised, at least partly, the use of marriage in establishing alliances in the world of Tswana politics.

Some of Sechele's children were baptised with him, although the relatives of his displaced wives became implacably hostile to Livingstone's evangelical efforts and his demands for monogamous unions. The Tswana viewed marriage as an alliance between domestic groups; the ideal family was the uterine household of mother and child. Missionary insistence on the nuclear family of father, mother and their offspring weakened those alliances between groups, discouraged intergenerational links, emphasised the loyalty of the couple to each other at the expense of kindred, and created a different concept of privacy. Tswana opposition to monogamy is quite understandable, for as later scholars have suggested:

> Not only did the polygamous household form the base of the polity; it also underpinned the symbolic construction of the social world. Indeed, when the Nonconformists later tried, as did most missionaries, to banish the 'barbarism' of plural marriage, they had scant idea what was at issue. Some, it is true, understood that the worldly authority of chiefs and royals would suffer. But none were quite aware how

Livingstone's manuscript of *Missionary Travels and Researches in South Africa* showing his conversation with a 'rain doctor'
Bound manuscript, 1857
33.8 x 45 cm (open)
PRIVATE COLLECTION
(cat. no. 2.40)

155

This is the original manuscript for Livingstone's great book, *Missionary Travels and Researches in South Africa*, published in 1857. Seen here is the opening of his account of his conversation with a Kwena healer, referred to by him as a 'rain doctor'. In the margin he has inserted a passage, adopted in the book, stressing that his readers need to understand the Kwena belief that 'all medicines act by a mysterious charm'.

profoundly they were tampering with the invisible
scaffolding of the sociocultural order.[21]

For all the multiple strands of this important encounter
between Livingstone and Sechele, his only convert, there
remains very little material evidence. In a letter of 1846,
to a correspondent in Glasgow, Livingstone listed the
contents of a box of African 'curios' from Chonwane.
This letter and some 'objects from Bechuanaland' were
exhibited at the then Royal Scottish Museum's Livingstone
centenary exhibition in 1913, when the artefacts were
described as a 'stool, club or image, rhinoceros horn stick,
sandals, carved ladle, native bottle, charms, needles in case,
rhinoceros tail. (Brought home by Livingstone: belonged
to the chief Sechele, an intimate friend of Livingstone.)'[22]

Livingstone's collections of items of material culture can
be misleading, however, if taken to represent the whole of
his ethnographic interests. In *Missionary Travels* he related
a conversation he had had with a Kwena healer whom he
referred to as a 'rain doctor'. It is in the form of a debate,
which begins with the Scottish 'medical doctor' asking,
'So you really believe that you can command the clouds?
I think that can be done by God alone.' To which the
Kwena 'rain doctor' replies, 'We both believe the very
same thing. It is God that makes the rain, but I pray to
him by means of these medicines, and, the rain coming,
of course it is then mine . . .'.[23]

Many missionaries came to consider such ritual specialists
as their enemies; those who converted them from
indigenous beliefs to Christian ones often kept the ritual
paraphernalia surrendered to them as tokens of successful
evangelical labours. Few such trophies appear in
Livingstone's collection. Throughout his conversation
with the Kwena healer Livingstone allows the African
'to confront him with the logical impasse of the mission.
The parallel use of the title "doctor" as much as the
symmetry of the actual debate, implies an ironic
conviction that the contest is being waged on equal
ontological grounds.'[24] It has been suggested that it was
through just such confrontations that the Tswana came
to have a more corporate 'ethnic' identity well beyond the
local community as they compared and contrasted their
cultural practices with those of Europeans.[25]

The two Africans with whom the Livingstone myth,
rather than the man, has been most closely connected are
James Chuma and Abdullah Susi. Often described in the
late-nineteenth-century literature as his 'faithful servants',
they are the most important individuals in the European
accounts of the transportation of Livingstone's embalmed

Below
James Chuma (*c.* 1850–1882)
By Maull & Co., 1874
Albumen carte-de-visite
10.2 x 6.2 cm
ROYAL GEOGRAPHICAL SOCIETY
(cat. no. 6.6)

James Chuma, a Yao released from
slavery in 1861, worked for the
Universities' Mission to Central
Africa until 1864. From there he
travelled to India where he was
baptised in 1865. He returned to
Africa to take part in Livingstone's
last journeys and was a member of
the party that carried his corpse to
the coast. After Livingstone's death
Chuma worked again for the UMCA.
He died in Zanzibar in 1882.

Abdullah Susi (**died 1891**)
By Maull & Co., 1874
Albumen carte-de-visite
10.2 x 6.2 cm
ROYAL GEOGRAPHICAL SOCIETY
(cat. no. 6.7)

Coming from Shupanga, Susi
joined the Zambezi expedition as a
wood-cutter in 1863. He became a
key figure in the later search for
the Nile, Stanley describing him as
the 'chief and confidential servant'
on this journey. After Livingstone's
death he worked for the Universities'
Mission to Central Africa and the
Church Missionary Society. He
was baptised in 1886, taking the
name David, and died five years
later in Zanzibar.

Opposite
James Chuma (*c.* 1850–1882)
By Maull & Co., 1874
Albumen cabinet print
15 x 10 cm (sight)
THE DAVID LIVINGSTONE CENTRE
(cat. no. 6.8)

This (and cat. no. 6.4) are from a
group of studio photographs by
Maull & Co., taken during Chuma
and Susi's visit to Britain in 1874.
They show the two men in
'African' dress against a painted
'African' backdrop.

James Chuma (*c.* 1850–1882)
and Abdullah Susi (**died 1891**)
By Maull & Co., 1874
Albumen cabinet print
15 x 10 cm (sight)
THE DAVID LIVINGSTONE CENTRE
(cat. no. 6.4)

body to the coast. Chuma and Susi were brought to Britain by James Young, and it was their recollections that Horace Waller used in constructing his scenes of the missionary's death. Although their lives were intertwined over a number of years, there is no clear evidence that Livingstone himself retained any mementoes of these two men. However, several objects either used or made by them do survive in British collections. Sometimes it is unclear which person was actually the owner or maker, as 'Chuma and Susi' seem to have been fused into a single persona in the mind of the British public.

Apart from these two men, Livingstone's name was most often linked with the Kololo. A Sotho group caught up in the disruptions and massive movements of peoples in southern Africa known as *Difaqane*, the Kololo had moved north by the time Livingstone crossed the Kalahari and first met them in 1851. He hoped for a mission to the 'Makololo' under their chief, Sebitwane, but shortly after their meeting, Sebitwane died. Livingstone described his grief in his journals and more publicly in *Missionary Travels*, where he wrote: 'He was decidedly the best specimen of a native chief I ever met. I never felt so much grieved by the loss of a black man before . . . .'.[26]

Livingstone was afraid that Sebitwane's successor, Sekeletu, would not be interested in a continuing partnership, but the Kololo hoped the missionary would be useful in ongoing political upheavals, during which the presence of Robert Moffat's son-in-law might afford some protection from the Ndebele of Mzilikazi, with whom Moffat had forged a close personal alliance.

Although Livingstone's mission never materialised, these people, whom he referred to as 'my faithful Makololo', supplied the carriers who accompanied him to Angola and along the Zambezi, guided him in 1855 to the Victoria Falls, formed a bodyguard on a trip to Lake Shirwa and frequently acted as translators. They also lent their knowledge to the collecting activites of the Zambezi expedition, describing the eggs of the tsetse fly for Livingstone, and gathering buaze fibres and insects. Livingstone noted that 'they enter into this work with spirit'.[27]

Yet there is very little identifiable material specifically from the Kololo in public collections. It may be that over the years they became such familiar companions that their possessions and manufactures lacked any 'curiosity' value. The disaster of the Helmore mission among them, and the deaths of missionary families for which at the time Livingstone was occasionally held to blame, may also have

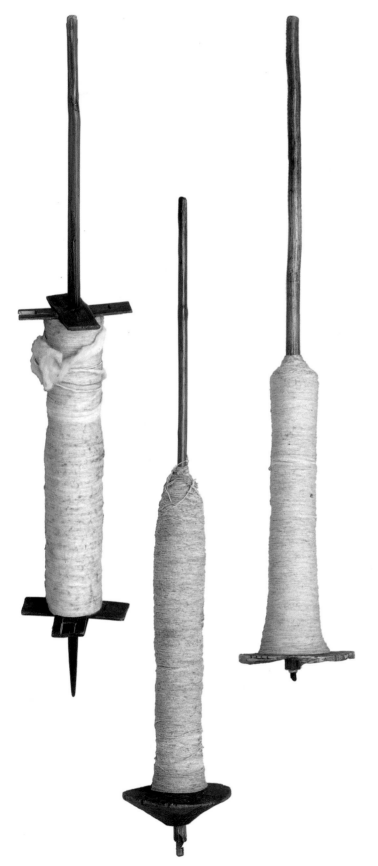

evoked painful feelings of failure that he would not seek to rekindle through objects. Most importantly, perhaps, the Kololo were replaced by the Mang'anja as the 'target' for Livingstone's plans to spread 'Christianity, Commerce and Civilisation' in Central Africa.

The Kololo did not survive as a political entity after the death of Sekeletu in 1864, and the Lozi (Barotse) re-established themselves as overlords in their own territories. Livingstone had, however, left some sixteen Kololo (although by this time most of them had been assimilated from other groups) on the River Shire. They had guns, which he had given them for hunting and for their own protection, and the experience of living in a more highly integrated political system than that of the people in the Shire Highlands. Marrying local women, they soon gathered followers, entered into the political scene and successfully established themselves among the Mang'anja. They, like Livingstone, were to become entangled in both mission politics and the intra-ethnic factionalism of the Mang'anja themselves.

Livingstone made several journeys into the Mang'anja homelands between 1859 and 1863, convinced that it was in their territory that his colonisation plans, based on the eradication of slavery and the substitution of legitimate commerce, would take place. Part of the argument made for government funding was that African cotton would be cheaper than the American, slave-grown, crop needed to keep the mills in Britain producing at full capacity.

Not surprisingly, the cotton plant, its cultivation and the indigenous objects associated with the production of cloth were collected and described in the journals, letters and publications sent home by members of the Zambezi expedition. For example, three Mang'anja spindles, each slightly different in design but full of cotton thread, were sent back by Kirk to Kew, possibly as part of a shipment of raw and spun cotton and associated instruments that he records in his journal for 12 January 1859. In a letter to Lord Malmesbury later in the year, Livingstone wrote that 'Everyone spins and weaves cotton. Even chiefs may be seen with the spindle and bag which serves as a distaff.'[28] The division of labour, with men more active in agricultural production than some neighbouring peoples, meant they were less likely to be away hunting or on the trail and thus even more amenable, to Livingstone's thinking, to providing the labour force for a European colony.

The Mang'anja were also noted metalworkers and it may be that some of the spears in the Glasgow Museum,

Left

Spindles with cotton thread collected from the Mang'anja on the River Shire by John Kirk
Maximum length 48.3 cm
LENT BY KIND PERMISSION OF THE TRUSTEES OF THE BRITISH MUSEUM
(cat. no. 3.35)

Livingstone noted that even chiefs were seen spinning cotton. He hoped that legitimate commerce, such as the cultivation of cotton and its manufacture into cloth, would eventually replace the slave trade.

'Native web, and Weaver smoking the huge tobacco pipe of the country'
From *Narrative of an Expedition to the Zambesi and its Tributaries*
By David and Charles Livingstone
Published by John Murray, London, 1865
QUENTIN KEYNES
(cat. no. 4.65)

While it cannot be assumed that it is the same object, John Kirk's description of weaving (in 1859) provides a valuable insight into how these looms functioned. He noted: 'The weaving is simple. The thread is passed from end to end between two horizontal bamboos supported in the ground. The upper ones are attached by Buaze or Musheo threads to an upper stick which serves to bring them up or down above the others, while a shuttle consisting of a stick, a little larger than the width of the cloth, and covered with the cotton thread, is passed from side to side, the thread unwinding as it passes.'

Right
**Figure smoking a pipe and
the leaf of a palm**
By Thomas Baines
19 November 1859
Watercolour over pencil on paper
38 x 26.2 cm
ROYAL GEOGRAPHICAL SOCIETY
(cat. no. 4.18)

According to Baines's inscription
the top drawing shows a 'native
smoking wild hemp in a water
pipe'. The lower drawing is of a
palm leaf. Sap for palm wine was
extracted from palm trees by the
local people.

**'Pelele, or Lip-ring of
Manganja woman'**
From *Narrative of an Expedition to the
Zambesi and its Tributaries*
By David and Charles Livingstone
Published by John Murray,
London, 1865
QUENTIN KEYNES
(cat. no. 4.65)

In his account of the Zambezi
expedition Livingstone describes
how such lip-rings were used. 'The
poorer classes make them of
hollow, or of solid, bamboo, but
the wealthier of ivory or tin. The
tin *pelele* is often made in the form
of a small dish. The ivory one is
not unlike a napkin-ring. No
woman ever appears in public
without the *pelele*, except in times of
mourning for the dead. It is
frightfully ugly to see the upper lip
projecting two inches beyond the
tip of the nose.'

160

identified only as having been collected by Livingstone on
the Zambezi, were made by them. Kirk, who drew some
of their spears in his journal, wrote on 26 March 1859 that
'The iron work of this region is very good. Yesterday the
Doctor bought a knife made of splendid iron, wrought
very thin and reduced to an elastic state by hammering.'[29]

Not all the objects that Livingstone collected among the
Mang'anja illustrate their potential usefulness to the
colonial endeavour, although they by no means provide a
complete inventory of Mang'anja material culture. One
cultural practice that Livingstone, like many other
Europeans at the time, found repulsive was the use of 'lip
rings'. He described them at some length in his published
account of the Zambezi expedition and also provided an
illustration of a woman wearing one. Calling it a
'curiosity', Kirk records in his journal for 5 January 1859
that Livingstone bought an ivory one; it may be the one
that he sent to his daughter Agnes in 1860. In a
companion letter he joked that the engineer from the
expedition, who was taking back various objects, would
show her how to wear it.

Livingstone was puzzled by this body alteration, which
he found ugly, and he was unable to accept that for the
Mang'anja it functioned as a marker of gender and status.
Instances of mutual incomprehension and cross-cultural
judgements can be found throughout Livingstone's writings;
his own ethnocentrism was most often unrecognised. African
examples of the same trait (he relates, for example, that a
group of pastoralists asked him how many cattle Queen
Victoria owned, as that was how they calculated their own
wealth) were probably included to induce a sense of
amused superiority on the part of British readers.

Perhaps in the same category of 'curiosity' as the lip rings
are several complex Mang'anja pipes (now at the Museum
of Mankind but formerly at Kew) brought back by the
Livingstone expedition. One, decorated with an animal
figure described as a 'crocodile', was said to be for
smoking *bhang* (cannabis). Both Kirk and Livingstone
commented on the widespread use of tobacco and hemp,
Kirk describing it as 'universal'.

Such items acted as confirmation for home audiences that
claims made by expedition members to be 'exploring'
were indeed true. As one scholar of material culture has
observed, 'what was important about collecting, was not
so much what could be said about or done with the
specimens collected but the way that collected material
attested to the fact of having visited remote places and
observed novel phenomena.'[30]

after Smithy — and theirs
in a water proba
Nov. 19th 59

There is a small hair between every division of the leaf
generally grow like a low bush. but sometimes has a stem
6 or 8 feet high and sometimes divided into four or five
branches each with a head of leaves — the fruit
is hard and very insipid — the natives cut down
the plants and [...] to the [...] a small earthen jar
[...]
Kongone

Manyema spears collected by Livingstone on his last journeys
Varying lengths, 142.7–189.3 cm
GLASGOW MUSEUMS
(cat. no. 1.4)

The only other group of named people, or more accurately peoples, from whom Livingstone collected significant numbers of objects are those he called the Manyuema or Manyema, whom he encountered between 1869 and 1871 in the course of his futile search for the sources of the Nile. Their homelands, which were also called Manyema, were often described as 'unknown territory' and Livingstone frequently extolled the physical beauty of the area. However, the whole basis of Manyema life was undergoing rapid and sometimes violent change owing to the expansion of Swahili trade and the incorporation of non-Swahili peoples into their sphere of commercial influence.[31] Stanley was to call the emerging economic frontier in Manyema an 'El Dorado'.

The Manyema had a reputation among the Swahili traders for cannibalism. At first Livingstone denied this allegation, attributing such reports to the gullibility of other travellers or the machinations of Manyema enemies. In a letter to his son Thomas, dated 24 September 1869, he reveals this scepticism:

> People laugh and say 'Yes we eat the flesh of men' and should they see the enquirer to be credulous enter into particulars. A black stuff smeared on the cheeks is the sign of mourning, and they told one of my people who believes all they say, that it is animal charcoal made of the bones of relatives they have eaten. They showed him the skull of one recently devoured, and he pointed it out to me in triumph. It was the skull of a gorillah – here called 'Soko' – and this they do eat . . . Many of the Arabs believe firmly in the cannibal propensities of the Manyuema, others who have lived long among them and are themselves three-quarters African blood deny them.

By 28 December 1870 he is writing of the Manyema that 'the love of high meat is the only reason I know for their cannibalism, but the practice is now hidden on account of the disgust that the traders expressed against open man-eating when they first arrived.'[32]

Members of Livingstone's party believed that one of their own men, called James, had been eaten by the Manyema. In his journal for 4 February 1871 Livingstone notes only that 'James was killed to-day by an arrow: the assassin was hid in the forest till my men going to buy food came up.'[33] It is Horace Waller, acting as editor of the *Last Journals*, who added a footnote at the end of the same page suggesting that 'The men gave indisputable proof that his body was eaten by the Manyuema who lay in ambush.'

A few days previously Livingstone had written, 'Their

Spearheads collected by Livingstone from 'Manyema country' during his last journeys
GLASGOW MUSEUMS
(cat. no. 5.60)

In 1871 Livingstone was ambushed by 'Manyema' warriors and narrowly missed being speared to death.

cannibalism is doubtful, but my observations raise grave suspicions. A Scotch jury would say "Not proven". The women are not guilty.'[34] Then on 21 April he noted:

> The men here deny that cannibalism is common. They eat only those killed in war, and, it seems, in revenge . . . Some west of Lualaba eat even those bought for the purpose of a feast; but I am not quite positive on this point: all agree in saying that human flesh is saltish, and needs but little condiment. And yet they are a fine-looking race; I would back a company of Manyuema men to be far superior in shape of head and generally in physical form too against the whole Anthropological Society.[35]

There is no suggestion that Livingstone witnessed any acts of cannibalism and it is unclear why he moved from his earlier assumption that such allegations were more likely to be about 'reputation' than 'reality'. One recent biographer concludes, '. . . the Manyema were purported to be cannibals though Livingstone never fully believed it, despite what Susi and Chuma said.'[36] No artefacts documenting this putative practice were collected by Livingstone.

Although the allegations of cannibalism were levelled indiscriminately at the Manyema, Livingstone was clearly aware of considerable variation in many cultural practices throughout the area and that the Manyema were made up of quite distinct peoples. Recent estimates are of some twenty-five groups in the present-day part of Zaire known as Maniema.[37] However, in his designation of artefacts Livingstone makes no such distinction, identifying them simply as of or from Manyema.

His collection from this area is composed largely of weapons – spears, short swords and knives. Why such a limited range of objects exists may be partly related to the nature of Livingstone's experiences there. In July 1871 he witnessed a massacre by slavers of several hundred Manyema, mostly women and children, at the large market in Nyangwe, an event that disturbed him profoundly.

> The terrible scenes of man's inhumanity to man brought on severe headache, which might have been serious had it not been relieved by a copious discharge of blood; I was laid up all yesterday afternoon, with the depression the bloodshed made, – it filled me with unspeakable horror. 'Don't go away,' say the Manyuema chiefs to me; but I cannot stay here in agony.[38]

Livingstone's party were themselves attacked on 8 August 1871 on their return to Ujiji. He believed that the Manyema had mistaken him for one of the market murderers, as he was wearing a red shirt or waistcoat like those worn by the slavers.[39] He records the attack in his journal for that day '. . . a large spear from my right lunged past and almost grazed my back, and stuck firmly into the soil . . . As they are expert with the spear I don't know how it missed, except that he was too sure of his aim and the good hand of God was upon me.'[40] The head of one of the spears that narrowly missed Livingstone is on display at the museum in Blantyre. Several Manyema weapons collected by Livingstone are in Glasgow; these may be the swords and spearheads that Livingstone packed up in a large tin box on 17 December 1871 'for transmission home by Mr Stanley'.[41] Several such weapons are illustrated in Stanley's account of how he found Livingstone, in which he enthuses, 'The Manyuema are the cleverest manufacturers of weapons.'[42]

Allegations of barbarity have often attracted collectors to certain kinds of artefacts. By acquiring objects associated with such practices – whether alleged, witnessed or just imagined – collectors could demonstrate their imaginary superiority at the top of an assumed social or evolutionary hierarchy. Along with the not uncommon practice of presenting finely crafted weapons to visitors judged of sufficent rank or importance, this may account for the significant presence of weapons in museum collections, including those donated by Livingstone. The partiality of this collection promoted or re-enforced stereotypical views of the peoples of Manyema.

Of course, 'the historical encounters between two social worlds – however circumscribed the one, or expansive the other – is always *dialectical*, that is, each works to transform the other. This is not to say that the process, or its social product, is determined in equal measure by both sides or that they have a commensurate impact on one another.'[43] In his Zambezi journal for 30 June 1858 John Kirk describes just such an interchange over a small dynamo or generator. 'The Doctor gets out his galvanic magnetic machine and gives a shock to the natives who come out today from the camp of Mariano the rebel. On feeling it, one of them at once said 'Oh Shynyessi' (the name of the electric fish). They then all recognized it as the same thing and gave the machine that name.'[44]

We might also ask if 'reverse' collections of 'Livingstoneia' developed. Certainly Livingstone records that the Africans preserved and displayed European artefacts. In *Missionary Travels* he tells how, having shown some of his own instruments, his host 'produced a jug, of English ware, shaped like an old man holding a can of beer in his hand, as the greatest curiosity he had to exhibit'.[45] What happened, one wonders, to the 'looking-glass' he pressed upon a woman who offered him food without expectation of payment? One mirror was preserved long enough by the African to whom it was given to constitute physical evidence of Livingstone's presence beyond the site of his alleged murder in 1866. Have any of the iron spoons and razors he often presented to local headmen survived? In 1860 he gave an accordion to the Kololo leader Sekeletu, who had also commissioned Livingstone to bring him 'any other beautiful thing you may see in your own country'.[46] Did it become a European 'curio', preserved, displayed or demonstrated for the amusement and edification of African viewers, thus establishing some parity in the mutual appropriation of material culture?

Livingstone and other Europeans on the Zambezi expedition sometimes 'exhibited' themselves as living objects: their hair, skin, clothing, feeding habits – and in the case of Commander Bedingfield, his false teeth – were of interest to visitors to their camp. Livingstone seems to have cheerfully demonstrated his shared humanity with Africans by occasionally lifting up his shirt to show his chest (albeit with untanned skin, which he once compared to 'blanched celery'). Kirk, however, was uncomfortable with this sort of display and complained in September 1861 that 'Our tent is pitched under the shade of a tree, a relief from the burning sun of the Autumn months, and here we have to pass the time as wild beasts in a show.'[47] A similar 'career' as a specimen or living exhibit may have been too much for the Kololo headman, whom Livingstone called Sekwebu; he accompanied Livingstone to England in 1856 but committed suicide at sea.

The reasons for that suicide remain obscure, as do, to some extent, Livingstone's reasons for sending particular objects back to nineteenth-century Britain. By looking at his collection as a cultural text, however, in which objects act as an expression not only of the views of those who chose to make and use them, but also of those who chose to collect them, it has become possible to understand something of the complexities of the Victorian encounter with Africa.

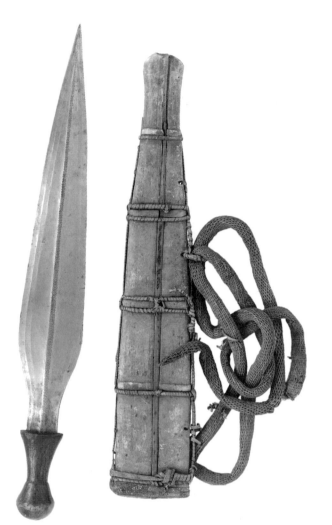

Sword, or dagger, and sheath collected by Livingstone in 'Manyema country' during his last journeys
Sheath, 59.3 cm; sword, 67.2 cm
GLASGOW MUSEUMS
(cat. no. 5.61)

165

Overleaf
Kudu in a landscape (detail)
By William Cornwallis Harris
c. 1837–1840
Watercolour and bodycolour over pencil on paper
30.2 x 41 cm
QUENTIN KEYNES
(cat. no. 2.16)

This striking watercolour was worked up by Harris after his visit to southern Africa. It was published as a lithograph in his folio volume of 1840, *Portraits of the Game Animals of Southern Africa.*

Discovery matches
Manufactured by Dixon, Son &
Evans, 1870s
Matchbox, 7 x 14.5 cm
THE DAVID LIVINGSTONE CENTRE
(cat. no. 5.56)

Tim Barringer

Fabricating Africa:
Livingstone and the Visual Image
1850–1874

5

'Livingstone and the Lion'
Magic lantern slide (glass positive)
From *The Life and Work of David
Livingstone*
Published by the London
Missionary Society, *c.* 1900
NATIONAL PORTRAIT GALLERY
LONDON
(cat. no. 6.12)

*The Life and Work of David
Livingstone*, a set of forty lantern
slides, reveals how the story of
Livingstone's life was transmitted
to later generations. This slide, in
the words of the pamphlet that
accompanies the set, shows
Livingstone's 'wonderful escape
from death in a lion encounter'. It
transforms the relatively passive
depiction of this famous incident
in *Missionary Travels and Researches
in South Africa* (see p. 178) into a
scene of high drama, with the lion
leaping through the air on to a
bloodied Livingstone.

Fabricating Africa:
Livingstone and the Visual Image
1850–1874

Visual representations played a crucial role in forming an idea of Africa in the imagination of the Victorian public. Livingstone attacked by a lion; the broad panorama of the Victoria Falls; the famous meeting of Livingstone and Stanley: such defining scenes of the Victorian encounter with Africa were memorialised in wood-engraved images that circulated throughout mid-Victorian Britain in illustrated books and newspapers. Images can portray people and landscapes with an immediacy that language struggles to emulate. As the earliest predecessors of the newspaper photographs, video news-footage and documentary films through which Africa is represented in Britain today, Victorian images of Africa retain much of the vividness that ensured their popularity with their original audiences. Nonetheless, they cannot be accepted at face value as simple reflections of things seen. Even the most rudimentary Victorian images of Africa are influenced by the attitudes of those who made them, by existing visual traditions and by the technologies with which they were produced. Looked at closely, such images are often as revealing about the Victorian culture that created them as about the African cultures and landscapes they claim to represent, giving visual form to contemporary ideas about race, gender, class and empire. The figures of explorers and missionaries appear in the same heroic, masterful vein as they do in the textual narratives: as the present exhibition attests, images could make a highly effective contribution to the construction of British popular heroes. They could also reveal competing ideas about the nature and value of African societies, and about the changes that could be achieved by colonisation.

In reading illustrated travel writing by explorers and missionaries, it is essential to remember how little was known of sub-Saharan Africa by the mid-Victorian public. African exploration generated considerable excitement, evidenced by the eager consumption of the publications of Livingstone, John Hanning Speke, Sir Samuel White Baker and Sir Richard Burton.[2] Their special impact derived from the fact that the African 'interior' was a blank space on the map, its people mysterious and threatening. It has recently been suggested that the modern science of ethnography 'is always caught up in the invention, not the representation, of cultures';[3] a similar mixture of invention and reportage characterises Victorian travelogues. It was from these texts, and their illustrations, that an idea of Africa and its inhabitants was fabricated in the collective imagination of Victorian Britain. This essay investigates illustrations to three contrasting contributions to this genre:[4] Speke's swashbuckling *Journal of the Discovery of the Source of the Nile* (1863) and David Livingstone's two major publications, the bestselling *Missionary Travels and Researches in South Africa* (1857) and *Narrative of an Expedition to the Zambesi and its Tributaries* (1865).

The White Explorer in the Dark Continent

At the heart of nineteenth-century African travel narratives lie accounts of direct encounters between Europeans and Africans. The contrast between the explorer – military man or missionary, upholding the values of European civilisation – and the Africans he met was habitually understood through binary oppositions, the most powerful of which was 'civilised' versus 'savage'. The idea of the savage is a familiar and recurring one,[5] constantly reinforced in Victorian popular and metropolitan culture through texts, exhibitions, illustrations and stage shows. Charles Dickens, writing in 1853, reacted to a group of 'Bushmen' recently exhibited in London[6] by concluding that savages were by no means noble, but rather 'cruel, false, thievish, murderous, addicted more or less to grease, entrails, and beastly customs'.[7] This relationship of the familiar and the unknown, the self and its other, is dramatically exhibited in book illustrations, where heroic representations of British explorers were contrasted with exaggerated and unflattering images of black figures, the medium itself lending extra directness to the contrast between black and white. These illustrations, often complex tableaux, enshrine the over-simplified polarities of civilised versus savage, clothed versus naked, Christian versus heathen, light versus dark, and white versus black, which shaped Victorian attitudes towards Africans.

This series of dichotomies can be seen very clearly in the wood engraving *Grant dancing with Ukulima* (fig. 7) from Speke's *Journal of the Discovery of the Source of the Nile* (1863). The *Journal* records that in 1861 Speke's travelling partner, James Augustus Grant, was recovering from a serious illness in the village of 'the great chief Ukulima (the Digger) of Nunda (the Hump)' in what is now the Nyamwezi district of Tanzania.[8] The source for the engraving was a drawing by Grant; it would then have been drawn on to a woodblock by a commercial artist in London, and finally engraved by a specialist wood engraver.[9] The image suggests the absolute difference between the European and the African in various ways: prominent in the foreground is Grant himself, dressed in a heavy checked shirt, linen or woollen knickerbockers and a cloth helmet,[10] juxtaposed with a stereotypical exoticised scene of 'savage' revelry. Grant's clothing and manner may

appear bizarre to the modern viewer, seeming singularly inappropriate for the heat of equatorial Africa. Yet the significance of his clothed state is that it contrasts with the semi-nakedness of the 'savages' surrounding him. Victorian attitudes to nakedness are clearly indicated in William Monk's Appendix to Livingstone's *Cambridge Lectures*, where the Batoka people are described as:

> the most complete savages with whom [Livingstone] has held intercourse in Africa . . . He found them a large-bodied race, fierce, blood-thirsty and the men entirely naked. They seemed to be more astonished at his dis[ap]proving of their nude condition, than ashamed of it.[11]

So deeply ingrained was the Victorian horror at the public exposure of the flesh of either sex that Livingstone automatically assumed the Batoka should have been ashamed of themselves. Nakedness was indexical of savagery. In *Grant dancing with Ukulima* black skin (male and female) is exposed where white skin remains covered.[12] It is ironic to recall that within the sphere of fine art the nude (male or female, but always white) occupied a privileged position.[13] For the Victorians the nakedness of the savage was the opposite of civilised nudity, which was itself permissible only under the regulated conditions of the life class.

The figure of Grant forms a cultural self-image, the explorer as the ambassador and personification of British civilisation. In spite of his actual powerlessness – he is isolated and unarmed – an asymmetry of power is written into the image. Grant's sternly expressionless downward gaze is met by the elderly Ukulima's timid, submissive half-smile: the figure of Ukulima bears none of the characteristics of Victorian manliness exhibited by Grant. Ukulima is, however, presented as a partially reformed character:

> a very kind and good man, though he did stick the hands and heads of his victims on the poles of his boma as a warning to others.[14]

Speke (presumably relying on Grant) also describes Ukulima's hospitality, represented in the plate:

> [He] received his guest and retainers with considerable ceremony, making all the men of the village get up a dance; which they did, beating the drums and firing off guns, like a lot of black devils let loose.[15]

The formal movements of European dance in the illustration are presented as contrasting with the untutored motion of the savage, most conspicuously signalled here

Fig. 7
'Grant dancing with Ukulima'
By J. B. Zwecker after a sketch by
James Augustus Grant
Wood engraving from *Journal of
the Discovery of the Source of the Nile*
Published by William Blackwood,
London, 1863
ROYAL GEOGRAPHICAL SOCIETY

Robert Moffat (1795–1883)
By George Baxter, *c.* 1842
Watercolour over pencil on paper
27.9 x 23.5 cm
NATIONAL PORTRAIT GALLERY
LONDON
(cat. no. 2.5)

Baxter made this portrait of
Moffat, with its depiction of a
'Bechuana Parliament' in the
background, during the
celebrated missionary's stay in
Britain from 1839 to 1843. A
pioneer of colour printing, Baxter
contributed the plates to Moffat's
*Missionary Labours and Scenes in
Southern Africa* (1842) while this
drawing formed the basis of an
engraving first issued in 1843.
There are notable differences
between the drawing and the
engraving. Moffat has been tidied
up in the print: his famous beard
removed and his open-neck shirt
replaced by a collar and stock.

Right
Robert Moffat (1795–1883)
By George Baxter, 1843
Baxtertype engraving
25.8 x 20.8 cm
NATIONAL PORTRAIT GALLERY
LONDON
(cat. no. 2.6)

by the satanic-looking figure – one of Speke's 'black devils'
– firing a gun in the air at the apex of the composition.[16]
The contrast between this figure and Grant is underlined
through the representation of skin colour as a stark and
absolute opposition of black and white. The heavy inking
of these commercial wood-engraved illustrations left little
opportunity for subtleties of shading, but the ideological
intention of the illustrations was to utilise skin colour to
maximise the difference between 'civilised' and 'savage'
figures. Here, Grant's face appears as white as the paper
on which the book is printed while the Africans' bodies
are an inky black.

The explorer was not always as placid in his behaviour as
Grant at Ukulima's court. Africa became the theatre for
the playing-out of European fantasies of masculinity,
evident in the travel literature's stylised accounts of
gallant escapes and perilous encounters with lions or
hostile natives, often matched by dramatic narrative plates.
'*Three Buffalo Charges in One Day, Mgunda Mkhali*' (fig. 8)[17]
exemplifies a common device whereby feats of
'sportsmanship' involving a tremendous carnage of
buffalo, rhinoceros or elephant are advanced as testimony
of the white man's superiority.[18] Three sequentially linked
vignettes by Johann Baptist Zwecker, after sketches by
Speke himself, form a narrative of the day's events in the
manner of the modern comic strip. In the language of the
mess-room Speke recounts that one of the buffalo 'plunged
headlong at us from his ambush, just, and only just, giving
me time to present my small 40-gauge Lancaster'.[19] The
illustration heightens the contrast between the masterful
bearded explorer, with his Sandhurst posture, and the
grossly caricatured, almost simian, representation of his
servant Suliman taking refuge in a tree.

While many of the explorers belonged to this military
culture, missionaries provided an alternative model for
interaction with the African population. The most
prominent of British missionaries in Africa before
Livingstone was Robert Moffat, Livingstone's father-in-law,
who for more than forty years from 1821 ran a mission at
Kuruman in what is now South Africa. Moffat achieved
very modest results: by 1850 there were only thirty converts
at Kuruman.[20] The title-page of Moffat's *Missionary Labours
and Scenes in Southern Africa* (1842),[21] which advertises the
author as 'thirty-three years an agent of the London
Missionary Society in that continent', depicts the
missionary at work, preaching from a covered wagon to
an attentive group of African villagers. The frontispiece
opposite, however, tells a somewhat different story and
illustrates the possibility of replicating the physical
and social structures of Western civilisation in Africa.

Fig. 8
**'Three Buffalo Charges in
One Day, Mgunda Mkhali'**
By Johann Baptist Zwecker
(after John Hanning Speke)
Wood engraving from *Journal of
the Discovery of the Source of the Nile*
Published by William Blackwood,
London, 1863
ROYAL GEOGRAPHICAL SOCIETY

175

Manuscript plan of the mission station at Kuruman

By Robert Moffat Jnr, 1850
Watercolour and black ink over pencil, with manuscript inscriptions, on paper laid on to linen
45.5 x 61.5 cm
COUNCIL FOR WORLD MISSION ARCHIVE, SCHOOL OF ORIENTAL AND AFRICAN STUDIES
(cat. no. 2.22)

This manuscript plan of the Kuruman mission station was drawn up by Robert Moffat's son in April 1850. As well as showing the mission's buildings, field layout and neighbouring villages, the plan also serves as a deed of ownership between the London Missionary Society and the local inhabitants. It records above the signatures of the elder Moffat and his fellow missionary, Robert Hamiltion, that the land was purchased – 'for sundry articles to the value of 50£ sterling' – in May 1824. Beside this, the document bears the marks of the successors of those who had agreed the 1824 sale.

The Mission Premises at the Kuruman Station, a colour print in the technique developed by George Baxter, who specialised in missionary images,[22] presents an idyll of colonialism almost indistinguishable from innumerable representations of Britain. Moffat, dressed in a blue jacket with tie and waistcoat, is seen discussing a religious text with another missionary. Their dominant foreground position suggests the vocabulary of ownership employed in eighteenth-century estate portraits, such as Thomas Gainsborough's *Mr and Mrs Andrews*, c. 1748.[23] In spite of his perilous profession and small income, the missionary is here able to affect, at least superficially, the lifestyle of the country gentry of the previous century. The inclusion of distant figures of labourers, source of his relative prosperity, and notoriously absent from Gainsborough's image,[24] is highly significant, for the labourers are clearly depicted as being black. Moffat, clothed, leisured, and foregrounded, seen as an individual, is portrayed in marked contrast to the generalised black figures in the distance, semi-naked and hard at work. While other images in *Missionary Labours* represent the possibility of religious salvation for Africans, the inclusion of these little figures indicates Africa's potential for providing a motivated and expert native workforce.

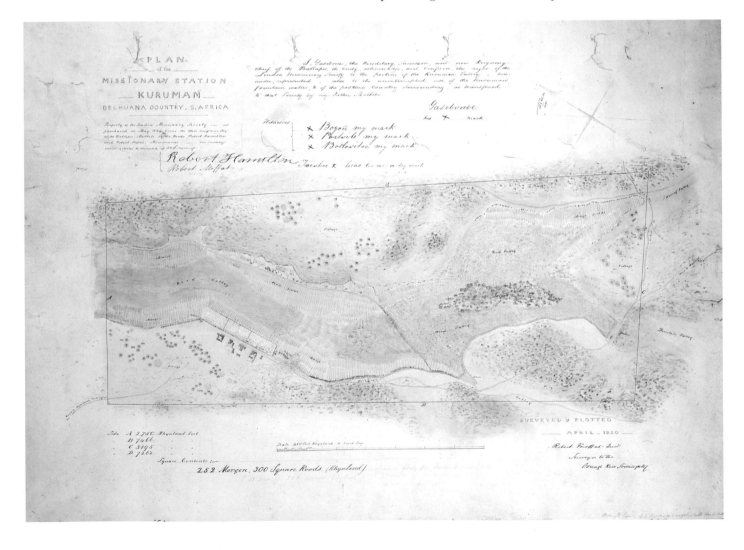

'Mount Stephanie, above Kebrabasa, Zambesi River'
By Thomas Baines, 9 March 1859
Oil on canvas, 46 x 65.7 cm
ROYAL GEOGRAPHICAL SOCIETY
(cat. no. 4.4)

The paintings and drawings of Thomas Baines, artist-storekeeper to the Zambezi expedition, provide an impressive record of the expedition's early stages. This painting, signed and dated 9 March 1859, is based on sketches made in late November 1858 when the party was reconnoitering the Kebrabasa (now Cabora Bassa) gorge. It shows Mount Stephanie, above the gorge, named by Livingstone after the young Queen of Portugal in deference to the help he received from Portuguese settlers in the area.

Frontispiece and title-page to *Missionary Labours and Scenes in Southern Africa*
By Robert Moffat
Published by John Snow, London, 1842
QUENTIN KEYNES
(cat. no. 2.48)

George Baxter's frontispiece to Moffat's book, engraved using his innovatory method of colour printing, shows Moffat engaged in discussion with a fellow missionary in front of the station at Kuruman. The title-page shows him preaching from a wagon.

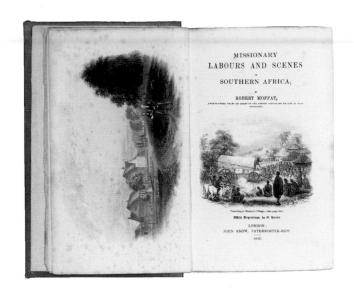

**'The Missionary's Escape
from the Lion'**
From *Missionary Travels and
Researches in South Africa*
By David Livingstone
Published by John Murray,
London, 1857
QUENTIN KEYNES
(cat. no. 1.3)

178

Livingstone's *Missionary Travels and Researches in South Africa*

In David Livingstone the intrepid and manly explorer was united with the Christian missionary, whose high moral purpose of bringing the gospel to the heathen provided an unshakeable justification for his presence in Africa. Livingstone's amalgam of active heroism and religious conviction singled him out as the ultimate muscular Christian[25] and was irresistible to the Victorian reading public. *Missionary Travels* captured the reader's attention with illustrations such as *'The Missionary's Escape from the Lion'*,[26] the famous scene in which: 'I saw the lion just in the act of springing upon me . . . Growling horribly close to my ear, he shook me as a terrier dog does a rat.'[27] Already present in this image were the elements of personal bravery, suffering and heroic fortitude in the face of adversity that contributed to the Livingstone myth. His blue peaked cap – his trademark at public appearances – can be seen in the right foreground.[28]

Livingstone's writing has a quite different tone from that of the military men, its underlying concerns being the moral reformation of Africa, the abolition of slavery and the mutual benefits that Westernisation could bring. With commerce and Christianity,[29] it seemed, would come the entire edifice of Victorian social beliefs: the ideal of respectability, the work ethic and strictly-regulated gender roles. As with Moffat's frontispiece, *Missionary Travels* graphically demonstrated the imposition of British social norms in Africa. *'Lake Ngami, Discovered by Oswell, Murray, and Livingstone'*[30] records Livingstone's visit in 1850 to the lake he had discovered in the previous year. Lake Ngami proved to be hardly a revelation: already well known to traders and to the local people, it turned out to be shallow and of little use for future commercial purposes.[31] The illustration was based on a drawing by Alfred Rider, who, Livingstone notes, had 'come to make sketches of this country and of the lake immediately after its discovery'[32] but had died of malaria before the Livingstone party arrived. The larger part of this illustration – all but the landscape – is therefore fictive. In spite of its title, the plate is concerned with culture, not geography. It is dominated by Livingstone pointing towards the lake, which he has discovered; but he figures also as a moral agent. This is achieved through the presence of Mary Livingstone, his wife, seated and nursing her baby. In a short passage in the 1865 *Narrative*, recording her death from malaria in 1862, Livingstone assessed his wife's role:

> Those who are not aware how this brave, good, English wife made a delightful home at Kolobeng, a thousand

Letter from David Livingstone to John Murray
22 May 1857
Manuscript letter, 18.3 x 21.9 cm
PRIVATE COLLECTION
(cat. no. 2.37)

In this letter to his publisher, Livingstone complains about the proof engraving for *Missionary Travels and Researches in South Africa*, illustrating the famous incident when he was mauled by a lion.

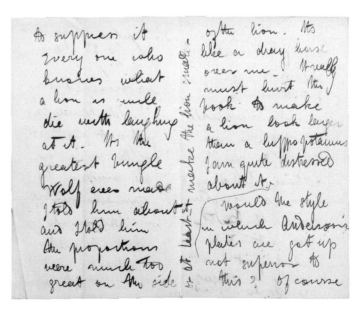

179

Stating that 'the lion encounter is absolutely abominable', Livingstone asks Murray to suppress the plate, since 'every one who knows what a lion is will die with laughing at it'. 'It's like a dray horse over me', he continues, 'it really must hurt the book to make a lion look larger than a hippopotamus. I am quite distressed about it'.

'Lake Ngami, discovered' by Oswell, Murray and Livingstone'
From *Missionary Travels and Researches in South Africa*
By David Livingstone
Published by John Murray,
London, 1857
QUENTIN KEYNES
(cat. no. 1.3)

'Reception of the Mission by Shinte'
Proof engraving for *Missionary Travels and Researches in South Africa*
(annotated by David Livingstone and John Murray)
Engraving with manuscript additions, 16 x 25.4 cm
PRIVATE COLLECTION
(cat. no. 2.28)

This plate illustrates Livingstone's account of the welcoming reception he received from Shinte in January 1854 during his coast-to-coast crossing. One of three surviving proof engravings for *Missionary Travels and Researches in South Africa*, it gives an insight into the production of the book. At the top Livingstone writes in pencil asking for the 'sheaves of arrows' to be shown hanging on the wearers' shoulders, not their backs, and that 'many more rings on the legs & arms of Shinte would be an improvement'. On the left, written in ink, Murray conveys the latter instruction to the engraver, Josiah Wood Whymper.

miles inland from the Cape, and as the daughter of Moffat and a Christian lady exercised most beneficial influence over the rude tribes of the interior, may wonder that she should have braved the dangers and toils of this down-trodden land. She knew them all, and, in the disinterested and dutiful attempt to renew her labours, was called to her rest instead.[33]

Great emphasis was placed on bringing the exemplary values of the Victorian family to African society. The British government's instructions for the 1858 Zambezi expedition, on which Mary Livingstone died, included the following passage:

> Her Majesty's Government attached . . . importance to the moral influence that might be exerted on the minds of the natives by a well regulated and orderly household of Europeans setting an example of consistent moral conduct to all who might witness it.[34]

In *'Lake Ngami'* the archetypal roles of the Victorian middle-class household are enacted: Livingstone, the paterfamilias, is at the top of a pyramid comprising his wife, children, servants and possessions. Mary Livingstone is seen enacting the stereotypical role of the 'Angel in the House', caring for the young and the sick. After the death of Alfred Rider from malaria, Livingstone recorded that 'by the aid of medicines and such comforts as could be made by the only English lady who ever visited the lake, the other [members of Rider's party] happily recovered.'[35] As in modern-life paintings of this period,[36] the line formed by the wife's body leads the eye towards the husband's head, indicating the approved hierarchy of power within the Victorian family. The Lake Ngami image reappears in a photograph made in 1857,[37] which restages the family grouping, though now with two sons and two daughters. Behind them is a screen (now lost) painted with scenes from the plates of *Missionary Travels*: carefully positioned to catch the light above the centre of the group is a copy of the *'Lake Ngami'* illustration. The ideal bourgeois family at home is juxtaposed with its representation (unchanged by the circumstances) in Africa.

The journey to Lake Ngami appears in a radically different light in the records of diaries and letters. Mary Livingstone was, at the time of their arrival at Lake Ngami in April 1850, five months pregnant with her fourth child. Livingstone's decision to take his young children and pregnant wife with him to explore a notably unhealthy region skirting the Kalahari Desert tempers the idyllic view of family bonds presented in the illustration. After four months the children became too weak to stand;

T. Picken, lith.

Published by John Murray, Albemarle S? May. 1857.

Day & Son, Lith? to the Queen.

LAKE NGAMI DISCOVERED BY OSWELL, MURRAY & LIVINGSTONE
From a Drawing made on the spot. 1850, by the late Alfred Ryder Esq.

could the artist not make the greaves or armlets on the boys shoulders as a soldier carries his musket & not on their necks & many more rings on the legs & arms of Shinte would seem important plenty of & beads round the necks of the women

Mr Whymper Please place more rings on the chiefs arms & legs – Up to the knees & elbow

Reception at Shinte's – Musicians in the foreground women on the chiefs left & two boys with sheaves of arrows on their shoulders on his right

Reception of the Mission by Shinte

Please & folk in the descriptions

J.W. WHYMPER SC

From a sketches by Capt. H Need R.N.

From a drawing by captain R. Stead H. M. Brig Linnet

River scenery on the West coast
The paddlers standing in the Barotse fashion

'River scenery on the West Coast'
Proof engraving for *Missionary Travels and Researches in South Africa* (annotated by David Livingstone and John Murray)
Engraving with manuscript additions, 16 x 25.4 cm
PRIVATE COLLECTION
(cat. no. 2.30)

Seen here is Livingstone's descriptive title for this proof engraving, which indicates that the paddlers of the canoe are 'standing in the Barotse fashion'. This was omitted from the published plate. The proof also shows how Murray shortened the credit for the drawing to Captain Henry Need. Need provided other drawings to illustrate Livingstone's account of the Angolan leg of his coast-to-coast journey for use in *Missionary Travels and Researches in South Africa*.

the new baby died shortly after it was born; and Mary Livingstone became ill with shivering and paralysis in her face.[38] Nonetheless, Livingstone decided in April the next year (1851) to take the family exploring again. He received a letter from Mary Moffat, his mother-in-law, indicting him for failing to fulfil the role of the responsible husband and father in which he is cast in the illustration. Learning in April 1851 that her daughter might once again be 'confined in the field', Mary Moffat wrote:

> O Livingstone what do you mean? Was it not enough that you lost one lovely babe, and scarcely saved the other, while the mother came home threatened with Paralysis? And will you again expose her and them in those sickly regions on an exploring expedition? All the world will condemn the cruelty of the thing not to say the indecorousness of it. A pregnant woman with three little children trailing about with a company of the other sex, through the wilds of Africa, among savage men and beasts![39]

This bitter criticism, of course, never appeared in the published accounts; it nonetheless indicates the extent to which idealised images of the Victorian family could diverge from actual experience.

While Livingstone had kept notes of his observations during his travels in Africa prior to the publication of *Missionary Travels* in 1857, he had little visual material, partly owing to his own lack of skill with the pencil.[40] Some of the engravings were made from drawings in London collections,[41] while others were made specially for the book: the 'spirited sketches' that Livingstone credits as sources for twelve of the wood engravings were fabricated by a draughtsman from verbal 'descriptions given to him by Major Vardon, Mr Oswell and myself'.[42] The artist charged with this task was Joseph Wolf, a German-born painter and commercial book illustrator, who specialised in botanical and zoological subjects and was regularly employed by Livingstone's publisher John Murray.[43] Wolf told his biographer that Livingstone's lack of knowledge of the possibilities of wood-engraved book illustration seriously hampered their collaboration, and that the explorer 'altogether lacked the power of vivid verbal description'.[44] The final form of the illustrations was reached by Livingstone commenting on and amending Wolf's entirely imaginary drawings. Some of these annotated proofs survive.[45] This process, akin to the production of illustrations for a work of fiction,[46] undermines any notion that the illustrations to *Missionary Travels* may contain useful scientific data.

183

184

An experienced traveller in
southern Africa and Australia,
Baines was appointed artist-
storekeeper to the Zambezi
expedition in January 1858. Like
other members of the expedition
he clashed with Charles
Livingstone and later with
Livingstone himself. He was
eventually dismissed in November
1859 on what now seem wholly
unfair charges of petty pilfering.
Nevertheless, the drawings and
paintings he made between 1858
and 1859 are remarkable records
of the expedition and the lower
Zambezi region.

Thomas Baines and the Zambezi Expedition

After his triumphant lecture series in 1857 and the
publication of *Missionary Travels*, which sold 70,000 copies,[47]
Livingstone ceased active work as a missionary and
embarked in 1858 upon a government-sponsored mission
to explore the Zambezi as a possible trading route into
Africa. This mission is documented in the *Narrative of an
Expedition to the Zambesi and its Tributaries*, published jointly
by David and Charles Livingstone. With the Zambezi
expedition's official status came the need to recruit
specialists to accompany Livingstone. As well as the
natural scientist Dr John Kirk and the geologist Richard
Thornton, the party included an artist, Thomas Baines,
who was also to act as storekeeper. Baines, a veteran of
expeditions in Australia and Africa, and recently elected
a Fellow of the Royal Geographical Society,[48] produced
an impressive series of paintings and drawings during the
first months of the expedition prior to his dismissal by
Livingstone on what can now be seen to have been a
wholly unfair set of charges.[49]

At the time of the Zambezi expedition significant changes
were occurring in visual culture as a result of the growing
importance of photography. Where previously an artist's
sketches would have been accepted as the most authentic
form of representation, it was increasingly clear that
photography (in spite of its technical limitations) would
soon supersede drawing as the best means of visual
reportage.[50] John Kirk and Livingstone's brother Charles
both took cameras on the Zambezi expedition and
significant tensions emerged between the graphic and the
photographic. These are explored in a painting by
Thomas Baines, worked up from sketches made on
Livingstone's Zambezi expedition in 1859: in *'Shibadda or
two channel rapid, above the Kebrabasa, Zambesi River'*,[51] Baines
represents himself in the foreground, sketchbook in hand,
with the view he has sketched arrayed behind him and
prominently featuring two Africans to the left. The artist,
he seems to claim, can represent landscape and figures
with equal effectiveness. In the extreme right corner,
menacing and immediately noticeable, is a tripod camera
with a black cloth and an anonymous operator. We know
from the context that these figures could be Charles
Livingstone and John Kirk.

In his painting Baines denies the photographer the
individuality allowed to the artist. Perhaps by placing
the photographer in a distant, perilous and marginal
perspective Baines was engaging in some humour at his
competitor's expense, reducing the biggest threat to his
hard-earned skills to a Lilliputian scale. Baines may also

'Shibadda, or two channel rapid, above the Kebrabasa, Zambesi River'
By Thomas Baines, January 1859
Oil on canvas, 46 x 65.7 cm
ROYAL GEOGRAPHICAL SOCIETY
(cat. no. 4.3)

Dated January 1859, this painting was probably worked up from sketches made in late November 1858 when Baines joined Livingstone's party to reconnoitre the rapids of the Kebrabasa (now Cabora Bassa) gorge. The painting shows Baines in the foreground, sketchbook in hand, and two of his companions in the bottom right-hand corner attempting to photograph the scene.

The *Ma Robert* on the Zambezi at Lupata
By John Kirk, *c.* 1858–1860
Albumen print, 13.2 x 20.6 cm
BY PERMISSION OF THE TRUSTEES OF THE NATIONAL LIBRARY OF SCOTLAND
(cat. no. 4.37)

Although Livingstone's brother Charles had been given the job of photographer to the Zambezi expedition, he proved to have little ability, and the only photographs to survive are by the medical officer and economic botanist, John Kirk. Kirk's photographs are limited to views of static subjects, such as this one of the steam launch the *Ma Robert*, but are nonetheless remarkable as the first photographs ever to be taken in the region.

Mary Livingstone's grave
By John Kirk, 1862
Albumen print, 14.5 x 19.8 cm
BY PERMISSION OF THE TRUSTEES OF THE NATIONAL LIBRARY OF SCOTLAND
(cat. no. 4.44)

Kirk's photograph of Mary Livingstone's grave, with the massive baobab tree behind, was later used as a guide for the plate that appeared in Livingstone's *Narrative of an Expedition to the Zambesi* (1864).

186

have wished to disparage Charles Livingstone, with whom he had clashed, and who was the architect of his expulsion from the expedition. On the other hand, Baines acknowledged elsewhere that 'in almost every [photograph] there is here and there some little bit of effective representation that I, as an artist, would give almost my right hand to be able to reproduce.'[52] Baines sympathetically enumerated 'the difficulties in the way of a photographer' in Africa:

> the restlessness of the sitters . . . the different conditions of atmosphere and intensity of the sun – the constant dust raised either by our people or the wind – the whirlwinds upsetting the camera . . . combine to frustrate the efforts of the operator.[53]

The photographers on the Livingstone expedition did indeed produce only very modest results: Charles Livingstone's attempts were a failure, and Kirk was only able to make a few photographs of large and static objects such as the baobab tree by Mary Livingstone's grave, and the steamer, the *Ma Robert*.[54]

Whatever their source, visual representations were not made purely for the purpose of illustrating narratives; they also formed an important part of the scientific evidence collected by the expedition. Livingstone had instructed his brother Charles to photograph the various tribes they encountered, selecting the 'better class of natives who are believed to be characteristic of the race',[55] as data for the science of ethnology, the early-Victorian 'Science of the Human Races'.[56] Livingstone made the same demand of Baines:

> You are required to furnish me . . . with a series of portraits of natives for the purposes of Ethnology, giving them if necessary in groups so as to show the shapes of the heads and bodies as accurately as you can . . . Birds and animals alive are also required.[57]

Baines provided this type of imagery very capably; an example is his vigorous figure study entitled '*A native of the country . . . on board the* Pearl',[58] which is inscribed with notes of ethnological interest ('height about 5 feet 6 – very stout and muscular'), although the inscription of a name[59] perhaps indicates an attempt to engage with the sitter as an individual rather than as a specimen of racial type. Probably influenced by an increasing personal animosity towards Baines, Livingstone rejected these studies in 1859:

> You have not got their true colours, nor in the drawings I have seen is the native countenance

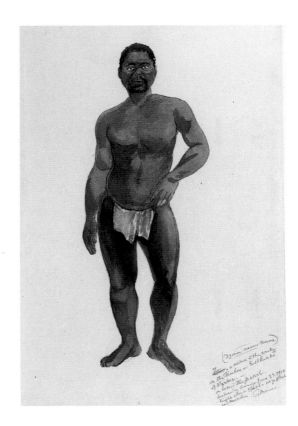

187

Tete: a house in which John Kirk and Livingstone stayed
By John Kirk, *c.* 1858–1863
Albumen print, 14.5 x 21.2 cm
(cat. no. 4.41)

Like Baines, Kirk made a number of records of Tete, the Portuguese colonial settlement and an important base during the Zambezi expedition.

African dwelling with a baobab tree in the background
By John Kirk, *c.* 1858–1863
Albumen print, 13.8 x 19.8 cm
(cat. no. 4.43)

Although Kirk's simple photographic technique was unable to capture images of the peoples of the Zambezi region, a number of his photographs show their dwellings.

Baobab tree, Shupanga
By John Kirk, *c.* 1858–1863
Albumen print, 15 x 20.6 cm
(cat. no. 4.36)

The majority of Kirk's surviving photographs record vegetation and tree types from the Zambezi region, revealing his interests as a botanist.

**'Shibante, a native of
Mazaro, boatman and pilot
belonging to Major Sicard'**
By Thomas Baines, 1859
Oil on canvas, 46 x 65.7 cm
ROYAL GEOGRAPHICAL SOCIETY
(cat. no. 4.8)

Baines accomplished portrait,
probably dating from July 1859,
shows Shibante (or Chibanti), the
slave of Major Sicard, the
Portuguese colonial governor of
Tete. Livingstone described him
in his *Narrative of an Expedition to
the Zambesi* as 'an intelligent active
young fellow'.

depicted except by the exaggeration of certain features.[60]

While only a handful of Baines's surviving drawings from this period are ethnographic studies, they do not seem to substantiate Livingstone's criticisms.

Other works by Baines speak of a qualitatively different relationship, with the subject seen as an individual, rather than a specimen or an example. These images are closer to portraits, a genre whose essence is acknowledgement of the subjectivity of the individual: portraiture provides images of the self rather than the other. *'Shibante, a native of Mazaro, boatman and pilot belonging to Major Sicard'*[61] acknowledges the individuality of the sitter, yet, unlike portraits, it was not commissioned by the subject and was not sold by Baines. While there is no attempt to Westernise the figure – to change his dress, for example – this is an image of a skilled and powerful named individual; in spite of Shibante's status as a slave 'belonging' to Major Sicard, the Portuguese colonial governor of Tete, he is holding an expertly manufactured basket signalling his own, or his people's, craft skills. Shibante's life history is recorded in the *Narrative*, where he is praised as a highly intelligent individual.[62]

Baines worked up several oil paintings based on subjects significant for Livingstone's project. An accomplished painting entitled *Working a coal seam near Tete, lower Zambezi*[63] records a visit Baines made to a coalmine owned by the Portuguese colonists,[64] his interest in the subject echoing Livingstone's description of the quality of African coal – with its explicitly colonialist agenda – in the *Narrative*. The direction of black labour by a white overseer is a paradigm of colonialism. It is perhaps appropriate that, in the shadowy areas of this image, the bodies of the black workers blend almost indistinguishably with the blackness of the raw coal. For the coloniser, labour as much as minerals constituted the black gold that Africa offered.

As a result of his dismissal from the expedition few of Baines's works were reproduced in the text of Livingstone's *Narrative*, which once again was illustrated with an eclectic series of images. Some were conjured up from Livingstone's sketches and descriptions by experienced draughtsmen and engravers in London;[65] two of Kirk's photographs were used;[66] and Livingstone also relied on four engravings by Horace Waller, who had joined the Zambezi expedition as part of the Universities' Mission in 1861.[67] Waller's drawings were used to illustrate Livingstone's accounts of the people he knew as the Mang'anja, whom he describes as:

Working a coal seam near Tete, lower Zambezi
By Thomas Baines, 1859
Oil on canvas, 46 x 65.7 cm
ROYAL GEOGRAPHICAL SOCIETY
(cat. no. 3.2)

Baines visited this coal mine, owned by the Portuguese colonists of Tete, in August 1859. For Livingstone the coal deposits of the lower Zambezi made it an ideal area for further settlement and offered the potential of providing fuel for as far away as the Cape Colony.

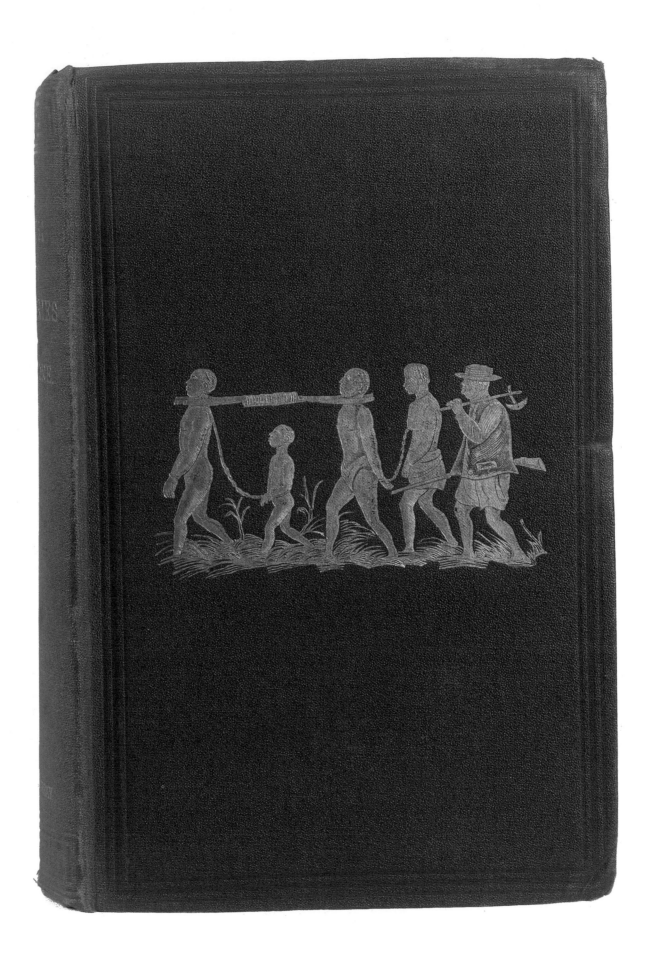

an industrious race; and in addition to working in iron, cotton, and basket-making, they cultivate the soil extensively . . . It is no uncommon thing to see men, women, and children hard at work, with the baby lying close by beneath a shady bush.[68]

The illustrations include 'Native web, and Weaver . . .' (see p. 159)[69] and 'Blacksmith's Forge and Bellows of Goatskin',[70] demonstrating the skills of the local craftsmen, clearly significant for Livingstone's plan to increase manufacturing and commercial activity in Africa. His admiration for the Mang'anja's propensity for labour, and consequent potential for being 'civilised', perhaps prompted Livingstone's ability to abandon temporarily the idea of racial difference:

> Many of the men are intelligent-looking, with well-shaped heads, agreeable faces, and high foreheads. We soon learned to forget colour, and we frequently saw countenances resembling those of white people we had known in England.[71]

Nonetheless, Livingstone reported that the Mang'anja were 'not a sober people',[72] and furthermore they maintained some 'savage' customs. This point is powerfully made by a plate depicting the 'Pelele, or Lip-Ring of Manganja woman'[73] (see p. 160), inserted in the upper lip, which Livingstone describes as 'frightfully ugly'.[74] The engraving shows a bust-length profile of a woman whose disembodied head is presented as a specimen, exemplifying a habit that ought to be changed, in contrast to her male counterpart, the blacksmith, whose healthy physique and industrious demeanour indicate the potential for Westernisation. The images of Africans labouring contentedly that punctuate the *Narrative* provide a concentrated, emblematic equivalent to the text's insistence on production and commerce as the key to 'improvement' among the peoples of Africa. This theme is highlighted through the prominent positioning of one illustration in particular: Waller's *Woman Grinding* is reproduced on the title-page (see p. 149).[75]

The central theme of Livingstone's work, the iniquity of the slave trade, appears in only one of the plates.[76] Addressing this shortcoming, Livingstone decided to emboss an emblem of slavery on the cover of the *Narrative* in gold, and asked Waller for:

> a small drawing for the outside of the book. I think a man in a slave stick with his hands tied behind and the slaver with a hold of the other end of the goree [slave stick] & a musket in his right hand will be best.[77]

Thus Livingstone ensured by visual means the recognition

of the main humanitarian theme of his work. The sole image of slavery inside the book is 'Gang of Captives met at Mbame's on their way to Tette',[78] drawn, probably from Livingstone's verbal description, by J. B. Zwecker and engraved by J. W. Whymper. The image is dominated by a frieze of black figures, the women and children chained and each of the men with 'his neck in the fork of a stout stick, six or seven feet long, and kept in by an iron rod which was riveted at both ends across the throat'.[79] One of the captors, also black, beats a captive with a stick, indicating the barbarity of the regime; another, wearing a European jacket and hat, holds a rifle and an axe.[80] The slaves, some completely naked, some clad in loin cloths, are presented here as innocents rather than savages, and the scene takes its place in a long tradition of anti-slavery imagery reaching back into the eighteenth century.[81]

193

'Blacksmith's Forge and Bellows of Goatskin'
From *Narrative of an Expedition to the Zambesi and its Tributaries*
By David and Charles Livingstone
Published by John Murray, London, 1865
QUENTIN KEYNES
(cat. no. 4.65)

Left
Gilt embossed binding of *Narrative of an Expedition to the Zambesi and its Tributaries*
By David and Charles Livingstone
Published by John Murray, London, 1865
QUENTIN KEYNES
(cat. no. 4.65)

'The Main Stream Came Up To Susi's Mouth'
From *The Last Journals of David Livingstone*
Edited by Horace Waller, volume 2
Published by John Murray,
London, 1874
QUENTIN KEYNES
(cat. no. 6.16)

Engraver's woodblock for 'The Main Stream Came Up To Susi's Mouth'
9.7 x 17.2 x 2 cm
PRIVATE COLLECTION
(cat. no. 6.19)

This is one of a collection of the engraver's woodblocks for the plates of *The Last Journals of David Livingstone*. *The Times* reviewer of the book considered this image, here seen in reverse, to be an emblem of Livingstone's martyrdom.

Martyrdom and Myth

While Speke more or less disappeared from public consciousness after his sudden death in 1864, and was memorialised only by a granite obelisk in Kensington Gardens,[82] wood-engraved illustrations continued to convey to a wide public the dramatic events of Livingstone's life up to and beyond the time of his death. The tremendous revival of interest in Livingstone after the announcement that Stanley had 'found' him was buttressed by some powerful images. Livingstone's portrait (taken from an earlier photograph), thought to be 'very welcome to our readers at this moment'[83] dominated the cover of the *Illustrated London News* of 3 August 1872, in the week when the story broke in England.[84] On 17 August a dramatic full-page illustration of Stanley and his highly armed convoy appeared, but the definitive illustration, captioned with the famous greeting 'Dr Livingstone, I presume?', appeared later in the year in Stanley's sensationalised bestselling account, *How I Found Livingstone*. The contrived formality of the occasion, as reported by Stanley, is well captured in the illustration, where the greeting is accompanied by a raising of hats.[85]

Livingstone graced the cover of the *Illustrated London News* for the last time in April 1874 with an elaborate full-page engraving of the arrival of his body at Southampton, while another large engraving documented his funeral in Westminster Abbey.[86] With Livingstone's reputation assured, these images emphasise the glossy regalia of Victorian official mourning. Only one black face appears among the pall-bearers, that of Jacob Wainwright, who, although he had been with Livingstone for only a year, had been a pupil at the Church Missionary Society's Nassick School, and thus exemplified the African brought within the pale of civilisation.[87] In spite of their absence from the funeral, the role played by Livingstone's servants, Susi and Chuma, in carrying his body 'during many months of a toilsome and dangerous journey of a distance of more than a thousand miles to the coast', was acknowledged in the paper's accompanying text as 'a grander and more touching memento of the great missionary explorer than any tomb'.[88] The last days of Livingstone's life provided the climax to Horace Waller's edition of *The Last Journals of David Livingstone*, published later in 1874, which insisted on the prominence of Susi and Chuma and relied on their testimony.[89]

The illustrations to the *Last Journals* enshrine a Livingstone myth based on ideas of self-sacrifice and bravery, rather than on specific successes as a missionary or an explorer. *'The Main Stream Came Up To Susi's Mouth'*[90] shows the

"THE MAIN STREAM CAME UP TO SUSI'S MOUTH."

enfeebled explorer carried across a flood on the shoulders of his faithful servant, while in *'Evening. Ilala. 29 April, 1873'*[91] Livingstone's dying body dimly echoes images of Christ's deposition from the cross. Although the scholarly George Birdwood described them as 'trashy and theatrical',[92] the significance of these images was readily understood. A reviewer in *The Times* fixed upon *'The Main Stream Came Up To Susi's Mouth'* as an emblem of Livingstone's martyrdom:

> The exhausted wanderer is represented to us borne through a mournful marsh. The rain is falling in torrents; in front, buried up to the neck in water, a stalwart negro with a bale as big as his body on his head, breasts the flood . . . On the shoulders of the faithful Susi the traveller is seated.

Even though the dying explorer was wholly reliant on Susi and Chuma, their role was conceived of by Livingstone, and by his biographers, as that merely of faithful servants. The chiaroscuro of racial difference coloured Livingstone's behaviour as surely as it dominated the visual and textual representations of his life and work.

Concluding his remarks on *'The Main Stream Came Up To Susi's Mouth'*, the *Times* reviewer reflected on the power of imagery to capture the essence of a text:

> There is a whole history in the four corners of this little sketch, and those who read the journals – and who will not who can! – will soon learn its moral for themselves.[93]

This was the great strength of wood-engraved illustrations of African subjects: their ability to encapsulate major issues in a format that was small, vivid and easily understood. While it would be misleading to consider the corpus of images discussed here as an accurate survey of the landscapes and peoples of mid-nineteenth-century Africa, they can be regarded as powerful emblems of one culture's view of another. However remotely connected to their African referent they might have been, these illustrations together fabricated an image of Africa for the mid-Victorian public that accorded with the central preoccupations of the age, mingling humanitarian concern with dreams of cultural and economic, if not yet explicitly imperial, expansion.

196

'Evening. Ilala. 29 April 1873'
Frontispiece to *The Last Journals of David Livingstone*
Edited by Horace Waller, volume 2
Published by John Murray,
London, 1874
QUENTIN KEYNES
(cat. no. 6.16)

'Evening. Ilala. 29 April 1873'
Frontispiece to *The Last Journals of David Livingstone*
Edited by Horace Waller, volume 2
Published by John Murray,
London, 1874
QUENTIN KEYNES
(cat. no. 6.16)

Overleaf
Town of Tete from the north shore of the Zambezi
By Thomas Baines, April 1859
Oil on canvas, 46 x 65.7 cm
ROYAL GEOGRAPHICAL SOCIETY
(cat. no. 4.6)

Dated on the reverse by Baines, this picture shows a distant view of the town of Tete. A significant Portuguese colonial settlement on the lower Zambezi, Tete was a base for the Zambezi expedition.

200

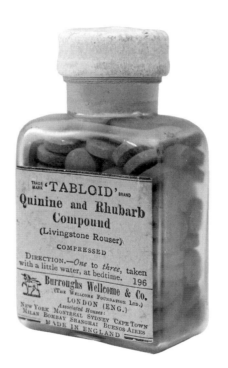

John M. MacKenzie

David Livingstone and
the Wordly After-Life:
Imperialism and Nationalism in Africa

David Livingstone
By Thomas Annan, 1861
Albumen print, 36.8 x 30.4 cm
SCOTTISH NATIONAL PORTRAIT
GALLERY
(cat. no. 5.12)

Dating from Livingstone's last
visit to Britain, this photograph by
the great Scottish photographer
was taken while Livingstone was
staying next door to the Annans
in Hamilton. Used as the wood-
engraved frontispiece in *The Last
Journals of David Livingstone*, it has
become one of the most famous
portraits of Livingstone.

Livingstone's Memorials

203

Few reputations have been as enduring, or as influential, as that of David Livingstone. The Victorians elevated certain of their contemporaries, invariably those associated with empire, to heroic status, and among these Livingstone was perhaps supreme. And while regard for many Victorian heroes declined in the twentieth century, particularly as imperial rule lost its impetus, respect for Livingstone remained surprisingly high. His name survived as a touchstone of selfless sacrifice and fearless endeavour, strengthened by his origins in a Scottish tradition of religious independency and working-class self-help and self-reliance. It was used in repeated appeals for action, not only throughout the partition of Africa in the late nineteenth century, but also through the missionary, educational and settler activities of the inter-war years. In that period it also became associated with a Scottish cultural resurgence. Even more surprisingly, Livingstone's reputation as a 'friend of the Africans' ensured that he was admired by black nationalists (often mission-educated) and that, uniquely among whites associated with nineteenth-century imperialism, he continued to be honoured by independent states.

Few people can have inspired as many memorials as Livingstone, not only statues, buildings, inscriptions, cairns and obelisks, but also Christian missions, towns, regions – even, in a sense, an entire country (Malawi). In Africa he is commemorated at the Victoria Falls, where the travel industry still uses his face and name as an inseparable adjunct of one of the greatest of natural phenomena. He is also commemorated at Nkotakota on Lake Malawi, where he visited the Jumbe or Muslim ruler and observed the slave trade; at Ujiji where he encountered Stanley; at Tabora where he lived for a time; and at Ilala where he died. More significantly, he is still honoured in Malawi as the inspiration of the mission and town of Blantyre, named after his birthplace in Lanarkshire, and of Livingstonia, the great mission and community at the northern end of Lake Malawi. In Zambia he is remembered through the town of Livingstone, the capital of the country until the 1930s. In a post-colonial age when statues have been knocked down and names changed throughout the world, it is a testimony to the extraordinary power of Livingstone's memory that these names, together with those of the mountains in Malawi and the island in the Zambezi named after him, have all survived.

In Scotland, in the 1870s, Livingstone statues were unveiled in both Edinburgh and Glasgow, and a memorial church and memorial library were built in Blantyre. His

'Carrying the Body to the Coast'
Magic lantern slide (glass positive) from *The Life and Work of David Livingstone*
Published by the London Missionary Society, *c.* 1900
NATIONAL PORTRAIT GALLERY LONDON
(cat. no. 6.12)

This is one of a set of forty lantern slides, which, along with the accompanying pamphlet, shows the Livingstone myth at its most potent. Livingstone, the pamphlet begins, 'made the way for liberty in Africa by his own daring and suffering'. Here Livingstone's body is carried by 'the faithful negroes, Jacob Wainwright, Chuma, and Susi'.

Section of the mpundu tree from the shores of Lake Bangweulu, under which Livingstone's heart was buried
Tree bark, carved by Jacob Wainwright, 1873
Approximately 100 cm (high)
ROYAL GEOGRAPHICAL SOCIETY
(cat. no. 6.29)

The inscription on the tree was cut by Jacob Wainwright at Ilala, apparently at Abdullah Susi's suggestion. Apart from Livingstone's name, it bears those of the three leading members of his party at the time of his death. Thought to be diseased, the tree was cut down in 1899. This inscribed section was then shipped to the Royal Geographical Society.

204

faithful followers Susi and Chuma were invited to Scotland to build a replica of the hut in which he had died.[1] His daughter and son-in-law were influential founders of the Royal Scottish Geographical Society in 1884–1885, initially designed (with branches in all the principal Scottish cities) as a means of perpetuating and developing his ideals and his quest for knowledge of Africa.[2] He was the subject of exhibitions in 1911 and 1913, and after the First World War his birthplace, formerly condemned to demolition, was saved by public subscription and opened in 1929 (by the Duchess of York, later Queen Elizabeth the Queen Mother) as the Scottish National Memorial to David Livingstone. Described as a 'place of pilgrimage' where the 'relics' had been gathered together, it confirmed Livingstone's status as a Protestant saint.[3] Meanwhile in Central Africa the Caledonian Societies raised the funds for the massive statue of Livingstone, sculpted by Sir W. R. Dick, which overlooks the Devil's Cataract of the Victoria Falls. It was unveiled in 1934, reflecting the extent to which Livingstone was viewed, together with Rhodes, as one of the founders of settler power in the region.[4]

Moreover, in his final years in Africa and in the decades after his death, Livingstone became the subject of a major biographical industry. Well over a hundred biographies were published, and Sunday Schools and youth organisations such as the Boy's Brigade handed them out as standard prizes throughout the land. As well as the famous entry in Samuel Smiles's *Self-Help* (and from the time of his death his photograph was used as the frontispiece of that much-reprinted work), he was prominently featured in all the Victorian books of heroes.[5] In 1907 Cambridge University held a commemorative meeting in a packed Senate House on the fiftieth anniversary of Livingstone's celebrated address to the University. In 1913 the centennial of his birth was celebrated in major events at the Royal Albert Hall, the Royal Geographical Society, St Paul's Cathedral and other cathedrals and churches. The Scottish composer Hamish McCunn wrote a cantata entitled 'Livingstone the Pilgrim'. On the centennial of his death in 1973 there was a fresh outburst of activity: conferences were held, books were published, and stamps were issued by no fewer than six independent African countries as well as the rebel white Rhodesia.[6]

This was the outward representation of Livingstone's major influence upon events in Africa, demonstrating the significance of the continent to Victorian ambitions and concerns. But why Livingstone? Why should one man have

exerted such extraordinary power from beyond the grave, a grave so symbolically divided between the pit beneath the tree in Chitambo's village and the place of honour in Westminster Abbey? To a large extent the answer lies in the Victorian capacity to create and manipulate major myths. Livingstone was perhaps the subject of the most powerful instrumental myth of the age.

Livingstone and the Heroic Myth

Heroic myths are not complete fabrications. They cannot be built out of men of straw. The legendary figures they celebrate are partially self-made through the genuine achievements of their lives, but their usefulness in the practical world is developed by successors who create the heroic after-life by emphasising, even exaggerating, the personal qualities, the seemingly selfless endeavours and the near-cosmic objectives of their subjects. Heroic myths in the epics of cultures throughout the world invariably involve lengthy journeys in which the hero vanishes from the present material domain and ultimately returns, personally transfigured and with the power to transfigure others. On his last journey Livingstone 'disappeared' for more than seven years. Apart from the celebrated encounter with Stanley, throughout that period he was the subject of many rumours, involving supposed disasters and triumphs, which had the effect of keeping the fascination of his name constantly before a captivated public. After some of Livingstone's followers emerged from Africa in 1867 with news of his supposed murder, the first of no fewer than six search expeditions was sent to Africa.[7] His disciple Horace Waller wrote to him in 1869: 'the interest in this country about you is as intense as ever I could wish it to be . . . The report of your murder, Sir Roderick's vehement denial, Young's most successful clear-up of Mousa's lie have all tended so to surround you with a halo of romance such as you can't imagine.'[8]

Waller had himself contrived to keep the name of Livingstone constantly in the public eye by writing, it has been estimated, no fewer than eighty-five letters to *The Times* during the last journey. The 'halo of romance' (the phrase represents an interesting combination of the religious and the secular) was transformed into near beatification by the ecstasies of Stanley after his return from basking in the aura of Livingstone's personality, which he considered almost Christ-like. Thus the myth was able to develop and mature over a period of years before the remarkable return of the body to Britain in early 1874. Livingstone had come back from his long period in the belly of the African whale as the most potent

Agnes and Tom Livingstone, Abdullah Susi, James Chuma and Horace Waller at Newstead Abbey
By R. Allen & Son, 1874
Woodbury-type photograph
14 x 19.8 cm
ROYAL GEOGRAPHICAL SOCIETY
(cat. no. 6.1)

This is one of a series of photographs taken in June 1874 at Newstead Abbey, the house of Livingstone's old friend William F. Webb, during the composition of the posthumous *Last Journals of David Livingstone*. In this photograph Livingstone's son and daughter, Abdullah Susi, James Chuma and Horace Waller, editor of the *Last Journals*, pose with Livingstone's maps and field notebooks.

206

hero of all, the dead hero, bereft of the human frailties that could have dented the massive reputation that was henceforth constructed from his life and work.

His final journals were carefully doctored and slanted for publication by Horace Waller, an Anglican priest.[9] He bowdlerised Livingstone's references to natural functions and sexual diseases; he excised what seemed to be favourable references to Muslims and Islam; he cut all criticisms of politicians and other explorers; and he omitted the impatient doctor's references to his own rages and despairs. A supremely saintly figure emerged from the journals rather than a weary traveller with very human foibles. Above all Livingstone is depicted as the fervent anti-slaver, concerned with the material and spiritual future of Africa and Africans, rather than as the failed explorer, always some distance from the elusive source of the Nile. Thus Livingstone was rewritten into a simple great man with a single high-minded objective rather than a disappointed, flawed and complicated figure convinced of his own failure. Moreover, by careful questioning of Susi and Chuma, Waller was able to create the powerful icon of Livingstone's death, kneeling in prayer in his hut at Chitambo's village.

Livingstone's qualities, achievements and objectives chimed perfectly with the prime concerns of the age. The exposure of slaving, the 'running sore' of the continent, contributed to a crusade that had kept entire departments of the Foreign Office and the Admiralty, as well as naval squadrons on both the West and East African coasts, busy for decades (the latter inspiring novels by Gordon Stables and R. M. Ballantyne). Livingstone's remarkable scientific observations – in entomology, botany, geology, ethnography and philology, as well as his geographical surveys – reflected not only the training and interests of Scots doctors in the early nineteenth century, but also the fascination with natural history and the earth sciences common at that time. What's more, ever since he had read the work of Dr Thomas Dick earlier in the century, Livingstone had had no problems reconciling science with religion, one of the major intellectual and spiritual dilemmas of the age.[10] Even more powerfully, he combined his scientific and religious interests with ideas about free trade, commerce, white emigration and a liberating and redemptive modern technology (the steam engine and the Western pharmacopoeia). He seemed to be both polymath and synoptic thinker, offering a programme that was both practical and moral, an economic order founded on Christian values.

In addition to all of this, he had emerged from a

207

Abdullah Susi, Horace Waller, James Chuma, Agnes Livingstone, Mrs Webb and William F. Webb, and Tom Livingstone at Newstead Abbey
By R. Allen & Son, 1874
Woodbury-type photograph
14 x 19.8 cm
ROYAL GEOGRAPHICAL SOCIETY
(cat. no. 6.2)

This shows the full party at Newstead including its owner William F. Webb and his wife. The lion skin probably belonged to Webb, a keen big-game hunter.

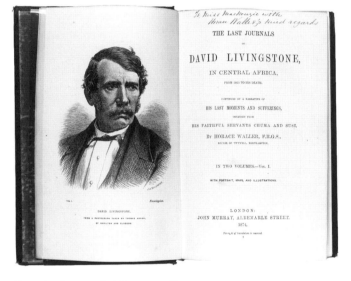

working-class background on the Celtic fringe, was largely self-made and self-taught and yet had been able to bend the English scientific and political Establishment to his own ends, influence Christian denominations that did not share his beliefs and inspire the well-bred inhabitants of Oxford and Cambridge to follow him. His capacity, through his fame as an explorer and his contemporaries' perception of an elevated moral character, to appeal across class and nation was immensely attractive to an otherwise class-conscious age. Even the disasters of the Zambezi expedition ultimately helped his reputation. Despite all setbacks, not least the personal ones arising from his inadequacy as a husband and a father, he triumphed through his epic final journey. Those who came after him were able to justify their own ambitions, inspire a public and personal following, and secure funding and political support by the repeated invocation of his name.

When H. M. Stanley, a very different figure,[11] heard of Livingstone's death on his return from the Ashanti campaign in the future Ghana in 1874, he pledged himself to 'be selected to succeed him in opening up Africa to the shining light of Christianity'.[12]

> The effect which this news had upon me, after the first shock had passed away, was to fire me with a resolution to complete his work, to be, if God willed it, the next martyr to geographical science . . . [13]

F. C. Selous, the great hunter who guided the Pioneer Column of Rhodes's British South Africa Company into Mashonaland (Zimbabwe) in 1890, wrote that he had been inspired to go to Africa by reading Livingstone's works.[14] Sir Harry Johnston, Consul in Mozambique and the first Commissioner of the British Central Africa Protectorate (Malawi) and later also of Uganda, depicted himself in his autobiography as continuing, indeed 'finishing', the work of Livingstone.[15] He also suggested that because of Queen Victoria's keen interest in the work of Livingstone she had been intrigued by the exploits of those who had followed him in Africa. The first survey of the partition of Africa, published by Sir John Scott Keltie of the RGS in 1893, described the death of Livingstone as having turned the 'scramble' for the continent into 'a kind of holy crusade'.[16]

It is a powerful phrase, neatly representing the extent to which the imperial thrust of the period could be dressed up in the language of moral improvement and religious effort. It also, perhaps, has echoes of the medieval and chivalric interests of the Victorian period, whose imagery was much invoked during imperial events like the Indian Mutiny in 1857. The example of Livingstone becomes that

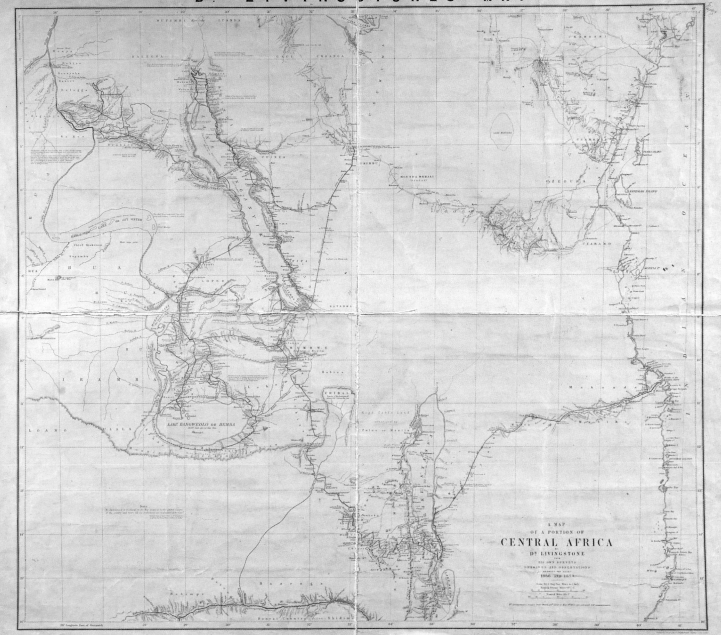

A MAP
OF A PORTION OF
CENTRAL AFRICA
BY
Dr LIVINGSTONE
FROM HIS OWN SURVEYS
DRAWINGS AND OBSERVATIONS
BETWEEN THE YEARS
1866 AND 1873.

of a shining knight, *'sans peur et sans reproche'*, fighting the dragon of the slave trade in Africa. It was just the kind of image to inspire those who followed, even those like the Reverend Dr James Stewart who had earlier fallen out with Livingstone and, in a fit of rage, thrown *Missionary Travels* into the Zambezi. It was through Stewart and others that major missions were to be founded in Livingstone's name in Central Africa, missions that would have considerable impact upon the political and cultural development of an entire region.

Many of Livingstone's most cherished ambitions could not be realised. The Zambezi was not navigable into the interior of Africa. The prospects of great cotton fields and white working-class migration were also chimerical. Even the missions founded at his behest (while Livingstone was struggling with the intractability of the Zambezi) were killed by over-optimism, bad management and fever. This was the fate of the missions of Helmore and Price to Linyanti on the upper Zambezi in 1858–1860 and of Bishop Mackenzie and the first party of the Universities' Mission to Central Africa (UMCA) near Lake Malawi in 1861–1862. Yet those that went out to Africa after Livingstone's death had very different outcomes.

The Livingstone Missions

One month after the funeral in Westminster Abbey in the spring of 1874 the presbytery of Jedburgh in the Scottish borders, prompted by one of its ministers, was petitioning the General Assembly of the Church of Scotland to establish a mission in Livingstone's favoured region of Lake Malawi. Livingstone had hoped for the establishment of a Scottish mission in the area as early as 1859; he had envisaged it as having a significant commercial role and suggested that it could be led by Scots artisans and laymen. His ideas then had been overtaken by the very different and ill-fated scheme of the Universities' Mission. Now it seemed as though the established Church of Scotland might create a mission along his own cherished lines. Its lay character occurred by default, for the fact was that the response in 1874 and early 1875 was non-existent. No minister could be induced to go, and, as a result, the faltering ambitions of the established Church were wholly overtaken by the more vigorous response of the Free Church of Scotland.[17]

The Reverend Dr James Stewart, who had been on the Zambezi with Livingstone and had later become the head of the notable educational mission at Lovedale in the Cape Colony, was well connected with the business community of western Scotland. His wife was a daughter of Alexander Stephen, the wealthy Clyde shipbuilder. In late 1874, at Stewart's request, prominent Glasgow businessmen were invited to a private meeting at the city's Queen's Hall. Within days, considerable donations had come from the shipbuilder Alexander Stephen; chemical manufacturers (James White and James Stevenson); the founder of the oil and shale industry James Young ('Paraffin Young', a friend and follower of Livingstone); the chairman of the British India Steam Navigation Company; Sir William Mackinnon; and others. By March 1876 £10,500 had been raised, a sizeable sum for the day and enough to kit out a considerable expedition to Lake Malawi (including a steam vessel, the *Ilala*). It was led by the Reverend Robert Laws (who was to spend more than half a century in Malawi and become one of the most admired and celebrated missionaries of the day) and guided by E. D. Young, leader of the search party that had sought evidence of Livingstone's survival in 1867. The mission was originally founded at Cape Maclear at the southern end of the Lake, but later moved to Bandawe, halfway up the Lake, and later again to Livingstonia further north. It was soon the centre for many outstations throughout the region.

Henry Henderson, the lay founder of the established Church's mission, who had formerly been a pioneer on the Queensland frontier in Australia, travelled with the Free Church party and surveyed the Lake with them from the *Ilala*. He decided to found his mission south of the Lake at what was to become Blantyre. At the beginning it was heavily dependent on the support of the larger and better-funded Free Church mission and could only muster laymen to staff it. By the end of 1877 the mission had been laid out and its gardens and workshops established by an engineer from India, another James Stewart, who was a cousin of Dr Stewart. Initially it sought to be an industrial and commercial mission on the lines of the communities created by the Church Missionary Society on the East African coast, where freed African slaves and people displaced by the internecine strife of the region could be encouraged to settle. But its lay leaders took on secular powers, and the scandalous abuse of judicial functions, involving floggings and an execution, led to its reorganisation under the leadership of the Reverend David Clement Scott. He built a notable church between 1888 and 1891 and turned the mission station into a major centre of education, language study and printing. Botanical experimentation was also conducted there and outstations were soon established elsewhere in the Highlands.

Nevertheless, the same group of wealthy Scots who had financed the Free Church expedition (and continued to

Livingstone's muzzle loader
118.2 cm (length)
THE DAVID LIVINGSTONE CENTRE
(cat. no. 5.48)

donate generously to it until the 1890s) also invested in a company designed to carry forward Livingstone's vision of Christianity and commerce. This was the African Lakes Company, founded by the brothers John and Fred Moir in 1878. Although it was a commercial failure until the twentieth century, it provided crucial support to all the mission stations and later to the incipient imperial administration in the region. Fred Moir, significantly, entitled his memoirs *After Livingstone*.[18] Meanwhile the Universities' Mission, originally inspired by Livingstone's address in the Senate House in Cambridge in 1857, had established itself on the island of Zanzibar and had built a cathedral on the site of the slave market. In 1879 the UMCA returned to its original field in Malawi and in 1885 it established a major mission on Likoma Island on the Lake, building another considerable cathedral there.

But Livingstone's influence spread out beyond his favourite area of Lake Malawi. In 1875 H. M. Stanley appealed in Livingstone's name for missionaries to enter Uganda, more than ten years before Mackinnon's Imperial British East Africa Company was established there in 1888. Moreover, the London Missionary Society and the Church Missionary Society increased their interest in East and Central Africa, particularly in the region of Lake Tanganyika. As missionary biographies and memoirs amply testify, all regarded themselves as in some way continuing the work of Livingstone.[19] Frederick Arnot, who travelled extensively across Central and southern Africa and established a mission in Katanga, the southern province of the Congo (Zaire), was proud of his connection with Livingstone's family, having played with the doctor's children when a child in Hamilton, near Blantyre.[20] Even Cardinal Lavigerie, the founder of the Catholic White Fathers' mission, acknowledged the role of Livingstone as pathfinder.

It can be argued that all of these events were as much influenced by the developing tempo of European interest in Africa, by the opening of the Suez Canal in 1869, by the establishment of a link between Aden and East Africa by the British India Steam Navigation Company in 1872 as by the memory of Livingstone. It has also been suggested that while he may have provided inspiration, his own programme for the missionary role in economic and commercial development was seldom followed.[21] What's more, all the early missions found it very difficult to escape violent involvement with the disturbed state of African politics around them, whether it was conflicts with Swahili and Yao slave traders in Malawi, the internecine strife of the court of King Mtesa of Buganda, or the patterns of dominance and subordination established by the Nguni

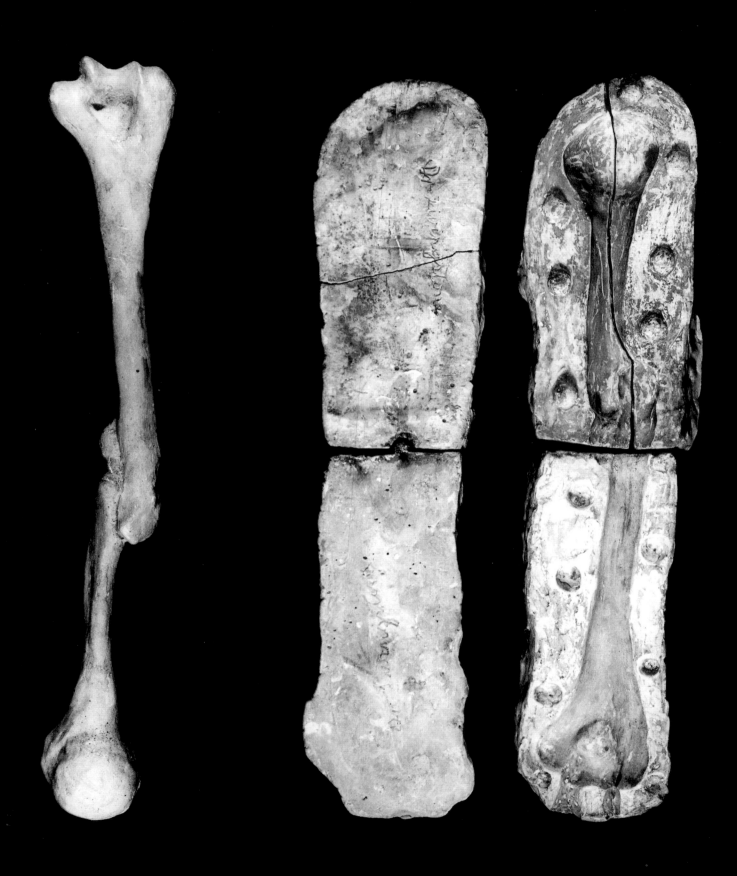

people (who had dispersed out of Natal in the early
nineteenth century) in parts of the modern Malawi,
Zambia, Zimbabwe and Tanzania. During these years of
upheaval the attempts of the missionaries to convert and
educate were greatly inhibited. It was only after
the institution of formal imperial rule that the missions
were able to pursue their ambitions, less hampered by
secular anxieties.

Livingstone and the Scramble for Africa

Missionary activity in the 1870s and early 1880s preceded
the establishment of European colonies in East and
Central Africa. (The missions were very much a part of
the quickening of the pace of interest in and the gathering
of information about Africa in that period.) By the early
1880s Europeans had begun to interfere increasingly with
the local politics, finance and commerce of North and
West Africa, and after Bismarck's Berlin Congress of
1884–1885 the process of treaty making and aggrandisement
speeded up in East and Central Africa as well. By 1890 the
British had used the device of chartered companies to
secure their position in what were to become Kenya and
Uganda (Sir William Mackinnon's Imperial British East
Africa Company) and Zambia and Zimbabwe (Cecil
Rhodes's British South Africa Company). By 1891 a
protectorate had also been declared in Malawi. By this
time King Leopold of the Belgians had carved out a vast
swathe of Central and Equatorial Africa (the Congo, now
Zaire) for his International Africa Association, the Germans
were firmly established in Tanganyika, and the Portuguese
had retained what they regarded as their historic rights
(though much reduced) in Angola and Mozambique,
where Livingstone had so famously travelled coast
to coast.

Livingstone's influence can be seen throughout this activity.
It was he who had first insisted on the maintenance of an
open route to the north from the Cape Colony through
what is now Botswana to Central Africa, bypassing the
Boer Republics of the Orange Free State and the
Transvaal.[22] Rhodes took up this cry. Zanzibar was
closely associated with Livingstone's name, as was the
Zambezi valley and of course the Lake Malawi area.
Throughout the international negotiations respecting the
partition of Africa, Livingstone's anxieties about the slave
trade and the 'moral improvement' of Africans remained
to the fore. They were incorporated, at the request of the
British, in the Berlin treaty and reappeared in subsequent
conventions.

**Plaster cast and moulds of
Livingstone's left humerus**
Cast, 36.5 cm (length);
moulds, 21 x 9 cm (length)
THE ROYAL COLLEGE OF
SURGEONS OF ENGLAND
(cat. nos. 6.27, 6.28)

After its arrival at Southampton
on 15 April 1874, Livingstone's
body was taken by train to
London and laid in the Savile
Row headquarters of the Royal
Geographical Society. A *post
mortem* was conducted that
evening by Sir William Fergusson.
Unrecognisable after its months in
transit, the body's identity was
verified by the deformation of the
left arm bone, dating from the
famous incident in February 1844
when Livingstone was mauled by
a lion. Several of these casts exist,
transformed from items of
medical curiosity into relics. The
moulds were probably made on
Fergusson's instructions.

A network of figures who regarded themselves as admirers and followers of Livingstone were closely involved with all these developments. Among them were Sir Bartle Frere, who led an anti-slavery diplomatic mission to the Sultan of Zanzibar, was subsequently Governor of the Cape, and acted as adviser to the Church Missionary Society and other missions; Sir Harry Johnston, virtually the founder of Malawi and later Commissioner in Uganda; and of course H. M. Stanley, who built his fame on the legendary encounter with Livingstone and was inseparably connected with both Leopold's exploits in the Congo and British interest in Uganda. Other less celebrated, but in some ways no less influential, figures included the Reverend John Mackenzie, missionary and colonial official in Botswana with keen interests in Central Africa; John Smith Moffat, Livingstone's brother-in-law, who also held official posts under the Crown; and the explorer and treaty maker Joseph Thomson. Sir William Mackinnon, with all his Scottish Presbyterian and shipping connections, was the founder of the East Africa Company, while Livingstone's son-in-law, Alexander Livingstone Bruce, was a director of both Mackinnon's chartered company and the Moirs' African Lakes Company. The Reverend Horace Waller, ever anxious for association with Livingstone and with many of the mission leaders, maintained close connections with those mentioned.

Yet the missions had a highly ambivalent relationship with formal imperial rule when it came. Originally they had not deemed it necessary at all: Livingstone himself had written of the need to maintain African freedoms in southern Africa.[23] Later, however, after years of disillusion in effecting converts and coping with local political turbulence, many of the missionaries considered imperial rule a helpful political adjunct to their cause. But it also produced anxieties over the drawing of imperial boundaries during the 'Scramble' and doubts about the acceptability of Protestant missions under a Catholic state like Portugal or vice versa. Relations between missions and the secular state, even when both were British, could also be tense. This was indeed the case in Malawi where the first Consul and Commissioner, Sir Harry Johnston, himself an atheist, often disapproved of the missions' tactics and was at pains to establish his capital at Zomba some forty miles from Blantyre, until then the principal settlement. Yet this same Johnston published a biography of Livingstone in 1891, at the request of Livingstone's daughter Agnes,[24] and visited the Vatican to assure the relevant Cardinal that Roman Catholic missions were safe in the hands of British colonial authorities.[25]

Moreover, Johnston was in the eye of one of the greatest storms to engulf the Scottish missions. In 1889 he was in Lisbon to negotiate a treaty with Portugal, and in its first draft he conceded the Shire Highlands to the Portuguese. This provoked outrage in Scotland. Public meetings were held and a monster petition was prepared to protest against this proposed abandonment of the area so dear to Livingstone. Lord Salisbury responded to this agitation by repudiating the treaty. From 1892 to 1893 there was fresh agitation over the collapse of the Imperial British East Africa Company as the ruler of Uganda. Once again Livingstone's name was invoked, providing a heightened emotional tone to the controversy. The Liberal government declared a protectorate.

However far reality diverged from the Livingstone ideal, not only in economics but also in terms of the much more sharply delineated racial ideas of the later nineteenth century, the Livingstone name remained both an inspiration to action and an emotional court of appeal that could fire public interest and anxiety and consequently influence government reactions. To understand the power of a personality, a sequence of events and a death in the Victorian mentality, it is only necessary to refer to that other great heroic myth, the one associated with the name of General Charles Gordon (who, though English, had Scottish ancestors). Gordon was seen by some as the inheritor of the Livingstone mantle. Indeed, the great mediator of the Livingstone myth, Horace Waller, tried to create a heroic apostolic succession by sending Gordon a strand of Livingstone's hair.[26]

Gordon's attacks upon the slave trade in the upper Nile, his utter fearlessness during his assignments in both China and Africa, his social conscience and perceptions of his elevated moral character, and, above all his martyrdom in Khartoum in early 1885 all served (despite his strangely unorthodox religious beliefs) to mark him out for mythic treatment. Queen Victoria was appalled at his fate and the Liberal government was seriously destabilised by the failure to rescue him. Like Livingstone he became a celebrated death icon, grandly defying the followers of the Mahdi at the top of the steps of the palace at Khartoum (see fig. 9). Indeed, the siege and Gordon's death were repeatedly recreated in popular culture, in plays and tableaux vivants, and many books were published about the events in the Sudan.[27] It has been argued that pressures on the British government for the reconquest of the Sudan between 1896 and 1898 were maintained by press and public agitation that Gordon's martyrdom should be avenged.[28] Yet Gordon was too eccentric and controversial for his celebrity, massive as it was from the 1880s to the 1920s, to survive far into the twentieth century. The final questions we must consider here are why Livingstone's reputation proved so durable and why it was available for adoption by Africans as well as by white settlers.

Livingstone's Reputation in the Twentieth Century

For white settlers and imperial rulers in Africa, Livingstone combined great moral distinction with the authorship of texts that marked him out as a complex apostle of empire. He had argued for white settlement, even if the form it took was to be severely criticised by many of his missionary followers, who viewed chartered rule and the settler treatment of Africans as distinctly remote from his ideal. The explanation for his reputation among Africans is much more complex. The glib answer might be that most Africans in the twentieth century received their education in mission schools, and for virtually all their teachers Livingstone remained the greatest hero and exemplar. It was perhaps inevitable that such admiration should rub off.

But it goes much deeper than this. Livingstone's own formative years occurred before the development of the sharper race consciousness of the later nineteenth century. While his racial attitudes have been much debated, generally he did view Africans as potentially the intellectual equals of, and as redeemable as, Europeans. He disliked the racist attitudes of Richard Burton, and in the Jamaican Governor Eyre controversy (that litmus test of racial views in the 1860s), he was sharply opposed to the governor's brutal suppression of the black rising in the Caribbean colony. His was a paternalistic approach. Second, he provided plentiful evidence of his concern for, and care of, his African followers, particularly the Kololo whom he so admired. This was usually reciprocated, and the extraordinary ending to his final journey seemed to constitute proof of the devotion of those who travelled closest to him. Third, although he did become embroiled in skirmishes, and was prepared to use firearms, unlike other explorers his was usually a non-violent progress across Africa. He even showed signs of some misgivings (rare in the period) over the shooting of African wildlife.[29] Fourth, while his relations with other Europeans were fraught with misunderstandings and often tempestuous disputes, as shown on the Zambezi expedition, Stanley offered strong evidence not only for his stoicism and resolution in his final years, but also for the mutual regard between him and his followers as well as the Muslims

Fig. 9
The Death of General Gordon
by G. W. Joy, *c.* 1893
Oil on canvas, 236 x 175 cm
REPRODUCED BY PERMISSION OF
LEEDS MUSEUMS AND GALLERIES
(CITY ART GALLERY)

215

Horace Waller's notebook,
recording Susi and Chuma's
account of Livingstone's death,
c. 1873–1874
Bound manuscript
21.8 x 13 cm (closed)
CURATORS OF THE BODLEIAN
LIBRARY, RHODES HOUSE LIBRARY
(cat. no. 6.14)

Shut door & went
out 4 air Majiwara
came to Susi as he
was afraid & said come
& see how the Doctor is
sleeping
Chun Susi, Muanyu,
Seri - Matthew - Crace
Saw Dr fallen forward
as if in the act of praying,
before cock crow, they
felt his cheeks & found
him dead

Horace Waller gained a first-hand
account of Livingstone's final days
through his interviews with Susi
and Chuma, who stayed with him
in Leytonstone during the summer
of 1874. He recorded the
interviews in this notebook and
published their narrative, in a
highly elaborated and doctored
form, in *The Last Journals of David
Livingstone*. Here he records their
account of finding Livingstone
dead.

216

among whom he lived on the shores of Lake Tanganyika.

While the instructions Livingstone drafted for the Zambezi expedition read like a colonial manifesto for Central Africa,[30] he did have some conception of future African freedoms. Although he naturally couched these in terms of freedom from slave raiding and freedom from what he saw as moral and economic backwardness, they were nevertheless freedoms that would ultimately offer the possibility of a new political dispensation. When missionaries moved around Central Africa in the later nineteenth century they repeatedly recorded affectionate tributes from elderly chiefs and headmen who had known Livingstone. While such traditions have to be treated with some reserve, 'Bwana Daudi' does seem to have left behind him a sense of what James Stewart called 'a kind of sanctified naturalness'.[31] It is interesting to learn that John Chilembwe, the leader of a black rising in Malawi during the First World War, had a biography of Livingstone in his possession.[32] It is highly likely that this was also the case with many of the leaders of African nationalism of a later period. Even if the African regard for Livingstone can be seen partly as the result of missionary influence, it can only have developed because Africans recognised in him a sympathetic figure who seemed to transcend so many of his contemporaries in his respect, concern and affection for so many of the peoples among whom he travelled.

While David Livingstone is no longer the household name he once was, echoes of his heroic reputation are still with us. In many ways it was a reputation that his successors partly manufactured and certainly manipulated to their own ends. Both his achievements and their success are represented by the fact that, more than 120 years after his death, he remains inseparably associated with the Africa that he regarded as his life's work and which made him the most celebrated figure of his day.

Replica of the hut in which Livingstone died, constructed at St John's Vicarage, Leytonstone
By an unknown photographer
c. 1910
Bromide print, 9.5 x 12.5 cm
THE COUNCIL FOR WORLD MISSION ARCHIVES
(cat. no. 6.11)

Long ago demolished, this replica hut was made by Susi and Chuma in the grounds of Horace Waller's vicarage at Leytonstone while they were staying with him in 1874. During their time in Britain, Susi and Chuma also made a similar replica on the highland estate of Livingstone's old friend, James Young.

Overleaf
Herd of hippopotami near the mouth of the Luabo River
By Thomas Baines, *c.* 1858–1859
Oil on canvas, 46 x 65.7 cm
ROYAL GEOGRAPHICAL SOCIETY
(cat. no. 4.1)

Although this was probably worked up later, Baines' painting records the early days of the Zambezi expedition when it was negotiating the waterways of the river's delta. The *Ma Robert* can be seen in the background, to the right of the picture.

NOTES

Chapter 1   David Livingstone: A Brief Biographical Account

The principal source is Tim Jeal, *Livingstone*, 1973 and 1993 (Pimlico).

1   Neil Livingstone's letters to the London Missionary Society (LMS), LMS Collection, School of Oriental and African Studies (LMS/SOAS); Agnes Livingstone's notes for Dr Blaikie, National Library of Scotland.
2   Wallis 1945, p. 42.
3   DL to LMS 5.9.1837, LMS/SOAS.
4   Blaikie 1880, p. 12.
5   *Ibid.*
6   Gutzlaff 1834.
7   R. Cecil to LMS 26.1.1839 and 23.2.1839, LMS/SOAS.
8   Seaver 1957, p. 27.
9   Blaikie 1880, p. 21.
10   R. Cecil to LMS 26.1.1839, LMS/SOAS.
11   DL to LMS 2.7.1839, LMS/SOAS.
12   DL to D. G. Watt 23.5.1845, LMS/SOAS.
13   DL to D. G. Watt 27.9.1843.
14   DL to LMS 2.12.1844, LMS/SOAS.
15   DL to D. G. Watt 2.4.1845, LMS/SOAS.
16   DL to J. S. Moffat 2.10.1858, Wallis 1945, p. 44.
17   DL to R. Moffat 12.5.1845, Schapera 1959, vol. 1, p. 118.
18   DL to Mr and Mrs N. Livingstone 14.5.1845, Schapera 1959, vol. 1, p. 122.
19   DL to LMS 10.4.1846, Schapera 1961, p. 91.
20   Schapera 1963, vol. 1, pp. 225–6.
21   Schapera 1963, vol. 2, p. 304.
22   DL to A. Murray 10.6.1847, State Archives, Pretoria.
23   DL to Janet Livingstone 31.1.1849, Schapera 1959, vol. 2, p. 19.
24   DL to R. Moffat 11.4.1849 and 4.5.1849, Schapera 1959, vol. 2, pp. 30, 43.
25   DL to LMS 17.3.1847, Schapera 1961, p. 108.
26   DL to Agnes and Janet Livingstone 30.3.1841, Schapera 1959, vol. 1, p. 31.
27   DL to LMS 26.5.1849, Schapera 1961, p. 130.
28   Schapera 1963, vol. 1, p. 157.
29   DL to LMS 3.9.1849, Schapera 1961, p. 133.
30   DL to LMS 17.3.1847, Schapera 1961, p. 108.
31   DL to R. Moffat 24.8.1850, Schapera 1959, vol. 2, pp. 101–2.
32   DL to R. Moffat 8.7.1850, Schapera 1959, vol. 2, pp. 83–5.
33   DL to Charles Livingstone 8.10.1851, *Atlantic Monthly*, July 1922.
34   DL to W. Thompson 27.9.1855, Schapera 1961, p. 286.
35   Schapera 1961, pp. 194, 247, 281.
36   Schapera 1960, p. 228.
37   DL to LMS 24.9.1853, Schapera 1961, p. 250.
38   Schapera 1960, p. 108.
39   Schapera 1963, vol. 2, pp. 373–4.
40   *The Times*, 8 August 1854.
41   DL to LMS 12.10.1855, Schapera 1961, p. 294.
42   Schapera 1963, vol. 2, p. 346.
43   Charles Livingstone to his wife, n.d., Livingstone Museum, Zambia.
44   LMS to DL 24.8.1855, Schapera 1961, p. 277.
45   DL to Sir R. Murchison 5.8.1856, Wallis 1956, vol. 1, p. xviii.
46   Blaikie 1880, p. 190.
47   Debenham 1957, pp. 129–30.
48   DL to N. Bendingfeld 28.6.1858, Wallis 1956, vol. 1, p. 18.
49   Foskett 1965, p. 301.
50   Foreign Office correspondence, Public Record Office, F. O. 63/871.
51   Robert Livingstone to DL, n.d., National Archives of Zimbabwe.
52   DL to Mrs Neil Livingstone 29.4.1862, Harryhausen Collection.
53   Wallis 1952, p. 62.
54   DL to Lord John Russell 28.4.1863, unpublished journal, p. 189, National Library of Scotland.
55   DL to T. Maclear 5.11.1863, National Archives of Zambia.
56   *The Times* 20.1.1863.
57   Blaikie 1880, p. 264.
58   Macnair 1940, p. 282.
59   DL to Agnes Livingstone 9.1869, British Museum Additional Manuscript, 50184.
60   DL to LMS 25.5.1865, LMS/SOAS.
61   Blaikie 1880, pp. 293–4.
62   *Ibid.*, p. 295.
63   Debenham 1957, pp. 293–4.
64   Blaikie 1880, p. 302.
65   Foskett 1964, p. 109.
66   Omitted from original by Horace Waller in Waller 1874, vol. 2, 19 April 1873 .
67   Waller 1874, vol. 1, pp. 13–14.
68   *Ibid.*, p. 346.
69   DL to Kirk 8.7.1868, Proceedings of the Royal Geographical Society, xiv, p. 8.
70   Stanley 1909, p. 274 (extract from diary 3.3.1872).
71   DL to Agnes Livingstone 23.8.1872, British Museum Additional Manuscript 50184.
72   McLynn 1989, p. 155.
73   *Ibid.*, p. 160.
74   DL to Agnes Livingstone 5.2.1871, British Museum Additional Manuscript 50184.
75   DL to Agnes Livingstone 1.7.1872, British Museum Additional Manuscript 50184.
76   Waller 1874, vol. 2, p. 93.
77   *Ibid.*, vol. 2, p. 269.
78   Jeal 1973, p. 362.
79   *Ibid.*, p. 363.

Chapter 2   Livingstone, Self-Help and Scotland

This essay is, of course, generally indebted to the biographies by Tim Jeal, *Livingstone* (1973) and Timothy Holmes, *Journey to Livingstone: Exploration of an Imperial Myth* (1993). I have tried, though, to base it on primary sources.

1   Foskett 1965, vol. 1, p. 193.
2   Boucher 1985, pp. 84, 100.
3   Carrington 1968, p. 308.
4   Wallis 1956, vol. 1, p. 137; Seaver 1957, pp. 341–2; Boucher 1985, p. 192.
5   Calder 1981, p. 246.
6   Cain 1986, p. 16.
7   Boucher 1985, p. 202.
8   Calder 1994, pp. 126–36.
9   Mostert 1992, p. 510 ff.
10   Seaver 1957, p. 456.
11   *Ibid.*, p. 288.
12   Smiles, *Self-Help*, 1882, pp. 290, 296.
13   Smiles 1905, pp. 325–6.
14   Smiles 1878, p. 429; for Dick's small place in what became a great area of scientific controversy, see Oldroyd 1990.
15   Smiles 1905, p. 327.
16   Smiles, *Thomas Edward*, 1882, pp. xvi, 298–9, 343–4, 380; Smiles 1905, p. 326.
17   Smiles, *Self-Help*, 1882, pp. 150–2.
18   For Miller, see Rosie 1981.
19   Smiles, *Self-Help*, 1882, pp. 101–2.
20   Smiles, *Thomas Edward*, 1882, pp. ix, xiv–xviii.
21   Seaver 1957, pp. 450, 459.

22 *Ibid.*, p. 440; Clendennen 1992, pp. 89–90; Boucher 1985, p. 131.

23 Clendennen 1992, p. 3.

24 Seaver 1957, pp. 27, 286–7.

25 Escott 1960, p. 21; Clendennen 1992, p. xix.

26 Escott 1960, pp. 45–96, 311–12.

27 Seaver 1957, pp. 288–9; Schapera 1963, vol. 2, p. 389.

28 Boucher 1985, p. 215.

29 Clendennen 1992, p. 63.

30 *Ibid.*, p. xix.

31 Morley 1906, pp. 672–4.

32 Smiles, *Self-Help*, 1882, pp. 242–4.

33 Clendennen 1992, p. xx.

34 Shapin 1983, pp. 155–6.

35 Siddle 1974, pp. 72–9.

36 Livingstone 1857, pp. 3–4.

37 Herbert 1994, p. 63.

38 Greene 1982, pp. 19–24.

39 Cannon 1978, pp. 75–7, 93, 105, 266–78 ff.

40 Boucher 1985, p. 41.

41 Clendennen 1992, p. 6.

42 Livingstone 1857, pp. 518–24.

Chapter 3   David Livingstone and the Culture of Exploration in Mid-Victorian Britain

1 Conrad 1926, pp. 19–20.

2 *Ibid.*, p. 134.

3 *Ibid.*, p. 25.

4 Mathews 1912.

5 Waller 1889, pp. 229–30.

6 Brantlinger 1985, p. 166.

7 Stafford 1989, pp. 28–9.

8 Winwood Reade 1873.

9 *Geographical Journal*, 120, 1954, p. 18.

10 Livingstone 1857, pp. 673–4.

11 Elston 1973, pp. 61–85.

12 McDonnell 1885, p. 3.

13 'Exeter Hall Pets', *Punch* 6, 1844, p. 240.

14 Thomson 1890, p. 345.

15 Helly 1987.

16 Waller's diaries for 1875 and 1876 are held at the Yale University Divinity School, New Haven, USA.

17 Conrad 1926, p. 2.

18 Becker 1874, pp. 332–4.

19 Stafford 1989, pp. 211–12.

20 Stanley 1885, p. 8.

21 Stanley 1909, p. 392.

22 Port 1995, pp. 258–9.

23 Gallagher and Robinson 1953, p. 1.

24 Cain and Hopkins 1993, p. 34.

25 *The Times*, 8 August 1854; cited in Jeal 1985, p. 158. In 1857 Livingstone was awarded the Society's Gold Medal.

26 Stafford 1989, pp. 162–8.

27 Coupland 1928, p. 103.

28 For an account of the official attitude towards Livingstone's subsequent and final expedition, see Bridges 1968, pp. 79–104.

29 Johnston 1913, p. 445.

30 Driver 1991, pp. 134–66. The following paragraph is based on this account.

31 *Anti-Slavery Reporter*, November 1878, pp. 118–9.

32 Stanley 1909, p. 295.

33 Middleton 1969, p. 8.

34 *Pall Mall Gazette*, 11 February 1878.

35 Waller 1891, p. 88.

36 *Geographical Journal*, 120, 1954, pp. 15–20.

37 Goldsworthy 1971, pp. 24–9, 205–53. More generally, see Rotberg 1966.

38 *Hansard*, vol. 522, 1953–4, col. 409.

Chapter 4   Doctor Livingstone Collects

1 Comaroff and Comaroff 1991, p. 88.

2 Wallis 1956, vol. 2, pp. 423–4.

3 Livingstone 1857, pp. 36, 397.

4 MacLaren 1991; MacLaren 1992.

5 Livingstone 1857, p. 261.

6 Holmes 1993, p. 161.

7 Wallis 1956, p. 359.

8 Foskett 1965, vol. 1, p. 63.

9 *Ibid.*, p. 174.

10 *Ibid.*, p. 45.

11 Livingstone 1857, p. 57.

12 Wallis 1956, vol. 2, p. 431.

13 *Ibid.*, p. 434.

14 Comaroff and Comaroff 1992, p. 227.

15 Livingstone 1857, pp. 198–9.

16 Thomas 1991, p. 103.

17 Livingstone 1857, p. 322.

18 Comaroff and Comaroff 1991, p. 185.

19 Wallis 1956, p. 261.

20 Holmes 1993, p. 40.

21 Comaroff and Comaroff 1991, p. 132.

22 Royal Scottish Museum 1913, p. 32.

23 Livingstone 1857, p. 23.

24 Comaroff and Comaroff 1991, p. 211.

25 Comaroff and Comaroff 1992.

26 Livingstone 1857, p. 90.

27 Wallis 1956, p. 62.

28 *Ibid.*, p. 318.

29 Foskett 1965, vol. 1, p. 165.

30 Thomas 1991, p. 141.

31 Oliver and Sanderson 1985, p. 553.

32 Waller 1874, pp. 92–3.

33 *Ibid.*, p. 99.

34 *Ibid.*, p. 98.

35 *Ibid.*, pp. 117–18.

36 Holmes 1993, p. 306.

37 Felix 1989.

38 Waller 1874, p. 139.

39 Holmes 1993, p. 311.

40 Waller 1874, p. 146.

41 *Ibid.*, p. 161.

42 Stanley 1872, p. 56.

43 Comaroff and Comaroff 1992, p. 97.

44 Foskett 1965, vol. 1, p. 48.

45 Livingstone 1857, p. 468.

46 *Ibid.*, p. 512.

47 Foskett 1965, vol. 2, p. 373.

Chapter 5 Fabricating Africa: Livingstone and the Visual Image 1850–1874

1 I would like to thank Felix Driver, Peter Funnell, Michaela Giebelhausen and Marcia Pointon for their comments on earlier drafts, and John Wells for applying his bibliographic and critical acumen to the present text. I have benefited from discussions of earlier versions given at the V&A/RCA Seminar in History of Design and at the 'Race and the Victorians' Conference organised by Shearer West at Leicester University. A fuller treatment of the images of African labour discussed here appears in my D.Phil. thesis 'Representations of Labour in British Visual Culture, 1850–1875', University of Sussex, 1994.

2 Brantlinger 1986, p. 195.

3 Clifford 1986, p. 2.

4 On the travelogue as a genre, see Youngs 1994.

5 Stocking 1987, pp. 208–19.

6 See Altick 1978, p. 282.

7 Dickens 1853, pp. 168–70, 338–9.

8 Speke 1863, p. 114; Maitland 1971, pp. 131–3.

9 See Anderson 1991, Fox 1988 and Wakeman 1973 on the techniques and significance of wood-engraved illustration during this period.

10 This dress is replicated in a photograph of *Grant in Dress Worn in Africa* (reproduced in Moorehead 1983, p. 53). I am grateful to Emma Taylor of the Textile and Dress Collection, V&A, for discussion of this issue.

11 Livingstone 1858, p. 99.

12 The only concession to the climate is that the knickerbockers Grant is wearing reach slightly below the knee, leaving a small part of the leg bare above the stockings. This would not have been acceptable dress in Britain.

13 Clark 1956, p. 67; Pointon 1990, pp. 12–14.

14 Speke 1863, p. 118.

15 *Ibid.*

16 Bloomfield 1990.

17 Speke 1863, opposite p. 66.

18 MacKenzie 1987.

19 Speke 1863, p. 65.

20 Jeal 1973, p. 98.

21 Moffat 1842. See also Northcott 1961.

22 Moffat 1842, frontispiece; see Lewis 1908, no. 91, p. 107; Mitzman 1978, no. 90, p. 129.

23 Thomas Gainsborough, *Mr and Mrs Andrews*, National Gallery, London.

24 Barrell 1980.

25 Vance 1985, pp. 2–3.

26 Livingstone 1857, opposite p. 13.

27 *Ibid.*, p. 12.

28 The illustration makes clear that it is through the agency of Mebalwe, a 'native schoolmaster' and a black man dressed in European clothes, that Livingstone's life was saved, although his gun misfired and he himself was also bitten by the lion.

29 Stanley 1983.

30 Livingstone 1857, opposite p. 66.

31 Jeal 1973, p. 92.

32 Livingstone 1857, p. 75.

33 Livingstone 1865, p. 417.

34 *Ibid.*, p. 11. Livingstone is here paraphrasing his official instructions as leader of the government-sponsored mission.

35 Livingstone 1857, p. 75.

36 Allwood and Treble 1982, no. 26, p. 32; Nead 1988, pp. 43–4. The children seen in the illustration are Robert (1846–1865), Agnes (1847–1912) and Thomas (1849–1875).

37 Livingstone Memorial, Blantyre: Glasgow Museums Service. Reproduced in Jeal 1973, plate 9, between pp. 128 and 129. This photograph is credited to F. Thurston in Fraser, 1913, opposite p. 48.

38 Jeal 1973, p. 91.

39 Mary Moffat to David Livingstone, n.d., in Schapera 1960, pp. 70–1.

40 Livingstone 1857, preface; Palmer 1895, p. 124, includes an anecdote concerning a sketch made by Livingstone of 'what he thought was a new species of monkey. But nobody could tell from the sketch, for what it was intended.'

41 Livingstone 1857, plate 7, opposite p. 56, *Hottentots – Women returning from the Water, and Men around a dead Harte-beest* is credited to 'a sketch at Stafford House in possession of the Duke of Sunderland'. A rather gothic vision of a *Bechuana Reed-Dance by Moonlight* is credited 'Sketched by Ford'. Livingstone 1857, opposite p. 225.

42 Livingstone 1857, preface; Palmer 1895, pp. 12–14, 311.

43 The plates are opposite pp. 13, 26, 27, 56, 71, 140, 142, 210, 242, 498, 562 and 588. Wolf's monogram appears on each. Palmer 1895, p. 312.

44 Palmer 1895, p. 124.

45 Murray archive.

46 Compare, for example, the negotiation between George Eliot and Frederic Leighton concerning the illustrations for *Romola*. See R. and L. Ormond, *Lord Leighton*, New Haven, 1975, pp. 57–9.

47 Brantlinger 1985, p. 195.

48 He was elected FRGS on 23 November 1857. Wallis 1941, p. 143.

49 Wallis 1941, pp. 168–82.

50 I am indebted to James Ryan for discussion of this issue.

51 Royal Geographical Society, London. Inscribed 'Tete Jan[uar]y 1859'.

52. Baines 1864, pp. 148–9.

53 *Ibid.*, p. 148. Baines was referring here to his experiences on an expedition, with James Chapman, to the Victoria Falls in 1861–1862.

54 Livingstone credits these with having 'materially assisted in the illustrations'. Livingstone 1865, p. vii. See also Coupland 1928.

55 Quoted in Helly 1987, p. 256.

56 Stocking 1987, pp. 47–53.

57 Livingstone to Baines, 11 July 1859, quoted in Wallis 1941, p. 171.

58 Royal Geographical Society, London. Annotation in pencil, lower right.

59 Baines appears to have made an attempt to find out his subject's name and notes that 'Dzina means name'; the word 'Teno' or 'Zeno', partially deleted, appears underneath and this may be the sitter's name.

60 Livingstone to Baines, 11 July 1859, quoted in Wallis 1941, p. 171.

61 Royal Geographical Society, London. 'Major Sicard' refers to Major Tito A. d'A. Sicard, the Portuguese colonial governor at Tete. See Livingstone 1865, p. 44.

62 Shibante or Chibanti, having sold himself into slavery to Major Sicard (a notoriously generous master) for a good price, himself bought slaves and ran a ferry business. Later he also traded slaves and ivory. Livingstone 1865, p. 49.

63 The watercolour on which this painting is based is reproduced in colour in Wallis 1956, vol. 2, plate 1, opposite p. 238.

64 Baines described the visit in *Cape Monthly Magazine*, vol. 7, March 1860, pp. 289–99, cited in Wallis 1941, p. 175.

65 One work by Joseph Wolf appears in Livingstone 1865, opposite p. 186. Engraved by Josiah Wood Whymper, this plate bears Wolf's monogram though it is not credited to him.

66 See *View of Steamer, Traps and Hippopotamus*, Livingstone 1865, p. 95, which may be based on Kirk's photograph of a *Hippopotamus Trap* [reproduced in Bensusan 1966, opposite p. 41]; the plate of *The Grave of Mrs Livingstone under the Baobab Tree*, near to Shupanga House, Livingstone 1865, opposite p. 31, probably relied on Kirk's photograph showing only the tree.

67 Jeal 1973, pp. 235–6; Helly 1987, no. 23, pp. 59–60.

68 Livingstone 1865, p. 110.

69 *Ibid.*, p. 112.

70 *Ibid.*, p. 113.

71 *Ibid.*, p. 114.

72 *Ibid.*, p. 117.

73 *Ibid.*, p. 115.

74 *Ibid.*, pp. 115–16.

75 *Ibid.*, p. 543 and title-page.

76 There is also an image of slave labour in Speke's *Journal of the Discovery of the Source of the Nile. Sirboko's Slaves carrying Fuel and cutting Rice*, drawn by Johann Baptist Zwecker – who also worked on Livingstone's volumes – depicts two chained gangs of slaves, supervised by an onlooker with a stick. Speke's own party was made up largely of slaves, whom he purchased.

77 Livingstone 1865, pp. 356–7.

78 *Ibid.*, opposite p. 356.

79 *Ibid.*, pp. 356–7.

80 A more explicit illustration appears in the posthumous volume of *The Last Journals of David Livingstone*, edited by Horace Waller. Waller prepared a sketch [Bodleian Library, Oxford, reproduced in Helly 1987, p. 148] from which J. B. Zwecker made a wood engraving [reproduced in Helly, p. 150]. An Arab slave trader is seen poised to split open the skull of a miscreant slave with an axe.

81 See for examples Pieterse 1992, pp. 52–63.

82 Maitland 1971, pp. 226–8.

83 *Illustrated London News*, 3 August 1872, p. 114.

84 *Ibid.*, title-page. The story first appeared in the *New York Herald*, 15 July 1872.

85 Stanley 1872, frontispiece.

86 *Illustrated London News*, 25 April 1874, pp. 381, 401.

87 Wainwright, more self-confident during his period in Britain than Susi and Chuma, was by no means universally admired. A chapter devoted to him in Fraser 1913 describes him as 'remarkably ugly, almost an exaggerated negro type' (p. 223) who, though 'in his way, and under proper control, a useful servant' (p. 221) had 'grown . . . above himself' (p. 223). Unwilling to accept a subordinate role when a guest of the Webb family at Newstead Abbey, he caused fierce resentment. I am grateful to Felix Driver for bringing this to my attention.

88 *Illustrated London News*, 25 April 1874, p. 383.

89 Helly 1987, pp. 107–29.

90 Engraving by J. B. Zwecker, Waller 1874, vol. 2, p. 268.

91 Engraved by J. W. Whymper in Waller 1874, frontispiece to vol. 2; also reproduced in Helly, 1987, p. 110, who notices (p. 111) that 'his attendants are drawn, presumably at the editor's [Horace Waller's] behest, as wearing both Arabic and African styles.'

92 *The Academy*, 13 February 1875, p. 161.

93 *The Times*, 7 January 1875, p. 7.

Chapter 6 David Livingstone and the Worldly After-Life: Imperialism and Nationalism in Africa

1 A further replica of this hut was built at the National Memorial at Blantyre. As late as 1972 it was reconstructed after a fire by Malawian students working in Britain! See Pachai 1973, p. 4.

2 One of the earliest achievements of the RSGS was the funding of Daniel Rankin's expedition that discovered the Chinde mouth of the Zambezi in 1889, enabling vessels of larger draught to enter the river, a cherished hope of Livingstone.

3 Macnair n.d.

4 The Federation of Rhodesia and Nyasaland issued a Livingstone stamp in 1955 on the centennial of his visit to the Victoria Falls.

5 One Victorian example of many will suffice: Hodder n.d., pp. 76–98.

6 John M. MacKenzie, 'David Livingstone: the construction of the myth', in Walker and Gallagher 1990.

7 Cole-King 1973.

8 Quoted in John McCracken, 'Livingstone and the Aftermath: the Origins and Development of the Livingstonia Mission', in Pachai 1973, p. 220.

9 Helly 1987; Waller 1874.

10 Thomas Dick's *Philosophy of a Future State* set out to reconcile science with religion and helped solve Livingstone's youthful crisis of faith.

11 Stanley wished to be buried in Westminster Abbey near Livingstone, but the Dean, the Reverend J. A. Robinson, refused to permit it. See Stanley 1909, p. 515.

12 Stanley 1909, p. 295.

13 Stanley 1880, p. 1.

14 Taylor 1989, pp. 4, 8–9.

15 Johnston 1923, pp. 330–1.

16 Keltie 1893, p. 114.

17 The best accounts of the origins of the two missions are to be found in Andrew C. Ross, 'Livingstone and the Aftermath: the Origins and Development of the Blantyre Mission' and John McCracken, 'Livingstone and the Aftermath: the Origins and Development of the Livingstonia Mission', both in Pachai 1973. See also McCracken 1977.

18 Moir 1923. Other books with Livingstone in the title included Dan Crawford, *Back to the Long Grass: My Link with Livingstone* (London, 1922) and Alfred Dolman, *In the Footsteps of Livingstone* (London, 1924). Authors and publishers clearly thought that the fame of the Livingstone name sold books.

19 Elmslie 1899, Hetherwick 1932 and Laws 1934 are but three examples.

20 Baker 1921, p. 18. 'Though only a boy, Fred there and then determined that "he would go and help that great man in his work".'

21 John McCracken, 'Livingstone and the Aftermath: the Origins and Development of Livingstonia Mission', in Pachai 1973.

22 Livingstone's views on keeping open the route to the north, expressed in a letter of December 1852, are quoted in Dachs 1972, p. 649.

23 During the eighth frontier war on the eastern Cape in the early 1850s Livingstone expressed his sympathies with the Xhosa people in an unpublished pamphlet: 'No nation ever secured liberty without fighting for it . . . we side with the weak against the strong.' Quoted in Holmes 1993, p. 66. Livingstone was also fiercely critical of the judicial excesses after the brutal suppression of the Kat River rebellion at the Cape.

24 Johnston 1891. For an account of the genesis of the project, see Johnston 1923, p. 288. Agnes Livingstone had been concerned by the neglect of Livingstone's scientific work in Waller's editing of *The Last Journals*.

25 Johnston 1923, p. 336.

26 Helly 1987, p. 106.

27 John M. MacKenzie, 'Heroic Myths of Empire', in MacKenzie 1992, pp. 125–30.

28 Johnson 1982, pp. 285–310.

29 Livingstone 1857, pp. 486, 562–3. For a discussion of Livingstone's approach to wildlife, see MacKenzie 1988, pp. 103–5.

30 Quoted in Bridglal Pachai, 'The Zambezi Expedition: New Highways for Old, 1858–64' in Pachai 1973, p. 31.

31 Quoted in Sheila Brock, 'James Stewart and David Livingstone', in Pachai 1973, p. 107.

32 George Shepperson, 'Livingstone and the Years of Preparation 1813–57', in Pachai 1973, p. 26.

Bibliography

Agthe 1985
Johanna Agthe, *Waffen Aus Zentral-Afrika*, Museum für Volkerkunde, Frankfurt, 1985.

Allwood and Treble 1982
Rosamond Allwood and Rosemary Treble, *George Elgar Hicks*, ILEA, Geffrye Museum, London, 1982.

Alpers 1975
Edward Alpers, *Ivory and Slaves: Changing Patterns of International Trade in East Central Africa in the late Nineteenth Century*, Heinemann, London, 1975.

Altick 1978
Richard Altick, *The Shows of London*, Belknap Harvard, Cambridge, MA, 1978.

Anderson 1991
Patricia Anderson, *The Printed Image and the Transformation of Popular Culture, 1790–1860*, Clarendon Press, Oxford, 1991.

Arens 1979
W. Arens, *The Man-Eating Myth: Anthropology and Anthropophagy*, Oxford University Press, New York, 1979.

Baines 1864
Thomas Baines, *Explorations in South-West Africa. Being an Account of a Journey in . . . 1861 and 1862 from Walvisch Bay, on the Western Coast, to Lake Ngami and the Victoria Falls*, Longmans, Green, London, 1864.

Baines 1946
Thomas Baines, *The Northern Goldfields Diaries of Thomas Baines . . .*, J. P. R. Wallis, ed., Chatto and Windus, London, Government Archives of Southern Rhodesia, Oppenheimer Series, no. 3, 1946.

Baker 1921
Ernest Baker, *The Life and Explorations of Frederick Stanley Arnot*, London, 1921.

Barrell 1980
John Barrell, *The Dark Side of the Landscape: The Rural Poor in English Painting 1730–1840*, Cambridge University Press, Cambridge, 1980.

Becker 1984
Bernard Becker, *Scientific London*, London, 1874.

Bensusan 1966
A. Bensusan, *Silver Images: History of Photography in Africa*, Howard Timmins, Cape Town, 1966.

Blaikie 1880
W. G. Blaikie, *The Personal Life of David Livingstone*, London, 1880.

Bloomfield 1990
Anne Bloomfield, 'Drill and Dance as Symbols of Imperialism' in J. A. Mangan, ed., *Making Imperial Mentalities: Socialisation and British Imperialism*, Manchester University Press, Manchester, 1990.

Boime 1990
Albert Boime, *The Art of Exclusion: Representing Blacks in the Nineteenth Century*, Thames and Hudson, London, 1990.

Boucher 1985
M. Boucher, ed., *Livingstone Letters 1843 to 1872: David Livingstone Correspondence in the Brenthurst Library Johannesburg*, Brenthurst Press, Johannesburg, 1985.

Bradlow 1975
Frank and Edna Bradlow, 'The English Vision in South Africa' in *Apollo*, vol. 102, no. 164, October 1975.

Brantlinger 1985
Patrick Brantlinger, 'Victorians and Africans: the Genealogy of the Myth of the Dark Continent' in *Critical Inquiry*, 12, 1985.

Brantlinger 1986
——, 'Victorians and Africans: the Genealogy of the Myth of the Dark Continent' in Gates 1986.

Brantlinger 1988
——, *Rule of Darkness: British Literature and Imperialism, 1830–1914*, Cornell University Press, Ithaca and London, 1988.

Bridges 1968
Roy Bridges, 'The Sponsorship and Financing of Livingstone's Last Journey' in *African Historical Studies*, 1, 1968.

Brown 1983
Paula Brown and Donald Tuzin, eds., *The Ethnography of Cannibalism*, Society for Psychological Anthropology, Washington, 1983.

Cain 1986
A. M. Cain, *The Cornchist for Scotland: Scots in India*, National Library of Scotland, Edinburgh, 1986.

Cain and Hopkins 1993
P. J. Cain and A. G. Hopkins, *British Imperialism: Innovation and Expansion, 1688–1914*, Longman, 1993.

Cairns 1965
H. Alan C. Cairns, *Prelude to Imperialism: British reactions to Central African Society, 1840–1890*, Routledge and Kegan Paul, London, 1965.

Calder 1981
A. Calder, *Revolutionary Empire . . .*, Jonathan Cape, London, 1981.

Calder 1994
——, 'Samuel Smiles: The Unexpurgated Version' in *Revolving Culture: Notes from the Scottish Republic*, I. B. Tauris, London, 1994.

Cannon 1978
S. F. Cannon, *Science in Culture: The Early Victorian Period*, Dawson, New York, 1978.

Carrington 1968
C. Carrington, *The British Overseas . . . Part 1: The Making of the Empire*, Cambridge University Press, Cambridge, 1968.

Chapman 1868
James Chapman, *Travels in the Interior of South Africa . . .*, 2 vols., Bell and Daldy, London, 1868.

Clark 1956
Kenneth Clark, *The Nude: a Study of Ideal Art*, John Murray, London, 1956.

Clendennen 1979
Gary W. Clendennen, assisted by Ian C. Cunningham, *David Livingstone; A Catalogue of Documents*, National Library of Scotland, Edinburgh, 1979.

Clendennen 1992
——, *David Livingstone's Shire Journal 1861–64*, Scottish Cultural Press, Aberdeen, 1992.

Clifford 1986
James Clifford and George E. Marcus, eds., *Writing Culture: the Poetics and Politics of Ethnography*, University of California Press, Berkeley, 1986.

Cole-King 1973
P. A. Cole-King, 'Searching for Livingstone: E. D. Young and Others' in Pachai 1973.

Comaroff and Comaroff 1991
Jean and John Comaroff, *Of Revelation and Revolution: Christianity, Colonialism, and Consciousness in South Africa*, University of Chicago Press, Chicago, 1991.

Comaroff and Comaroff 1992
——, *Ethnography and the Historical Imagination*, Westview Press, Boulder, 1992.

Conrad 1926
Joseph Conrad, *Last Essays*, R. Curle, ed., Dent, London, 1926.

Coombes 1994
Annie Coombes, *Reinventing Africa: Museums, Material Culture and Popular Imagination*, Yale University Press, New Haven, 1994.

Coupland 1928
Reginald Coupland, *Kirk on the Zambesi: A Chapter of African History*, Clarendon Press, Oxford, 1928.

Dachs 1972
Anthony J. Dachs, 'Missionary Imperialism – the case of Bechuanaland' in *Journal of African History*, XIII, 1972.

Debenham 1957
F. Debenham, *The Way to Ilala*, London, 1957.

Debrunner 1979
Hans Werner Debrunner, *Presence and Prestige: Africans in Europe*, Basler Afrika Bibliographien, Basel.

Dickens 1853
Charles Dickens, 'The Noble Savage' in *Household Words*, vol. 7, 11 June 1853.

Driver 1991
Felix Driver, 'Henry Morton Stanley and his Critics: Geography, Exploration and Empire' in *Past and Present*, no. 133, 1991.

Elmslie 1899
W. A. Elmslie, *Among the Wild Ngoni*, Edinburgh, 1899.

Elston 1973
Philip Elston, 'Livingstone and the Anglican Church' in Pachai 1973.

Escott 1960
H. Escott, *A History of Scottish Congregationalism*, Congregational Union of Scotland, Glasgow, 1960.

Felix 1989
Marc Felix, *Maniema*, Fred Jahn, Munich, 1989.

Flint 1970
E. Flint, 'Trade and Politics in Barotseland during the Kololo Period' in *Journal of African History*, 11, 1970.

Foskett 1964
Reginald Foskett, *The Zambezi Doctors*, Edinburgh, 1964.

Foskett 1965
_____, ed., *The Zambesi Journal and Letters of Dr John Kirk 1858–63*, 2 vols., Oliver and Boyd, Edinburgh, 1965.

Fox 1988
Celina Fox, *Graphic Journalism in England during the 1830s and 40s*, Garland, New York, 1988.

Fraser 1913
Augusta Zelia Fraser, *Livingstone and Newstead*, John Murray, London, 1913.

Gallagher and Robinson 1953
John Gallagher and Ronald Robinson, 'The Imperialism of Free Trade' in *Economic History Review*, 6, 1953.

Gates 1986
Henry Louis Gates, Jr., ed., *'Race', Writing and Difference*, University of Chicago Press, Chicago, 1986.

Goldsworthy 1971
David Goldsworthy, *Colonial Issues in British Politics, 1945–1961*, Oxford University Press, Oxford, 1971.

Greene 1982
M. T. Greene, *Geology in the Nineteenth Century*, Cornell University Press, Ithaca, 1982.

Gutzlaff 1834
Karl Gutzlaff, *A Journal of Three Journeys along the Coast of China in 1831, 1832 and 1833*, London, 1834.

Hair 1973
P. E. H. Hair, 'Livingstone as African Historian' in *David Livingstone and Africa: Proceedings of a Seminar held on the occasion of the centenary of the death of David Livingstone*, African Studies Centre, University of Edinburgh, 1973.

Helly 1987
Dorothy O. Helly, *Livingstone's Legacy: Horace Waller and Victorian Mythmaking*, Ohio University Press, Athens, OH, 1987.

Herbert 1994
W. N. Herbert, *The Testament of the Reverend Thomas Dick*, Arc, Todmorden, 1994.

Hetherwick 1932
Alexander Hetherwick, *The Romance of Blantyre*, London, 1932.

Hodder n.d.
Edwin Hodder, *Heroes of Britain in Peace and War*, London, n. d., vol. 2.

Holmes 1990
Timothy Holmes, ed., *David Livingstone: Letters and Documents 1841–1872*, Livingstone Museum, Livingstone, 1990.

Holmes 1993
_____, *Journey to Livingstone: Exploration of an Imperial Myth*, Canongate Press, Edinburgh, 1993.

Honour 1989
Hugh Honour, *The Image of the Black in Western Art*, Harvard University Press for the Menil Foundation, Cambridge, MA, 1989.

Isaacman 1989
A. F. Isaacman, 'The countries of the Zambezi basin' in J. F. Ade Ajayi, ed., *General History of Africa, VI, Africa in the Nineteenth Century until the 1880s*, UNESCO, Paris, 1989.

Jack 1991
Anthony Jack, *Africa: Relics of the Colonial Era*, Michael Graham-Stewart, London, 1991.

JanMohammed 1986
Abdul JanMohammed, 'The Economy of Manichean Allegory: the Function of Racial Difference in Colonialist Literature', in Gates 1986.

Jeal 1973
Tim Jeal, *Livingstone*, Heinemann, London, 1973.

Jeal 1985
_____, *Livingstone*, Penguin, Harmondsworth, 1985.

Johannesburg Art Gallery 1991
Johannesburg Art Gallery, *Art and Ambiguity: Perspectives on the Brenthurst Collection of Southern African Art*, Johannesburg Art Gallery, 1991.

Johnson 1982
Douglas Johnson, 'The death of Gordon: a Victorian Myth' in *Journal of Imperial and Commonwealth History*, X, 1982.

Johnston 1891
H. H. Johnston, *Livingstone and the Exploration of Central Africa*, London, 1891.

Johnston 1913
_____, 'Livingstone as an Explorer' in *Geographical Journal*, 41, 1913.

Johnston 1923
_____, *The Story of My Life*, London, 1923.

Keltie 1893
J. Scott Keltie, *The Partition of Africa*, London, 1893.

Kimambo 1989
I. N. Kimambo, 'The East African coast and hinterland, 1845–80' in J. F. Ade Ajayi, ed. *General History of Africa VI, Africa in the Nineteenth Century until the 1880s*, UNESCO, Paris, 1989.

Laws 1934
Robert Laws, *Reminiscences of Livingstonia*, Edinburgh, 1934.

Lewis 1908
C. T. Courtney Lewis, *George Baxter, Colour Printer: His Life and Work: A Manual for Collectors*, Sampson Low, Marston and Co., London, 1908

Livingstone 1857
David Livingstone, *Missionary Travels and Researches in South Africa*, John Murray, London, 1857.

Livingstone 1858
_____, *Dr Livingstone's Cambridge Lectures*, William Monk, ed., Deigton Bell & Co., Cambridge, 1858.

Livingstone 1865
David and Charles Livingstone, *Narrative of an Expedition to the Zambesi and its Tributaries; and of the Discovery of the Lakes Shirwa and Nyassa. 1858–1864*, John Murray, London, 1865.

Lovelace 1991
Antonia Lovelace, 'The African Collections at the Glasgow Art Gallery and Museum' in *Journal of Museum Ethnography*, 3, 1991.

MacCracken 1977
John MacCracken, *Politics and Christianity in Malawi 1875–1940: the Impact of the Livingstonia Mission in the Northern Province*, Cambridge, 1977.

McDonnell 1885
W. McDonnell, *Exeter Hall: a Theological Romance*, 10th edition, Boston, 1885.

MacKenzie 1987
John M. MacKenzie, 'The Imperial Pioneer and Hunter and the British Masculine Stereotype in late-Victorian and Edwardian Times' in Mangan and Walvin, 1987.

MacKenzie 1988
_____, *The Empire of Nature*, Manchester, 1988.

MacKenzie 1992
_____, ed., *Popular Imperialism and the Military*, Manchester, 1992.

MacLaren 1991
I. S. MacLaren, 'Samuel Hearne's Accounts of the Massacre at Bloody Fall, 17 July 1771' in *Ariel*, 22, 1991.

MacLaren 1992
_____, 'Exploration/Travel Literature and the Evolution of the Author' in *International Journal of Canadian Studies / Revue internationale d'études canadiennes*, 5, 1992.

McLynn 1989
F. McLynn, *Stanley*, London, 1989.

Macnair 1940
James I. Macnair, *Livingstone the Liberator*, London, 1940.

Macnair n. d.
_____, *The Story of the Scottish National Memorial to David Livingstone*, Blantyre, n.d.

Maitland 1971
Alexander Maitland, *Speke*, Constable, London, 1971.

Mangan 1990
J. A. Mangan, ed., *Making Imperial Mentalities: Socialisation and British Imperialism*, Manchester University Press, Manchester, 1990.

Mangan and Walvin 1987
J. A. Mangan and J. Walvin, *Manliness and Morality: Middle-Class Masculinity in Britain and America, 1800–1940*, Manchester University Press, Manchester, 1987

Marks 1976
Stuart Marks, *Large Mammals and a Brave People: Subsistence Hunters in Zambia*, University of Washington Press, Seattle, 1976.

Mathews 1912
Basil Mathews, *Livingstone the Pathfinder*, Oxford University Press, London, 1912.

Middleton 1969
Dorothy Middleton, ed., *The Diary of A. J. Mounteney Jephson, Emin Pasha Relief Expedition, 1887–1889*, Cambridge University Press, Cambridge, 1969.

Mitzman 1978
Max E. Mitzman, *George Baxter and the Baxter Prints*, David and Charles, Newton Abbot, 1978.

Moffat 1842
Robert Moffat, *Missionary Labours and Scenes in Southern Africa*, John Snow, London, 1842.

Moir 1923
F. L. M. Moir, *After Livingstone, an African Trade Romance*, London, 1923.

Moorehead 1983
Alan Moorehead, *The White Nile*, Penguin Books, Harmondsworth, 1983.

Morley 1906
J. Morley, *The Life of Richard Cobden*, T. Fisher Unwin, London, 1906 edition.

Mostert 1992
N. Mostert, *Frontiers: the Epic of South Africa's Creation and the Tragedy of the Xhosa People*, Jonathan Cape, 1992.

National Museums of Zambia 1965
National Museums of Zambia, *The Life and Work of David Livingstone*, National Museums of Zambia, Livingstone, 1965.

Nead 1988
Lynda Nead, *Myths of Sexuality: Representations of Women in Victorian Britain*, Basil Blackwell, Oxford, 1988.

Newitt 1973
M. D. D. Newitt, *Portuguese Settlement on the Zambesi*, Longman, London, 1973.

Ngcongco 1989
L. D. Ngcongco, 'The Mfecane and the rise of new African States' in J. F. Ade Ajayi, ed., in *General History of Africa VI, Africa in the Nineteenth Century until the 1880s*, UNESCO, Paris, 1989.

Northcott 1961
Cecil Northcott, *Robert Moffat: Pioneer in Africa, 1817–1870*, Lutterworth Press, London, 1961.

Ntara 1973
Samuel Josia Ntara, *The History of the Chewa*, Franz Steiner Verlag GMBH, Wiesbaden, 1973.

Oliver and Sanderson 1985
Roland Oliver and G. N. Sanderson, eds., *The Cambridge History of Africa from 1870–1905*, vol. 6, Cambridge University Press, Cambridge, 1985.

Oldroyd 1990
D. R. Oldroyd, *The Highland Controversy: Constructing Geological Knowledge . . .* , Chicago University Press, Chicago, 1990.

Pachai 1973
Bridglal Pachai, ed., *Livingstone: Man of Africa, Memorial Essays, 1873–1973*, Longman, London, 1973.

Page 1973
Melvin E. Page, 'David Livingstone, the Arabs and the Slave Trade' in Pachai 1973.

Page 1974
_____, 'The Manyema hordes of Tippu Tip' in *International Journal of African Historical Studies*, 7, 1974.

Palmer 1895
A. H. Palmer, *The Life of Joseph Wolf, Animal Painter*, Longmans, Green, London, 1895.

Parssinen 1982
Carol Ann Parssinen, 'Social Explorers and Social Scientists: The Dark Continent of Victorian Ethnography' in Jay Ruby, ed., *A Crack in the Mirror*, University of Pennsylvania Press, Philadelphia, 1982.

Phillipson 1975
D. W. Phillipson, ed., *Mosi-oa-tunya: A Handbook to the Victoria Falls Region*, Longman, London, 1975.

Pieterse 1992
Jan Nederveen Pieterse, *White on Black: Images of Africa and Blacks in Western Popular Culture*, Yale University Press, New Haven, 1992.

Pointon 1990
Marcia Pointon, *Naked Authority: the Body in Western Painting, 1830–1908*, Cambridge University Press, Cambridge, 1990.

Pointon 1993
——, *Hanging the Head: Portraiture and Social Formation in Eighteenth-Century England*, Yale University Press, New Haven, 1993.

Port 1995
Michael H. Port, *Imperial London: Civil Government Building in London, 1851–1915*, Yale University Press, New Haven, 1995.

Pratt 1992
Mary Louise Pratt, *Imperial Eyes: Travel Writing and Trans-culturation*, Routledge, London, 1992.

Prichard 1848
James Cowles Prichard, *The Natural History of Man comprising Inquiries into the Modifying Influence of Physical and Moral Agencies on the different Tribes of the Human Family*, H. Ballière, London, revised 3rd edition, 1848.

Rangeley 1959
W. H. J. Rangeley, 'The Makalolo of Dr. Livingstone' in *Nyassaland Journal*, XII, 1959.

Reynolds 1968
Barrie Reynolds, *The Material Culture of the Peoples of the Gwembe Valley*, Manchester University Press, Manchester, 1968.

Richards 1990
Thomas Richards, *The Commodity Culture of Victorian England: Advertising and Spectacle 1851–1914*, Stanford University Press, Stanford, 1990.

Roberts 1973
A. D. Roberts, 'Livingstone's Value to the Historian of African Societies' in *David Livingstone and Africa: Proceedings of a Seminar held on the occasion of the centenary of the death of David Livingstone*, Centre of African Studies, University of Edinburgh, 1973.

Rosie 1981
G. Rosie, *Hugh Miller: Outrage and Order*, Mainstream, Edinburgh, 1981.

Rotberg 1966
Robert Rotberg, *The Rise of Nationalism in Central Africa*, Harvard University Press, Cambridge, MA, 1966.

Rotberg 1970
_____, ed., *Africa and Its Explorers: Motives, Methods and Impact*, Harvard University Press, Cambridge, MA, 1970.

Royal Scottish Museum 1913
Royal Scottish Museum, A Guide to the Livingstone Centenary Exhibition, HMSO, Edinburgh, 1913.

Sanday 1986
Peggy Reeves Sanday, *Divine Hunger: Cannibalism as a Cultural System*, Cambridge University Press, Cambridge, 1986.

Schapera 1959
Isaac Schapera, ed., *David Livingstone: Family Letters, 1841–1856 . . .* , 2 vols., Chatto and Windus, London, 1959.

Schapera 1960
_____, ed., *Livingstone's Private Journals, 1851–53*, Chatto and Windus, London, 1960.

Schapera 1961
_____, ed., *Livingstone's Missionary Correspondence, 1841–1856*, Chatto and Windus, London, 1961.

Schapera 1963
_____, ed., *Livingstone's African Journal, 1853–6*, 2 vols., Chatto and Windus, London, 1963.

Schapera 1974
_____, ed., *David Livingstone: South African Papers 1849–1853*, Van Riebeeck Society, Capetown, 1974.

Schoffeleers 1973
J. M. Schoffeleers, 'Livingstone and the Mang'anja Chiefs' in Pachai 1973.

226

Schoffeleers 1975
_____, 'The Interaction of the M'Bona Cult and Christianity, 1859–1963' in T. O. Ranger and John Weller, eds., *Themes in Christian History in Central Africa*, Heinemann, London, 1975.

Seaver 1957
George Seaver, *David Livingstone: His Life and Letters*, Lutterworth Press, London, 1957.

Shapin 1983
S. Shapin, 'Nibbling at the Teats of Science . . .' in I. Inkster and J. Morrell, eds., *Metropolis and Province: Science in British Culture, 1780–1850*, Hutchinson, London, 1983.

Shepperson 1965
George Shepperson, ed., *David Livingstone and the Rovuma*, University Press, Edinburgh, 1965.

Siddle 1973
D. J. Siddle, 'David Livingstone: Mid-Victorian Field Scientist' in *David Livingstone and Africa: Proceedings of a Seminar held on the occasion of the centenary of the death of David Livingstone*, Centre of African Studies, University of Edinburgh, 1973.

Siddle 1974
_____, 'David Livingstone: A Mid-Victorian Field Scientist' in *Geographical Journal*, vol. 140, part. 1 1974.

Sieber 1980
Roy Sieber, *African Furniture and Household Objects*, Indiana University Press, Bloomington, 1980.

Simpson 1973
Donald H. Simpson, 'The Magic Lantern and Imperialism', Library Notes, The Royal Commonwealth Society, vol. 191 (NS), 1973.

Simpson 1975
_____, *Dark Companions: The African contribution to the European exploration of East Africa*, Paul Elek, London, 1975.

Smiles 1878
S. Smiles, *Robert Dick – Baker of Thurso: Geologist and Botanist*, John Murray, London, 1878.

Smiles, *Self-Help*, 1882
_____, *Self-Help* (revised edition), John Murray, London, 1882.

Smiles, *Thomas Edward*, 1882
_____, *The Life of a Scottish Naturalist: Thomas Edward*, (second edition), John Murray, London, 1882.

Smiles 1905
_____, *Autobiography*, John Murray, London, 1905.

Smith 1956
Edwin W. Smith, 'Sebetwane and the Makololo' in *African Studies*, 15, 1956.

Speke 1863
John Hanning Speke, *Journal of the Discovery of the Source of the Nile*, William Blackwood, London, 1863.

Spring 1993
Chris Spring, *African Arms and Armour*, British Museum Press, London, 1993.

Stafford 1989
Robert Stafford, *Scientist of Empire: Sir Roderick Murchison, Scientific Exploration and Victorian Imperialism*, Cambridge University Press, Cambridge, 1989.

Stanley 1872
Henry Morton Stanley, *How I Found Livingstone . . .*, Sampson and Low, London, 1872.

Stanley 1880
_____, *Through the Dark Continent*, London, 1880.

Stanley 1885
_____, 'Central Africa and the Congo Basin; or, The Importance of the Scientific Study of Geography' in *Journal of the Manchester Geographical Society*, 1, 1885.

Stanley 1983
Brian Stanley, '"Commerce and Christianity": Providence Theory, the Missionary Movement, and the Imperialism of Free Trade, 1842–1860' in *Historical Journal*, vol. 26, no. 1, 1983.

Stanley 1909
Dorothy Stanley, ed., *The Autobiography of Henry Morton Stanley*, London, 1909.

Stocking 1987
George W. Stocking, *Victorian Anthropology*, Free Press, New York, 1987.

Tabler 1963
Edward C. Tabler, *The Zambezi Papers of Richard Thornton*, 2 vols., Chatto & Windus, London, 1965.

Taylor 1989
Stephen Taylor, *The Mighty Nimrod: the Life of Frederick Courtney Selous*, London 1989.

Terashima 1980
Hideaki Terashima, 'Hunting Life of the Bambote: An Anthropological Study of Hunter-gatherers in a Wooded Savanna' in *Senri Ethnological Studies*, 6, 1980.

Thomas 1991
Nicholas Thomas, *Entangled Objects: Exchange, Material Culture and Colonialism in the Pacific*, Harvard University Press, Cambridge, MA, 1991.

Thomas 1994
_____, *Colonialism's Culture*, Princeton University Press, Princeton, 1994.

Thomson 1890
Joseph Thomson, 'The Results of European Intercourse with the African' in *Contemporary Review*, March, 1890.

Thornton 1983
Robert Thornton, 'Narrative Ethnography in Africa, 1850–1920: The Creation and Capture of an Appropriate Domain for Anthropology' in *Man* (NS) 18, 38, 1983.

Tibbles 1994
Anthony Tibbles, ed., *Transatlantic Slavery: Against Human Dignity*, HMSO and National Museums and Galleries on Merseyside, London, 1994.

Vance 1985
Norman Vance, *The Sinews of the Spirit: the Ideal of Christian Manliness in Victorian Literature and Religious Thought*, Cambridge University Press, Cambridge, 1985.

Vaughan 1991
Megan Vaughan, *Curing their ills: Colonial Power and African Illness*, Polity Press, Cambridge, 1991.

Vellut 1989
J. L. Vellut 'The Congo Basin and Angola' in J. F. Ade Ajayi, ed., *General History of Africa*, VI, *Africa in the Nineteenth century until the 1880s*, UNESCO, Paris, 1989.

Wakeman 1973
Geoffrey Wakeman, *Victorian Book Illustration: The Technical Revolution*, David and Charles, Newton Abbott, 1973.

Walker and Gallagher 1990
Graham Walker and Tom Gallagher, *Sermons and Battle Hymns: Protestant Popular Culture in Scotland*, Edinburgh, 1990.

Waller 1874
Horace Waller, ed., *The Last Journals of David Livingstone in Central Africa . . .*, 2 vols, John Murray, London, 1874.

Waller 1889
_____, 'The Universities Mission to Central Africa' in *Quarterly Review*, 168, 1889.

Waller 1891
_____, *Ivory, Apes and Peacocks: An African Contemplation*, London, 1891.

Wallis 1941
J. P. R. Wallis, *Thomas Baines of King's Lynn: Explorer and Artist 1820–1875*, Jonathan Cape, London, 1941.

Wallis 1945
_____, ed., *The Matabele Mission: A Selection from the Correspondence of John and Emily Moffat, David Livingstone and Others 1858–1875*, London, 1945

Wallis 1952
_____, ed., *The Zambesi Journal of James Stewart 1862–1863*, London, 1952

Wallis 1956
_____, ed., *The Zambezi Expedition of David Livingstone, 1858–1863*, 2 vols., Chatto and Windus, London, 1956.

White 1987
Landeg White, *Magomero*, Cambridge University Press, Cambridge, 1987.

Winwood Reade 1873
William Winwood Reade, *An African Sketch-Book*, London, 1873.

Youngs 1994
Youngs, Tim, *Travellers in Africa: British Travelogues, 1850–1900*, Manchester University Press, Manchester, 1994.

Exhibition List

Items are listed according to the six main sections of the exhibition, ordered by medium and then alphabetically by artist or author.

Measurements are given in centimetres, height before width.

*Scotland only
† London only

Introduction

1.1
David Livingstone (1813–1873)
By Henry Wyndham Phillips, 1857
Oil on canvas
71.8 x 59 oval
PRIVATE COLLECTION

1.2
Manuscript map of Lake Shirwa (now Chilwa) and the River Shire
By David Livingstone, c. 1859
Ink and watercolour on squared paper laid on to linen, 100 x 67.2
ROYAL GEOGRAPHICAL SOCIETY
(Malawi S5)

1.3
Missionary Travels and Researches in South Africa
By David Livingstone
Published by John Murray, London, 1857
Printed book, 23 (spine height)
QUENTIN KEYNES

1.4
'Manyema' spears collected by Livingstone on his last journeys
Iron and wood with plant fibres and skins, 142.7–189.3 (length)
GLASGOW MUSEUMS
(1877.21.a/b/c/e/f)

1.5
Kafue ivory bracelet collected by Livingstone and given to Agnes Livingstone, 1859
THE DAVID LIVINGSTONE CENTRE
(810)

Early Years and Travels in Southern Africa

2.1
Herd of buffalo opposite Garden Island, Victoria Falls
By Thomas Baines, c. 1862–1865
Oil on canvas, 46 x 65.7
ROYAL GEOGRAPHICAL SOCIETY
(Baines 38)

2.2
Bird's-eye view of the Victoria or Mosioatunya – 'smoke sounding' – Falls
By Thomas Baines, 1866
Oil on canvas, 30.8 x 46.4
ROYAL GEOGRAPHICAL SOCIETY
(Baines 37)

2.3
James Young (1811–1883)
Attributed to Sir John Watson Gordon, 1850s
Oil on canvas, 76.3 x 63.2
PRIVATE COLLECTION

2.4
Robert Moffat (1795–1883) with John Mokoteri and Sarah Roby
By William Scott, 1842
Oil on canvas, 53.4 x 45.7
SCOTTISH NATIONAL PORTRAIT GALLERY (PG 2035)

2.5
Robert Moffat (1795–1883)
By George Baxter, c. 1842
Watercolour over pencil on paper 27.9 x 23.5
NATIONAL PORTRAIT GALLERY, LONDON (6312)

2.6
Robert Moffat (1795–1883)
By George Baxter, 1843
Baxtertype engraving, 25.8 x 20.8
NATIONAL PORTRAIT GALLERY, LONDON (D4432)

2.7
Blantyre
By Bruce Cameron, c. 1920
Etching, 18.6 x 26.5
SCOTTISH NATIONAL GALLERY OF MODERN ART (148)

2.8
'Meribohwhey, Chief Town of the Tammakas'
By John Campbell
Pencil, ink and grey wash on paper, 12.8 x 19.5
COUNCIL FOR WORLD MISSION ARCHIVE, SCHOOL OF ORIENTAL AND AFRICAN STUDIES
(Box 3, Campbell, folder 4;32)

2.9
'King's District in the city of Lattakoo'
By John Campbell, 1813/1820
Watercolour over pencil on paper 12.6 x 19
COUNCIL FOR WORLD MISSION ARCHIVE, SCHOOL OF ORIENTAL AND AFRICAN STUDIES
(Box 3, Campbell, folder 4;33)

2.10
Southern African Sketches
By John Campbell, May 1813
Grey wash over pencil on paper 16.5 x 21 (open)
COUNCIL FOR WORLD MISSION ARCHIVE, SCHOOL OF ORIENTAL AND AFRICAN STUDIES
(Box 3, Campbell)

2.11
Southern African Sketches
By John Campbell, June 1813
Watercolour over pencil on paper 16.5 x 21 (open)
COUNCIL FOR WORLD MISSION ARCHIVE, SCHOOL OF ORIENTAL AND AFRICAN STUDIES
(Box 3, Campbell)

2.12
Southern African Sketches
By John Campbell, October 1813
Grey wash over pencil on paper 16.5 x 21 (open)
COUNCIL FOR WORLD MISSION ARCHIVE, SCHOOL OF ORIENTAL AND AFRICAN STUDIES
(Box 3, Campbell)

2.13
Mzilikazi, King of the Ndebele
By William Cornwallis Harris 25 October 1836
Watercolour over pencil on paper 38 x 28.6
QUENTIN KEYNES

2.14
Mzilikazi with Ndebele warriors
By William Cornwallis Harris 1836
Watercolour over pencil on paper 27.8 x 37.5
QUENTIN KEYNES

2.15
Gnu in a landscape
By William Cornwallis Harris c. 1837–1840
Watercolour and bodycolour over pencil on paper, 31 x 41.2
QUENTIN KEYNES

2.16
Kudu in a landscape
By William Cornwallis Harris, c. 1837–1840
Watercolour and bodycolour over pencil on paper, 30.2 x 41
QUENTIN KEYNES

2.17
John Campbell (1766–1840)
By Thomas Hodgetts (after John Renton), 1819
Mezzotint, 35.5 x 25.5
NATIONAL PORTRAIT GALLERY, LONDON (D1189)

2.18
Manuscript map of Livingstone's route from Sesheke to Luanda
By David Livingstone, 1854
Pencil and ink on paper laid on to card and backed with linen 74.8 x 46
ROYAL GEOGRAPHICAL SOCIETY
(Africa S.S.53)

2.19
Manuscript map of part of Livingstone's route from Luanda to Quelimane, showing the Victoria Falls
By David Livingstone, 1856
Brown ink on paper laid on to linen, 33 x 42.5
ROYAL GEOGRAPHICAL SOCIETY
(Zambia S.S.2)

2.20
Sketch of the Victoria Falls
By David Livingstone (?)August 1860
Watercolour over pencil, inscribed in ink, on card 12.6 x 15.3
ROYAL GEOGRAPHICAL SOCIETY
(DL/3/5/1)

2.21
Reverend Ralph Wardlaw (1779–1853)
By Sir Daniel MacNee
Ink and wash on paper 17.8 x 11.2
SCOTTISH NATIONAL PORTRAIT GALLERY (2420)

2.22
Manuscript plan of the mission station at Kuruman
By Robert Moffat Jnr, 1850
Watercolour and black ink on paper, 45.5 x 61.5
COUNCIL FOR WORLD MISSION ARCHIVE, SCHOOL OF ORIENTAL AND AFRICAN STUDIES
(Maps E78:30 Kuruman)

2.23
David Livingstone
By Sarah Newell, 1840
Watercolour on ivory, 7.5 x 5.4
COUNCIL FOR WORLD MISSION ARCHIVE, SCHOOL OF ORIENTAL AND AFRICAN STUDIES

2.24
Reverend John Philip (1775–1851)
By Thompson (after Wildman)
Steel engraving, 22.1 x 14
NATIONAL PORTRAIT GALLERY, LONDON

2.25
William John Burchell
(?1782–1863)
By Mrs Dawson Turner
(after John Sell Cotman), 1816
Etching, 17.6 x 14.2
NATIONAL PORTRAIT GALLERY,
LONDON

2.26
Sir John Barrow (1764–1848)
By an unknown artist, c. 1795
Watercolour on ivory, 4.4 x 3.5
NATIONAL PORTRAIT GALLERY,
LONDON (769)

2.27
Engraver's sketch of a section
of a gorge cut by the Zambezi
at the Victoria Falls
(annotated by David Livingstone)
Pencil with manuscript additions
on paper, 16 x 25.4
PRIVATE COLLECTION

2.28
'Reception of the Mission
by Shinte'
From *Missionary Travels and
Researches in South Africa*
(annotated by David Livingstone
and John Murray)
Proof engraving with manuscript
additions, 16 x 25.4
PRIVATE COLLECTION

2.29
'Scene at a Sleeping-place
in Angola'
From *Missionary Travels and
Researches in South Africa*
(annotated by David Livingstone)
Proof engraving with manuscript
additions, 16 x 25.4
PRIVATE COLLECTION

2.30
'River scenery on the West Coast'
From *Missionary Travels and
Researches in South Africa*
(annotated by David Livingstone
and John Murray)
Proof engraving with manuscript
additions, 16 x 25.4
PRIVATE COLLECTION

2.31
John Murray (1808–1892)
By David Octavius Hill & Robert
Adamson, 1840s
Calotype print, 20.5 x 15.2
NATIONAL PORTRAIT GALLERY,
LONDON (X26046)

2.32
Dr Thomas Graham (1805–1869)
By Maull & Polyblank, c. 1855
Albumen print, 20 x 14.6
(arched top)
NATIONAL PORTRAIT GALLERY,
LONDON (P106[9])

2.33
Mary Livingstone,
née Moffat (1821–1862)
Photogravure after an earlier
photograph (photographer
unknown, late 1850s), 36 x 29
THE DAVID LIVINGSTONE CENTRE
(056)

2.34
William Cotton Oswell (1818–1893)
Photogravure after an earlier
photograph (photographer
unknown, c. 1850), 16 x 12.4
THE DAVID LIVINGSTONE CENTRE
(077)

2.35
Letter from David Livingstone to
John Arundel, 5 September 1837
Manuscript letter, 22.8 x 18.4
COUNCIL FOR WORLD MISSION
ARCHIVE, SCHOOL OF ORIENTAL
AND AFRICAN STUDIES

2.36
Letter from David Livingstone
to Sir Roderick Impey
Murchison, 25 January 1856
Manuscript letter, 24.5 x 18.3
ROYAL GEOGRAPHICAL SOCIETY
(DL/2/8/2)

2.37
Letter from David Livingstone
to John Murray, 22 May 1857
Manuscript letter, 18.3 x 21.9
PRIVATE COLLECTION

2.38
Letter from Mary Livingstone
to the directors of the London
Missionary Society, 21 July 1854
Manuscript letter, 18 x 11.2
COUNCIL FOR WORLD MISSION
ARCHIVE, SCHOOL OF ORIENTAL
AND AFRICAN STUDIES

2.39
Analysis of the language of the
Bechuanas
By David Livingstone, c. 1852–1858
Bound manuscript, 25 x 44 (open)
PRIVATE COLLECTION

2.40
*Missionary Travels and Researches
in South Africa*
By David Livingstone, 1857
Bound manuscript
33.8 x 45 x 12 (open)
PRIVATE COLLECTION

2.41
Sporting Journal
By Thomas Montrose Steele, 1843
Bound manuscript
c. 22.5 x 18.5 (closed)
BY PERMISSION OF THE TRUSTEES
OF THE NATIONAL LIBRARY OF
SCOTLAND (MS20320)

2.42
*Travels in the Interior of
Southern Africa*
By William John Burchell,
volume 2
Published by Longman & Co.,
London, 1824
Printed book, 29 (spine height)
QUENTIN KEYNES

2.43
Travels in South Africa
By John Campbell, volume 2
Published by the London
Missionary Society, London, 1822
Printed book, 26.3 (spine height)
QUENTIN KEYNES

2.44
Wild Sports of Southern Africa
By William Cornwallis Harris
Published by Pelham Richardson,
London, 4th edition, 1844
Printed book, 25.5 (spine height)
QUENTIN KEYNES

2.45
*Five Years of a Hunter's Life in
the Far Interior of Southern Africa*
By R. Gordon Cumming
Published by John Murray,
London, 1850
Printed book, 21 (spine height)
QUENTIN KEYNES

2.46
An Introduction to Arithmetic
(with Livingstone's signature)
By James Gray
Published in Edinburgh, 1825
Printed book with manuscript
additions, 14.5 (spine height)
THE DAVID LIVINGSTONE CENTRE
(388)

2.47
*Missionary Travels and Researches
in South Africa*
By David Livingstone
Published by John Murray,
London, 1857
Printed book, 23 (spine height)
QUENTIN KEYNES

2.48
*Missionary Labours and Scenes
in Southern Africa*
By Robert Moffat
Published by John Snow,
London, 1842
Printed book, 23.3 (spine height)
QUENTIN KEYNES

2.49
Researches in South Africa
By John Philip, volume 1
Published by James Duncan,
London, 1828
Printed book, 24 (spine height)
QUENTIN KEYNES

2.50
*Illustrations of the Zoology of
South Africa, Aves*
By Sir Andrew Smith
Published by Smith, Elder & Co.,
London, 1838–1849
Printed book, 32.3 (spine height)
QUENTIN KEYNES

2.51
*A Description of an Extensive
Collection of Rare, and Undescribed
Specimens of Natural History;
Collected and Conveyed to this
Country at Considerable Expense*
By Andrew Steedman, 1833
Printed leaflet, 21 x 10 (closed)
BY PERMISSION OF THE TRUSTEES
OF THE NATIONAL LIBRARY OF
SCOTLAND (APS.3.78.21)

2.52
Livingstone's certificates from the
Andersonian University, Glasgow,
1836–1838
Five printed cards with
manuscript additions
Each 7.6 x 11.3
THE DAVID LIVINGSTONE CENTRE
(1403, 1405, 1406, 1407, 1410)

2.53
Tswana *New Testament* (1840)
Translated by Robert Moffat, 1841
Printed book, 18.7 (spine height)
BRITISH AND FOREIGN BIBLE
SOCIETY COLLECTIONS (385 E40)

2.54
Old Testament extracts printed
at Kuruman
Translated by Robert Moffat
Printed pamphlet
21.2 x 13.8 (closed)
BRITISH AND FOREIGN BIBLE
SOCIETY COLLECTIONS (385 E47)

2.55
Basin given to Sechele
by Livingstone, c. 1852
Brass, 40 (diameter)
THE DAVID LIVINGSTONE CENTRE
(145)

2.56
Boat's compass used by
Livingstone on his first journey
down the Zambezi
Manufactured by Dubas, Nantes
Metal and glass in wooden box
24 (diameter)
ROYAL GEOGRAPHICAL SOCIETY
(213/5)

2.57
Livingstone's magic lantern
55 x 40.7 x 15
THE DAVID LIVINGSTONE CENTRE
(343)

2.58
Snuff box of Tswana design
collected by Robert Moffat
in South Africa
Ivory, wood and (?)leather
20.3 (height)
LENT BY KIND PERMISSION OF
THE TRUSTEES OF THE BRITISH
MUSEUM (Af1910–384.a)

2.59
Spirally curved elephant's tusk,
presented by Livingstone to
Sir Richard Owen
Approximately 87 x 18.2
THE DAVID LIVINGSTONE CENTRE
(267)

2.60
Rope of African manufacture
brought back from Lake Ngami
by Livingstone
Plant fibre, 82 (length)
THE DAVID LIVINGSTONE CENTRE
(119)

Return to Britain

3.1
Women making panellas for
sugar, at Katipo, near Tete
By Thomas Baines, 12 August 1859
Oil on canvas, 46 x 65.7
ROYAL GEOGRAPHICAL SOCIETY
(Baines 34)

3.2
Working a coal seam near Tete,
lower Zambezi
By Thomas Baines, 1859
Oil on canvas, 46 x 65.7
ROYAL GEOGRAPHICAL SOCIETY
(Baines 35)

3.3
The Slave Trade
By François-Auguste Biard
c. 1840
Oil on canvas, 162.5 x 228.6
WILBERFORCE HOUSE MUSEUM
– HULL CITY MUSEUMS, ART
GALLERIES AND ARCHIVES

3.4
Lord Palmerston (1784–1865)
By Francis Cruikshank, c. 1855
Oil on canvas, 49.2 x 39.7
NATIONAL PORTRAIT GALLERY,
LONDON (3953)

3.5
Thomas Guthrie (1803–1873)
By James Edgar, 1862
Oil on millboard, 54.7 x 45.7
SCOTTISH NATIONAL PORTRAIT
GALLERY (2633)

3.6
4th Earl of Clarendon
(1800–1870)
By Sir Francis Grant, 1843
Oil on canvas, 61 x 50.7
EARL OF CLARENDON

3.7
David Livingstone
By Monson of Cambridge
December 1857
Oil on board, 16.5 x 12.5
ROYAL GEOGRAPHICAL SOCIETY
(358/0.1)

3.8
Sir Roderick Impey Murchison
(1784–1871)
By Stephen Pearce, 1856
Oil on canvas, 38.7 x 32.4
NATIONAL PORTRAIT GALLERY,
LONDON (906)

3.9
Samuel Smiles (1812–1904)
By Sir George Reid, c. 1877
Oil on canvas, 62.2 x 45.7
NATIONAL PORTRAIT GALLERY,
LONDON (1377)

3.10
Samuel Wilberforce (1805–1873)
By George Richmond, c. 1864
Oil on paper, 44.5 x 33.3
NATIONAL PORTRAIT GALLERY,
LONDON (1054)

3.11
Baroness Burdett-Coutts
(1814–1906)
By an unknown artist, c. 1840
Oil on panel, 33 x 27.1
NATIONAL PORTRAIT GALLERY,
LONDON (6181)

3.12
Sir William Jackson Hooker
(1785–1865)
By Thomas Woolner, 1859
Marble bust, 62 (height)
ROYAL BOTANIC GARDENS, KEW

3.13
Sir Thomas Fowell Buxton
(1786–1845)
By Benjamin Robert Haydon, 1840
Chalk on paper, 52.4 x 40.6
NATIONAL PORTRAIT GALLERY,
LONDON (3782)

3.14
William Wilberforce (1759–1833)
By George Richmond, 1833
Watercolour on paper, 43.8 x 33
NATIONAL PORTRAIT GALLERY,
LONDON (4997)

3.15
Sir Joseph Dalton Hooker
(1817–1911)
By Julia Margaret Cameron, c. 1868
Albumen print, 31.8 x 25.4
THE ROYAL PHOTOGRAPHIC
SOCIETY, BATH (RPS 2064 PF9)

3.16
David Livingstone
By Maull & Polyblank, 1857
Albumen print, 19.8 x 14.7
(arched top)
NATIONAL PORTRAIT GALLERY,
LONDON (AX7279)

3.17
Sir Richard Owen (1804–1892)
By Maull & Polyblank, 1856
Albumen print, 19.8 x 14.6
(arched top)
NATIONAL PORTRAIT GALLERY,
LONDON (P106[15])

3.18
David Livingstone
By an unknown photographer
1856–1858
Ambrotype, 14.4 x 10
SCOTTISH NATIONAL PORTRAIT
GALLERY (PGP 78)

3.19
Letter from David Livingstone
to Sir William Jackson Hooker
5 February 1857
Manuscript letter, 17.9 x 22.2
ROYAL BOTANIC GARDENS, KEW
(Afr.Letts. 1844–58 [LIX] f189)

3.20
Letter from David Livingstone
to Sir Joseph Dalton Hooker
28 July 1857
Manuscript letter, 17.9 x 22.2
ROYAL BOTANIC GARDENS, KEW
(Eng.Letts. 1865–1900 [22]
ff128–129)

3.21
Letter from David Livingstone
to Sir Richard Owen
29 December 1860
Manuscript letter, 21.3 x 36.5
BY PERMISSION OF THE TRUSTEES
OF THE NATURAL HISTORY
MUSEUM (OC62 ff415&416)

3.22
Letter from David Livingstone to
Lord Palmerston, 15 January 1861
Manuscript letter, 32.2 x 20
BY PERMISSION OF THE TRUSTEES
OF THE NATIONAL LIBRARY OF
SCOTLAND (MS10768 ff47–8)

3.23
Hints to Travellers
By Francis Galton *et al.*
Published by the Royal
Geographical Society, London, 1854
Printed pamphlet, 22 x 14 (closed)
ROYAL GEOGRAPHICAL SOCIETY

3.24
Proof dedication page to
*Missionary Travels and Researches
in South Africa*
By David Livingstone
Published by John Murray,
London, 1857
Printed sheet with manuscript
additions, 22 x 14
PRIVATE COLLECTION

3.25
Dr Livingstone's Cambridge Lectures
By William Monk
Published by Deighton Bell & Co.,
Cambridge and London, 1858
Printed book, 19.2 (spine height)
QUENTIN KEYNES

3.26
Livingston Fund, 5 January 1857
Printed pamphlet, 26.2 x 19.2
(closed)
ROYAL BOTANIC GARDENS, KEW
(Afr.Letts. 1844–58 [LIX] f187)

3.27
Microscope given to Livingstone
by Baroness Burdett-Coutts
45 x 31.8
THE DAVID LIVINGSTONE CENTRE
(273)

3.28
The Royal Geographical Society
Gold Medal, awarded to
Livingstone in 1855 and presented
to him on 15 December 1856
By William Wyon, 1856
Gold medal, 5.4 (diameter)
THE DAVID LIVINGSTONE CENTRE
(686)

3.29
Silver-gilt casket presented by
the city of Glasgow to Livingstone
in 1857
Silver-gilt, 14 x 19 x 6.5
THE DAVID LIVINGSTONE CENTRE
(684)

3.30
Elephant tusk collected in Africa
by Livingstone
110 x 15 x 35
GLASGOW MUSEUMS (1900.159.a)

3.31

Wooden yoke removed by
Livingstone from the neck
of a slave
158 x 15.5
THE DAVID LIVINGSTONE CENTRE
(560)

3.32

Wrought-iron slave chains and
shackles brought from Africa
by Livingstone
ROYAL GEOGRAPHICAL SOCIETY
(103X [RGS 314])

3.33

Mang'anja loom with cotton,
collected by Livingstone
Wood and cotton fibre
101.5 x 91.5
COURTESY OF THE TRUSTEES
OF THE NATIONAL MUSEUMS
OF SCOTLAND (RMS 762.2)

3.34

Sample of sugar
(*Gramineae/Saccharum officinarum L.*)
Glass jar containing crude sugar,
15.7 (height)
ROYAL BOTANIC GARDENS, KEW
(40591)

3.35

Three spindles with cotton thread
collected from the Mang'anja
on the River Shire by John Kirk
Wood and cotton, 45.7, 47, 48.3
(length)
LENT BY KIND PERMISSION OF
THE TRUSTEES OF THE BRITISH
MUSEUM (Af.2894/5/6)

The Zambezi Expedition

4.1

Herd of hippopotami near
the mouth of the Luabo River
By Thomas Baines, *c.* 1858–1859
Oil on canvas, 46 x 65.7
ROYAL GEOGRAPHICAL SOCIETY
(Baines 23)

4.2

'Wounded hippopotamus above
Kebrabasa, Zambesi River'
By Thomas Baines, *c.* 1858–1859
Oil on canvas, 46 x 65.7
ROYAL GEOGRAPHICAL SOCIETY
(Baines 28)

4.3

'Shibadda, or two channel rapid,
above the Kebrabasa, Zambesi
River'
By Thomas Baines, 1859
Oil on canvas, 46 x 65.7
ROYAL GEOGRAPHICAL SOCIETY
(Baines 24)

4.4

'Mount Stephanie, above
Kebrabasa, Zambesi River'
By Thomas Baines, 9 March 1859
Oil on canvas, 46 x 65.7
ROYAL GEOGRAPHICAL SOCIETY
(Baines 27)

4.5

'Elephant in the Shallows of
the Shire River, the steam
launch firing'
By Thomas Baines, 1859
Oil on canvas, 46 x 65.7
ROYAL GEOGRAPHICAL SOCIETY
(Baines 29)

4.6

Town of Tete from the north
shore of the Zambezi
By Thomas Baines, April 1859
Oil on canvas, 46 x 65.7
ROYAL GEOGRAPHICAL SOCIETY
(Baines 30)

4.7

'Conde, a Native of Tete'
By Thomas Baines, 1859
Oil on canvas, 46 x 65.7
ROYAL GEOGRAPHICAL SOCIETY
(Baines 32)

4.8

'Shibante, a native of Mazaro,
boatman and pilot belonging
to Major Sicard'
By Thomas Baines, 1859
Oil on canvas, 46 x 65.7
ROYAL GEOGRAPHICAL SOCIETY
(Baines 36)

4.9

Hoisting the foremost section of
the steam launch, the *Ma Robert*
By Thomas Baines, 16 May 1858
Pencil on paper, 19.3 x 27.4
ROYAL GEOGRAPHICAL SOCIETY
(X343/022607)

4.10

Hoisting the central section of
the *Ma Robert*
By Thomas Baines, 16 May 1858
Pencil on paper, 19.1 x 27.5
ROYAL GEOGRAPHICAL SOCIETY
(X343/022605)

4.11

The *Ma Robert* aground
By Thomas Baines, 24 May 1858
Watercolour over pencil on paper
19.2 x 27.7
ROYAL GEOGRAPHICAL SOCIETY
(X343/022606)

4.12

'Tom Jumbo, the head Krooman
of the *Ma Robert* inviting natives
to come on board'
By Thomas Baines, 25 May 1858
Watercolour over pencil on paper
19.8 x 28
ROYAL GEOGRAPHICAL SOCIETY
(X343/022613)

4.13

The *Pearl* passing through the
Kongone Canal
By Thomas Baines, 10 June 1858
Watercolour over pencil on paper
19.5 x 27.2
ROYAL GEOGRAPHICAL SOCIETY
(X343/022608)

4.14

The *Pearl* ashore in the Kongone
Canal
By Thomas Baines, 11 June 1858
Pencil on paper, 19.5 x 27.7
ROYAL GEOGRAPHICAL SOCIETY
(X343/022612)

4.15

'Electric Fish' from the Zambezi
Delta
By Thomas Baines, 13 June 1858
Watercolour over pencil on paper
19.4 x 27.2
ROYAL GEOGRAPHICAL SOCIETY
(X343/022611)

4.16

'A native of the country . . . on
board the *Pearl*'
By Thomas Baines, 23 June 1858
Watercolour over pencil on paper
32.2 x 22.2
ROYAL GEOGRAPHICAL SOCIETY
(X341/022600)

4.17

Earthenware pots for catching
palm sap
By Thomas Baines
(?)28 November 1859
Watercolour over pencil on paper
26.6 x 37.9
ROYAL GEOGRAPHICAL SOCIETY
(X229/021894)

4.18

Figure smoking a pipe and the
leaf of a palm
By Thomas Baines
19 November 1859
Watercolour over pencil on paper
38 x 26.2
ROYAL GEOGRAPHICAL SOCIETY
(X229/021895)

4.19

Mangrove at the mouth of
the Kongone
By Thomas Baines
2 December 1859
Watercolour over pencil on paper
36.4 x 26.5
ROYAL GEOGRAPHICAL SOCIETY
(X229/021899)

4.20†

'Dzomba from the East'
By John Kirk, 19 April 1859
Watercolour over pencil on paper
7.2 x 12
BY PERMISSION OF THE TRUSTEES
OF THE NATIONAL LIBRARY OF
SCOTLAND (MS10750 sheet 2)

4.21†

'Mongazi Village'
By John Kirk, April 1859
Watercolour over pencil on paper
7.2 x 12
BY PERMISSION OF THE TRUSTEES
OF THE NATIONAL LIBRARY OF
SCOTLAND (MS10750 sheet 2)

4.22†

Sketch map of River Shire
and Lake Shirwa (now Chilwa)
By John Kirk, April 1859
Watercolour and ink over pencil
on paper, 19.7 x 12.6
BY PERMISSION OF THE TRUSTEES
OF THE NATIONAL LIBRARY OF
SCOTLAND
(MS10750 sheet 3)

4.23

Sketch of Lake Shirwa
(now Chilwa)
By John Kirk, 18 April 1859
Watercolour, pencil and ink
on paper, 19.3 x 51.8
ROYAL GEOGRAPHICAL SOCIETY
(DL3/5/2)

4.24

Four botanical drawings of
Barringtonia racemosa (L.) Spreng.
By John Kirk, May 1859–March
1860
Pencil, watercolour and ink
on paper, each 18.1 x 12.4
(maximum)
ROYAL BOTANIC GARDENS, KEW
(105)

4.25

Sketch map of Lake Nyasa
By John Kirk, June 1862
Manuscript map, black ink and
watercolour on paper, 38.5 x 27.1
ROYAL BOTANIC GARDENS, KEW
(African Letters 1859–1865 [LX],
ff160–161)

4.26†
David and Charles Livingstone,
John Kirk and Charles Meller
visiting Bishop Mackenzie's grave
By Charles Meller, 1863
Watercolour over pencil on paper
17.5 x 25
THE UNITED SOCIETY FOR THE
PROPAGATION OF THE GOSPEL
AND RHODES HOUSE LIBRARY
(Album 37)

4.27*
'Fruit of the Potamus'
By Charles Meller, 2 March 1863
Watercolour over pencil on paper
17.5 x 25
THE UNITED SOCIETY FOR THE
PROPAGATION OF THE GOSPEL
AND RHODES HOUSE LIBRARY
(Box AI[I]A, UMCA)

4.28†
'Last Visit to Chibisa'
By Charles Meller, 15 July 1863
Watercolour over pencil on paper
17.5 x 25
THE UNITED SOCIETY FOR THE
PROPAGATION OF THE GOSPEL
AND RHODES HOUSE LIBRARY
(Box AI[I]A, UMCA 7–18)

4.29*
View of Chibisa
By Charles Meller, 15 July 1863
Watercolour over pencil on paper
17.5 x 25
THE UNITED SOCIETY FOR THE
PROPAGATION OF THE GOSPEL
AND RHODES HOUSE LIBRARY
(Box AI[I]A, UMCA 7–18)

4.30†
'An Evening Halt'
By Charles Meller, 19 July 1863
Watercolour over pencil on paper
17.5 x 25
THE UNITED SOCIETY FOR THE
PROPAGATION OF THE GOSPEL
AND RHODES HOUSE LIBRARY
(Box AI[I]A, UMCA)

4.31*
The hut in which Bishop
Mackenzie died
By Charles Meller (after Henry
Rowley), August 1863
Watercolour over pencil on paper
17.5 x 25
THE UNITED SOCIETY FOR THE
PROPAGATION OF THE GOSPEL
AND RHODES HOUSE LIBRARY
(Box AI[I]A, UMCA 7–18)

4.32†
'Missionaries Buying Food at
Magomero'
By Charles Meller (after Henry
Rowley), August 1863
Watercolour over pencil on paper
17.5 x 25
THE UNITED SOCIETY FOR THE
PROPAGATION OF THE GOSPEL
AND RHODES HOUSE LIBRARY
(Box AI[I]A, UMCA 7–18)

4.33*
'An Evening Halt'
By Charles Meller, c. 1862
Watercolour over pencil on paper
17.5 x 25
THE UNITED SOCIETY FOR THE
PROPAGATION OF THE GOSPEL
AND RHODES HOUSE LIBRARY
(Box AI[I]A, UMCA 7–18)

4.34
Engraver's watercolour sketch
of Mary Livingstone's grave
(annotated by David Livingstone)
1864–1865
Grey and black wash with white
bodycolour on paper, 21.8 x 30.8
PRIVATE COLLECTION

4.35
Thomas Baines (1822–1875)
By James Chapman, c. 1861–1864
Albumen print, 7 x 7.2
ROYAL GEOGRAPHICAL SOCIETY
(PR/050113)

4.36†
Baobab tree, Shupanga
By John Kirk, c. 1858–1863
Albumen print, 15 x 20.6
BY PERMISSION OF THE TRUSTEES
OF THE NATIONAL LIBRARY OF
SCOTLAND
(9942/40 [3])

4.37†
The *Ma Robert* on the Zambezi
at Lupata
By John Kirk, c. 1858–1860
Albumen print, 13.2 x 20.6
BY PERMISSION OF THE TRUSTEES
OF THE NATIONAL LIBRARY OF
SCOTLAND (9942/40 [10])

4.38†
Vegetation at Lupata
By John Kirk, 1859
Albumen print, 15.5 x 20.6
BY PERMISSION OF THE TRUSTEES
OF THE NATIONAL LIBRARY OF
SCOTLAND (9942/40 [13])

4.39†
Dwellings in the village at Luabo
By John Kirk, 1859
Albumen print, 12.3 x 19.8
BY PERMISSION OF THE TRUSTEES
OF THE NATIONAL LIBRARY OF
SCOTLAND (9942/40 [15])

4.40†
Pandanus trees
By John Kirk, 1859
Albumen print, 14.8 x 19
BY PERMISSION OF THE TRUSTEES
OF THE NATIONAL LIBRARY OF
SCOTLAND (9942/40 [16])

4.41†
Tete: a house in which John Kirk
and Livingstone stayed
By John Kirk, c. 1858–1863
Albumen print, 14.5 x 21.2
BY PERMISSION OF THE TRUSTEES
OF THE NATIONAL LIBRARY OF
SCOTLAND (9942/40 [17])

4.42†
Shupanga: the *Lady Nyassa*
By John Kirk, 1862
Albumen print, 14.5 x 19.8
BY PERMISSION OF THE TRUSTEES
OF THE NATIONAL LIBRARY OF
SCOTLAND (9942/40 [26])

4.43†
African dwelling with
a baobab tree in the background
By John Kirk, c. 1858–1863
Albumen print, 13.8 x 19.8
BY PERMISSION OF THE TRUSTEES
OF THE NATIONAL LIBRARY OF
SCOTLAND (9942/40 [27v])

4.44†
Mary Livingstone's grave
By John Kirk, 1862
Albumen print, 14.5 x 19.8
BY PERMISSION OF THE TRUSTEES
OF THE NATIONAL LIBRARY OF
SCOTLAND (9942/40 [24])

4.45†
William George Tozer
(?1829–1899)
By Liddell Sawyer, c. 1868
Albumen cabinet print
16.5 x 10.5
THE UNITED SOCIETY FOR THE
PROPAGATION OF THE GOSPEL
AND RHODES HOUSE LIBRARY
(Photos 63)

4.46
John Kirk (1832–1922)
Albumen cabinet print after an
earlier photograph (photographer
unknown, c. 1857), 12.3 x 8.7 (oval)
ROYAL BOTANIC GARDENS, KEW
(44489)

4.47
Charles Frederick Mackenzie
(1825–1862)
By an unknown photographer
Late 1850s
Albumen print, 19.5 x 14.8
THE UNITED SOCIETY FOR THE
PROPAGATION OF THE GOSPEL
AND RHODES HOUSE LIBRARY
(Album 37, p15)

4.48
Henry Rowley (died c. 1907)
and Horace Waller (1833–1896)
By an unknown photographer
1860s
Albumen carte-de-visite, 9.4 x 5.9
NATIONAL PORTRAIT GALLERY,
LONDON (AX68135)

4.49
George Rae (?1831–1865)
By an unknown photographer
Early 1860s
Albumen carte-de-visite, 7.5 x 5.7
THE DAVID LIVINGSTONE CENTRE
(236)

4.50
Charles Livingstone (1821–1873)
By an unknown photographer, 1860s
Albumen carte-de-visite, 8.5 x 4.8
THE DAVID LIVINGSTONE CENTRE
(243)

4.51
Thomas Baines (1822–1875)
By an unknown photographer, 1860s
Albumen carte-de-visite, 9.8 x 5.3
ROYAL GEOGRAPHICAL SOCIETY
(PR/05011)

4.52
William George Tozer
(?1829–1899)
By an unknown photographer
c. 1861
Albumen print, 9.1 x 5.7
THE UNITED SOCIETY FOR THE
PROPAGATION OF THE GOSPEL
AND RHODES HOUSE LIBRARY
(Photos 63)

4.53
Letter from Holloway Helmore to
Olive Helmore, 29 January 1859
Manuscript letter, 22.5 x 18.4
COUNCIL FOR WORLD MISSION
ARCHIVE, SCHOOL OF ORIENTAL
AND AFRICAN STUDIES
(Africa personal box 1, Holloway
Helmore papers, no. 12)

4.54
Letter from Lizzie Helmore to
Olive Helmore, 4 December 1860
Manuscript letter, 18 x 11.3
COUNCIL FOR WORLD MISSION
ARCHIVE, SCHOOL OF ORIENTAL
AND AFRICAN STUDIES
(Africa personal box 1, Holloway
Helmore papers, no. 27)

4.55
John Kirk's notebook containing
meteorological observations,
9 May–12 November 1860
Bound manuscript, 18.5 x 12.8
(closed)
BY PERMISSION OF THE TRUSTEES
OF THE NATIONAL LIBRARY OF
SCOTLAND (9942/22)

4.56
'List of Specimens of Natural
History packed for transmission
to England'
By John Kirk, June 1862
Bound manuscript, 34 x 46 (open)
ROYAL BOTANIC GARDENS, KEW

4.57
Sketchbook given to Horace
Waller by John Kirk, May 1863
Leatherbound sketchbook
14.5 x 26.5 (closed)
CURATORS OF THE BODLEIAN
LIBRARY, RHODES HOUSE
LIBRARY (MSS.Afr.s.16.5[22])

4.58
*Narrative of an Expedition to the
Zambesi and its Tributaries*
By Charles Livingstone with
revisions by David Livingstone
1864 (chapters 1–3)
Bound manuscript, 33.3 x 41
(open)
PRIVATE COLLECTION

4.59
Letter from David Livingstone to
the Commander of Her Majesty's
Ship, 25 May 1859
Manuscript letter, 32.2 x 40
QUENTIN KEYNES

4.60
Letter from David Livingstone to
the editor of *The Times*
17 March 1862
Manuscript letter, 13.6 x 21.2
BY PERMISSION OF THE TRUSTEES
OF THE NATIONAL LIBRARY OF
SCOTLAND
(Manuscript Dep 237)

4.61
Letter from David Livingstone to
Agnes Livingstone, 29 April 1862
Manuscript letter, 22.9 x 18.5
BY PERMISSION OF THE TRUSTEES
OF THE NATIONAL LIBRARY OF
SCOTLAND (MS10704 ff17–20)

4.62
Manuscript sheet with a sketch
of a fish from Lake Nyasa
(now Lake Malawi)
By David Livingstone
c. 1868–1870
Pencil and ink on paper
19.2 x 27.5
PRIVATE COLLECTION

4.63
Horace Waller's field journal 1861
Bound manuscript, 15.8 x 9.5
(closed)
CURATORS OF THE BODLEIAN
LIBRARY, RHODES HOUSE
LIBRARY (MSS.Afr.s.16/4[9])

4.64
Account book of the Zambezi
expedition, March 1858–April
1864
Bound manuscript, 19 x 14 x 2.5
(closed)
THE DAVID LIVINGSTONE CENTRE
(1116)

4.65
*Narrative of an Expedition to the
Zambesi and its Tributaries*
By David and Charles
Livingstone
Published by John Murray,
London, 1865
Printed book, 23 (spine height)
QUENTIN KEYNES

4.66
'On the Birds of the Zambesi
Region of Eastern Tropical
Africa'
By John Kirk
From *Ibis*, volume 6, series 1, 1864
Printed book, 22.7 (spine height)
BY PERMISSION OF THE TRUSTEES
OF THE NATURAL HISTORY
MUSEUM

4.67
*The Story of the Universities' Mission
to Central Africa*
By Henry Rowley
Published by Saunder's, Otley
& Co., London, 1866
Printed book, 20 (spine height)
QUENTIN KEYNES

4.68
Mary Livingstone's copy of
*Le Nouveau Testament de notre
Seigneur Jesus Christ*
(inscribed by David Livingstone)
Published in London, 1859
Printed book, 11 (spine height)
THE DAVID LIVINGSTONE CENTRE
(109)

4.69
Sextant used by Livingstone in
Central Africa
Brass, iron, glass
Approximately 25 x 23
ROYAL GEOGRAPHICAL SOCIETY
(285/6)

4.70
Three spears collected on
the Zambezi by Livingstone
Iron, wood and plant fibre
148.9–165 (length)
GLASGOW MUSEUMS
(1877.21.ia/ka/ma)

4.71
Knife and sheath of Shona
design collected by Livingstone
from the Zambezi
Iron, wood and sinew; knife 28
(length), sheath 21.5 (length)
GLASGOW MUSEUMS (1877.21.qa)

4.72
Two arrows shot into Livingstone
and Kirk's boat when exploring
the Rovuma
Iron and wood, each 72 (length)
ROYAL GEOGRAPHICAL SOCIETY
(0.2 [RGS 244])

4.73
Copper wire collected by
Livingstone in Central Africa
Copper wire coil with fibre
wrapping, 24 (diameter)
COURTESY OF THE TRUSTEES OF
THE NATIONAL MUSEUMS OF
SCOTLAND (RMS 762.4)

4.74
Hand mill for grinding corn,
collected by Livingstone, c. 1861
Stone bowl and maul, 10 x 43
COURTESY OF THE TRUSTEES OF
THE NATIONAL MUSEUMS OF
SCOTLAND (RMS 762.1)

4.75
Earthenware pot for catching
palm sap collected by John Kirk
on the Zambezi expedition
11.5 x 11.5
LENT BY KIND PERMISSION OF
THE TRUSTEES OF THE BRITISH
MUSEUM (Af.1960.20.46)

4.76
Wooden headrest from the
Zambezi Delta
15.5 x 18.5
COURTESY OF THE TRUSTEES
OF THE NATIONAL MUSEUMS OF
SCOTLAND
(RMS 538.3)

4.77
Mang'anja pipe collected by John
Kirk on the Zambezi expedition
Bamboo, 40.7 x 43.2
LENT BY KIND PERMISSION OF
THE TRUSTEES OF THE BRITISH
MUSEUM (Af.2685 a/b)

4.78
Camwood collected by
Livingstone from Bemba,
Central Africa
2.1 x 3.6 x 12.7
GLASGOW MUSEUMS (1877.21.da)

4.79
Two sections of an antelope net
collected by Livingstone during
the Zambezi expedition
Bark from the baobab tree
a) approximately 488 x 183
COURTESY OF THE TRUSTEES OF
THE NATIONAL MUSEUMS OF
SCOTLAND (RMS–594)
b) approximately 122 x 274
ROYAL BOTANIC GARDENS, KEW

4.80
Fish net made from buaze bark
(*Polygalaceae/Securidaca
longipedunculata*)
25.5 x 18.5 x 11
ROYAL BOTANIC GARDENS, KEW
(66905)

4.81
Fly whisk used by Livingstone
on the Zambezi expedition
Shredded plant fibre, 38 x 15
THE DAVID LIVINGSTONE CENTRE
(358)

4.82
Cordage of African manufacture
collected in 1858 by John Kirk
on the Zambezi expedition
Palm leaf, 38.2 x 17.8
LENT BY KIND PERMISSION OF
THE TRUSTEES OF THE BRITISH
MUSEUM (Af.1979.1.2472)

4.83
Basket
Palm fibre
Approximately 9 (height)
COURTESY OF THE TRUSTEES
OF THE NATIONAL MUSEUMS
OF SCOTLAND (RMS 538.2)

4.84
Two baskets collected by John
Kirk on the Zambezi expedition
Palm leaf; 48.3 x 28, 24.2 x 39.4
LENT BY KIND PERMISSION OF
THE TRUSTEES OF THE BRITISH
MUSEUM (Af.1960.20.48 & 51)

4.85
Two rubber balls
Each approximately 6.4 (diameter)
GLASGOW MUSEUMS
(1877.21.ea/fa)

4.86
Ivory armring worn by
the Mang'anja, collected
by Livingstone in 1859
9.3 (diameter)
GLASGOW MUSEUMS (1877.21.ha)

4.87
Hippopotamus canine tooth
collected by Livingstone and
given to his friend James Young
GLASGOW MUSEUMS (1900.159.c)

4.88
Elephant molar collected
by Livingstone
BY PERMISSION OF THE TRUSTEES
OF THE NATURAL HISTORY
MUSEUM (DEPARTMENT OF
ZOOLOGY) (59.12.29.3)

4.89
Ivory lip-ring used by Mang'anja
women, collected by Livingstone
in 1859
10 (diameter)
THE DAVID LIVINGSTONE CENTRE
(809)

4.90
Two sets of female waist beads
collected by John Kirk on the
Zambezi expedition
Seeds and cord; 30.5, 35.5
LENT BY KIND PERMISSION OF
THE TRUSTEES OF THE BRITISH
MUSEUM (Af.1960.20.54 & 56)

4.91
Female waist beads, probably
of Toka design, collected by
Livingstone
Glass beads, clam shell, cowries
and wood, approximately 22 x 20
THE DAVID LIVINGSTONE CENTRE
(705)

4.92
Herbarium specimen of
Barringtonia racemosa (L.) Spreng.
collected by John Kirk, October
1862
ROYAL BOTANIC GARDENS, KEW

4.93
Portion of stem
(*Apocynaceae/Adenium obesum*)
collected by John Kirk
Plant fibre, 18 x 5 x 3
ROYAL BOTANIC GARDENS, KEW
(49490)

4.94
Fruit and seeds from the Rovuma
River (*Sterculiaceae/Sterculia sp.*)
collected by John Kirk
20.3 x 15.3 x 5.7 (mounted)
ROYAL BOTANIC GARDENS, KEW
(65036)

4.95
Oil nuts from the Shire Highlands
(*Euphorbiaceae/Schinziophyton rautenii
Schinz*) collected by John Kirk
3 x 2.3
ROYAL BOTANIC GARDENS, KEW
(44489)

4.96
Dickinson's kestrel (*Falco
dickinsoni*) collected by John Kirk
BY PERMISSION OF THE TRUSTEES
OF THE NATURAL HISTORY
MUSEUM (63.12.30.3)

4.97
Livingstone's turaco (*Tauraco
Livingstonii*) collected by Charles
Livingstone
BY PERMISSION OF THE TRUSTEES
OF THE NATURAL HISTORY
MUSEUM (63.12.8.2)

4.98
Blue-cheeked bee-eater
(*Merops superciliosus persicus*)
collected by John Kirk
BY PERMISSION OF THE TRUSTEES
OF THE NATURAL HISTORY
MUSEUM (86.6.24.79)

4.99
Scarlet-chested sunbird (*Nectarinia
senegalensis gutturalis*) collected
by John Kirk
BY PERMISSION OF THE TRUSTEES
OF THE NATURAL HISTORY
MUSEUM (63.12.30.20)

4.100
Malachite kingfisher (*Alcedo
cristata*) collected by John Kirk
BY PERMISSION OF THE TRUSTEES
OF THE NATURAL HISTORY
MUSEUM (63.12.30.28)

4.101
Red-billed hornbill (*Tockus
erythrorhynchus*) collected on
the Zambezi expedition
BY PERMISSION OF THE TRUSTEES
OF THE NATURAL HISTORY
MUSEUM (60.12.31.51)

4.102
Lesser pied kingfisher (*Ceryle rudis*)
collected on the Zambezi
expedition
BY PERMISSION OF THE TRUSTEES
OF THE NATURAL HISTORY
MUSEUM (60.12.31.118)

4.103
Scarlet-chested sunbird
(*Nectarinia senegalensis gutturalis*)
collected by John Kirk
BY PERMISSION OF THE TRUSTEES
OF THE NATURAL HISTORY
MUSEUM (84.2.6.26)

4.104
Genet (*Genetta tigrina*) collected
by John Kirk
BY PERMISSION OF THE TRUSTEES
OF THE NATURAL HISTORY
MUSEUM (DEPARTMENT OF
ZOOLOGY) (64.1.9.3)

4.105
Lake Nyasa Left-handed Apple
Snail '*Lanistes sp.*' *Lanistes nyassanus*
(Dohrn, 1865) collected by John
Kirk, 1861
BY PERMISSION OF THE TRUSTEES
OF THE NATURAL HISTORY
MUSEUM (1862.9.25.2)

4.106
Pfeiffer's Freshwater Mussel
'*Iridina wahlbergi*' *Aspatharia
pfeifferiana* (Bernardi, 1860)
collected by John Kirk, 1861
BY PERMISSION OF THE TRUSTEES
OF THE NATURAL HISTORY
MUSEUM (1862.9.25.3)

4.107
Robertson's Lake Snail '*Paludina
sp.*' *Bellamya robertsoni*
(Frauenfeld, 1865) collected
by John Kirk, 1861
BY PERMISSION OF THE TRUSTEES
OF THE NATURAL HISTORY
MUSEUM (1862.9.25.5)

4.108
Elliptical Left-handed Apple
Snail '*Ampullaria lusitanica*' *Lanistes
ellipticus* (Martens, 1866) collected
by John Kirk, 1861
BY PERMISSION OF THE TRUSTEES
OF THE NATURAL HISTORY
MUSEUM (1862.9.25.6)

The Search for the Nile's Source and the Last Journeys

5.1
John Hanning Speke (1827–1864)
and James Augustus Grant
(1827–1892) with Timbo
By Henry Wyndham Phillips
c. 1864
Oil on canvas, 127 x 157.5
P. G. H. SPEKE

5.2
'The Last Charge, Latooka,
17 April 1863'
By Samuel White Baker
c. 1863–1866
Watercolour over pencil on paper
22.5 x 31.3
ROYAL GEOGRAPHICAL SOCIETY
(x851/34)

5.3
'The Start from M'rooli for the
Lake, February 1864'
By Samuel White Baker
c. 1864–1866
Watercolour over pencil on paper
22.5 x 31.3
ROYAL GEOGRAPHICAL SOCIETY
(x851/45)

5.4
'The Albert N'yanza, March
1864'
By Samuel White Baker
c. 1864–1866
Watercolour over pencil on paper
22.5 x 31.3
ROYAL GEOGRAPHICAL SOCIETY
(x851/46)

5.5
'The Welcome on our Return to
Shooa, 21 November 1864'
By Samuel White Baker
c. 1864–1866
Watercolour over pencil on paper
22.5 x 31.3
ROYAL GEOGRAPHICAL SOCIETY
(x851/49)

5.6
Album of Nile sketches
By James Augustus Grant
1860–1863
Album of watercolours on paper
32.8 x 39 (closed)
BY PERMISSION OF THE TRUSTEES
OF THE NATIONAL LIBRARY OF
SCOTLAND (MS17919)

5.7
Manuscript map of Lake
Tanganyika
By David Livingstone, 1873
Pencil on ruled mapping paper
on linen, 100.5 x 68.5
THE DAVID LIVINGSTONE CENTRE
(808 [Map 7])

5.8
James Gordon Bennett Jnr
(1841–1915)
By 'Nemo'
(Constantine von Grimm),
Vanity Fair, 15 November 1884
Chromolithograph, 38.8 x 26.3
NATIONAL PORTRAIT GALLERY,
LONDON

5.9
Mutesa, Kabaka of Buganda
By John Hanning Speke, 1862
From an album of watercolours
by John Hanning Speke and
James Augustus Grant
Watercolour over pencil on paper
in a bound volume
24.8 x 16.2 x 2 (closed)
ROYAL GEOGRAPHICAL SOCIETY
(Libr Mss Speke JH(b)I)

5.10
Manuscript map of Burton
and Speke's route, 1857–1858
By John Hanning Speke
1858–1859
Ink and watercolour on paper,
squared in pencil and laid on
to linen, 44.5 x 35.5
ROYAL GEOGRAPHICAL SOCIETY
(Tanzania S/s.16)

5.11
Manuscript map of Speke and
Grant's route from Zanzibar
to the Nile
By John Hanning Speke, 1863
Ink and watercolour on ruled
paper laid on to linen, 38.2 x 30.5
ROYAL GEOGRAPHICAL SOCIETY
(Tanzania S/S.12)

5.12
David Livingstone
By Thomas Annan, 1864
Albumen print, 36.8 x 30.4
SCOTTISH NATIONAL PORTRAIT
GALLERY (PGP 78)

5.13
Majid bin Said
By (?)Hurrychund Cintamow
(?)1869
Hand-coloured albumen print
23.2 x 19.2
ROYAL GEOGRAPHICAL SOCIETY
(PRO 26687)

5.14
Sir Richard Francis Burton
(1821–1890)
By Ernest Edwards, April 1865
Albumen print, 8.7 x 6.8
NATIONAL PORTRAIT GALLERY,
LONDON (AX14771)

5.15
'Album of Photographs of
Zanzibar'
By John Kirk, 1868–1874
Album of platinum prints
51 x 31.3 (open)
BY PERMISSION OF THE TRUSTEES
OF THE NATIONAL LIBRARY OF
SCOTLAND (9942/43)

5.16
Henry Morton Stanley (1841–1904)
By London Stereoscopic
Company, 1872
Albumen carte-de-visite, 8.7 x 6.4
NATIONAL PORTRAIT GALLERY,
LONDON
(X32118)

5.17
Henry Morton Stanley (1841–1904)
By London Stereoscopic
Company, c. 1872
Albumen carte-de-visite, 8.7 x 6.4
NATIONAL PORTRAIT GALLERY,
LONDON (X46623)

5.18
Henry Morton Stanley (1841–1904)
and Kalulu (c. 1864–1877)
By London Stereoscopic
Company, c. 1872
Albumen carte-de-visite, 9 x 6.2
NATIONAL PORTRAIT GALLERY,
LONDON (X45981)

5.19
Sir Samuel White Baker
(1821–1893)
By Maull & Co., 1860s
Albumen carte-de-visite, 8.9 x 6.1
NATIONAL PORTRAIT GALLERY,
LONDON (X8353)

5.20
Sir Samuel White Baker
(1821–1893)
By Maull & Co., 1860s
Albumen carte-de-visite, 8.9 x 6.1
NATIONAL PORTRAIT GALLERY,
LONDON (X47500)

5.21
Sir Samuel White Baker
(1821–1893)
By Maull & Co., 1860s
Albumen carte-de-visite, 8.9 x 6.1
NATIONAL PORTRAIT GALLERY,
LONDON (X47501)

5.22
Lady Baker (née Florence von
Saas)
By Maull & Co., 1860s
Albumen carte-de-visite, 8.9 x 6.1
NATIONAL PORTRAIT GALLERY,
LONDON (X47503)

5.23
Henry Morton Stanley (1841–1904)
By C. H. Nedey of Alexandria
(after an earlier photograph)
c. 1867–1870
Albumen carte-de-visite, 9.1 x 5.4
QUENTIN KEYNES

5.24
Lieutenant W. J. Grandy's party
before the start of the search
for Livingstone
By J. Silviera, 1873
Albumen print, 14.5 x 19.2
ROYAL GEOGRAPHICAL SOCIETY
(PRO 26867)

5.25
The meeting of the British
Association for the Advancement
of Science, Bath, September 1864
By an unknown photographer 1864
Albumen print, 10.8 x 7.2
BATH ROYAL LITERARY AND
SCIENTIFIC INSTITUTION (BRLSI/3)

5.26
Members of the meeting of
the British Association for the
Advancement of Science,
Bath, 1864
By an unknown photographer
1864
Albumen print, 10.8 x 7.2
BATH ROYAL LITERARY AND
SCIENTIFIC INSTITUTION
(BRLSI/4)

5.27
William Oswell Livingstone
(1851–1892)
By an unknown photographer, 1860s
Albumen carte-de-visite, 8.8 x 5.7
THE DAVID LIVINGSTONE CENTRE
(207)

5.28
Agnes Livingstone, Livingstone's
sister (1823–1895), and Anna
Mary, his daughter (1858–1939)
By an unknown photographer
c. 1870
Albumen carte-de-visite, 8.8 x 5.7
THE DAVID LIVINGSTONE CENTRE
(207)

5.29
Anna Mary Livingstone
(1858–1939)
By an unknown photographer, 1860s
Albumen carte-de-visite, 8.8 x 5.7
THE DAVID LIVINGSTONE CENTRE
(207)

5.30
Lieutenant D. S. Dawson and
Lieutenant W. Henn discussing
the Livingstone search expedition
with William Oswell Livingstone
By an unknown photographer
c. 1871–1872
Albumen print, 10.3 x 6.5
ROYAL GEOGRAPHICAL SOCIETY
(PRO 050668)

5.31
James Augustus Grant's journal
showing a list of 'African Kit'
1858–1863
Bound manuscript, 23 x 19 x 3.5
(closed)
BY PERMISSION OF THE TRUSTEES
OF THE NATIONAL LIBRARY OF
SCOTLAND (MS17915)

5.32
Livingstone's field notebook,
2 July–4 September 1866
Bound manuscript, 15 x 9.5 x 7.5
(closed)
THE DAVID LIVINGSTONE CENTRE
(1142)

5.33
Envelope with Livingstone's
observations and journal entries
for March–September 1871
Manuscript sheet, 22 x 38.8
BY PERMISSION OF THE TRUSTEES
OF THE NATIONAL LIBRARY OF
SCOTLAND (MS10703)

5.34
Letter from David Livingstone
to Agnes Livingstone
12 December 1871
Manuscript letter, 18 x 22.8
THE BRITISH LIBRARY BOARD
(Add Ms 50,184 f.176)

5.35
'List of men and goods from
Zanzibar to Mr H. M. Stanley'
By David Livingstone
(?)March 1872
Manuscript sheet, 15.7 x 20.1
BY PERMISSION OF THE TRUSTEES
OF THE NATIONAL LIBRARY OF
SCOTLAND (MS10705)

5.36
The Albert N'yanza
By Samuel White Baker, volume 2
Published by Macmillan & Co.,
London, 1866
Printed book, 23 (spine height)
QUENTIN KEYNES

5.37
The Lake Regions of Central Africa
By Richard Francis Burton,
volume 2
Published by Longman & Co.,
London, 1860
Printed book, 23.4 (spine height)
QUENTIN KEYNES

5.38
'The Meeting of Livingstone and
Stanley in Central Africa'
By G. Durand (after Henry
Morton Stanley), *The Graphic*,
3 August 1872
Wood engraving, 40.2 x 61
NATIONAL PORTRAIT GALLERY,
LONDON

5.39
John Hanning Speke's revised
proofs of *Journal of the Discovery
of the Source of the Nile*, 1863
Bound volume of proof sheets
with manuscript additions
30.2 x 52 (open)
BY PERMISSION OF THE TRUSTEES
OF THE NATIONAL LIBRARY OF
SCOTLAND (MS4874)

5.40
*What Led to the Discovery of the
Source of the Nile*
By John Hanning Speke
(annotated by John Hanning
Speke)
Published by Blackwoods,
Edinburgh and London, 1863
Printed book, 23 (spine height)
QUENTIN KEYNES

5.41
*What Led to the Discovery
of the Source of the Nile*
By John Hanning Speke
Published by Blackwoods,
Edinburgh and London, 1863
Printed book, 23 (spine height)
QUENTIN KEYNES

5.42
How I Found Livingstone; travels, adventures and discoveries in Central Africa
By Henry Morton Stanley
Published by Sampson Low & Co., London, 1872
Printed book, 22.2 (spine height)
QUENTIN KEYNES

5.43
The Search after Livingstone
By E. D. Young, revised by Horace Waller
Published by Letts, Son & Co., London, 1868
Printed book, 18.3 (spine height)
QUENTIN KEYNES

5.44
A Map of a Portion of Central Africa by Dr Livingstone
Published by John Murray for Stanford's Geographical Establishment, London, 1874
Printed map (proof), 80 x 87.9
ROYAL GEOGRAPHICAL SOCIETY (Africa Div.97)

5.45
The East African Lakes, showing their relations to the Source of the Nile
Published by John Murray, London, 1868
Printed map, 22 x 62.5
ROYAL GEOGRAPHICAL SOCIETY (Uganda S/S 21)

5.46
Sir Samuel White Baker's muzzle loader
Manufactured by H. Holland
c. 1860, 119 x 16
ROYAL GEOGRAPHICAL SOCIETY (358/0.1)

5.47
Winchester rifle (no. 25377H), Calibre .44 Henry Rimfire
1866 patent
LOANED BY COURTESY OF THE DIRECTOR, NATIONAL ARMY MUSEUM (6312–251–74)

5.48
Livingstone's muzzle loader
118.2 (length)
THE DAVID LIVINGSTONE CENTRE (519)

5.49
Livingstone's prismatic compass
Manufactured by Cary, London
Brass, approximately 7.5 (diameter)
ROYAL GEOGRAPHICAL SOCIETY (5.1 [RGS 552])

5.50
Livingstone's mapping ruler
62.9 (length)
THE DAVID LIVINGSTONE CENTRE (326)

5.51
Bottle of Livingstone's Rousers pills
8 (height)
THE DAVID LIVINGSTONE CENTRE (305)

5.52
Livingstone's pocket surgical instrument case
21 x 26.1 (open)
THE DAVID LIVINGSTONE CENTRE (312)

5.53
Medicine chest used by Livingstone on his last journeys
1860s
Leather case with glass bottles containing drugs and medical implements, 12 x 17.5 x 32
COURTESY OF THE TRUSTEES OF THE SCIENCE MUSEUM (A642570)

5.54
Livingstone's clasp knife, mirror and pen
ROYAL GEOGRAPHICAL SOCIETY (113/103.1)

5.55
Inkwell used by Livingstone on his last journeys
3.5 x 4.5
THE DAVID LIVINGSTONE CENTRE (301)

5.56
Discovery matches
Manufactured by Dixon, Son & Evans, 1870s
Matchbox, 7 x 14.5
THE DAVID LIVINGSTONE CENTRE (078)

5.57
Livingstone's cap
ROYAL GEOGRAPHICAL SOCIETY (Hat 1 [RGS 138])

5.58
Stanley's helmet
ROYAL GEOGRAPHICAL SOCIETY (Hat 2 [RGS 139])

5.59
Snuff box presented to Stanley by Queen Victoria
Gold, enamel and precious stones, 3.7 x 8 x 6
NATIONAL MUSEUM AND GALLERY, CARDIFF (A 50,500)

5.60
Three spearheads collected by Livingstone from 'Manyema country' during his last journeys
Iron and copper, 34–56 (length)
GLASGOW MUSEUMS (1877.21.g/h/i)

5.61
Sword, or dagger, and sheath collected by Livingstone in 'Manyema country' during his last journeys
Iron and leather, cane, snake or crocodile skin; sword 67.2 (length), sheath 59.3 (length)
GLASGOW MUSEUMS (1877.21.m)

5.62
Iron ingot collected by Livingstone from the market in Nyangwe
5.5 x 51 x 12
GLASGOW MUSEUMS (1877.21.p)

5.63
Horns from a 'bush buck' said to have been shot by Livingstone
19 (length)
GLASGOW MUSEUMS (1877.21.za)

The Myth Begins

6.1
Agnes and Tom Livingstone, Abdullah Susi, James Chuma and Horace Waller at Newstead Abbey
By R. Allen & Son, 1874
Woodbury-type print, 14 x 19.8
ROYAL GEOGRAPHICAL SOCIETY (PR/026870)

6.2
Abdullah Susi, Horace Waller, James Chuma, Agnes Livingstone, Mrs Webb and William F. Webb, and Tom Livingstone at Newstead Abbey
By R. Allen & Son, 1874
Woodbury-type print, 14 x 19.8
ROYAL GEOGRAPHICAL SOCIETY (PR/026871)

6.3
Livingstone's coffin at the Royal Geographical Society's headquarters in Savile Row
By London Stereoscopic Company, 1874
Albumen print, 18.6 x 23.5
THE DAVID LIVINGSTONE CENTRE (228)

6.4
James Chuma (c. 1850–1882) and Abdullah Susi (died 1891)
By Maull & Co., 1874
Albumen cabinet print, 15 x 10
THE DAVID LIVINGSTONE CENTRE (081)

6.5
James Chuma (c. 1850–1882) and Abdullah Susi (died 1891)
By Maull & Co., 1874
Albumen cabinet print, 15 x 10
THE DAVID LIVINGSTONE CENTRE (081)

6.6
James Chuma (c. 1850–1882)
By Maull & Co., 1874
Albumen carte-de-visite, 10.2 x 6.2
ROYAL GEOGRAPHICAL SOCIETY (PRO 50464)

6.7
Abdullah Susi (died 1891)
By Maull & Co., 1874
Albumen carte-de-visite, 10.2 x 6.2
ROYAL GEOGRAPHICAL SOCIETY (PRO 52200)

6.8
James Chuma (c. 1850–1882)
By Maull & Co., 1874
Albumen cabinet print, 15 x 10
THE DAVID LIVINGSTONE CENTRE (081)

6.9
Verney Lovett Cameron (1844–1894)
By Maull & Fox, c. 1870
Albumen cabinet print, 16.3 x 10.4
ROYAL GEOGRAPHICAL SOCIETY (PRO 50399)

6.10
Jacob Wainwright on board the *Malva* with Livingstone's coffin
By an unknown photographer
1874
Albumen print, 16.6 x 20.5
QUENTIN KEYNES

6.11
Replica of the hut in which Livingstone died, constructed at St John's Vicarage, Leytonstone
By an unknown photographer
c. 1910
Bromide print, 9.5 x 12.5
THE COUNCIL FOR WORLD MISSION ARCHIVES

6.12
The Life and Work of David Livingstone
Published by the London Missionary Society, c. 1900
40 magic lantern slides (glass positives) and printed pamphlet
NATIONAL PORTRAIT GALLERY, LONDON

6.13
Letter from Verney Lovett
Cameron to the Secretary of
the Royal Geographical Society,
16 October 1873
Manuscript letter, 26.8 x 21.2
ROYAL GEOGRAPHICAL SOCIETY
(DL/5/1/1)

6.14
Horace Waller's notebook
recording Susi and Chuma's
account of Livingstone's death
c. 1865–1874
Bound manuscript, 21.8 x 13
(closed)
CURATORS OF THE BODLEIAN
LIBRARY, RHODES HOUSE
LIBRARY
(MSS.Afr.x.16/4 [24])

6.15
Notebook with James Chuma's
signature
Bound manuscript, 13.5 x 10.7
(closed)
PRIVATE COLLECTION

6.16
*The Last Journals of David
Livingstone*
Edited by Horace Waller
2 volumes
Published by John Murray
London, 1874
Printed book, 22.1 (spine height)
QUENTIN KEYNES

6.17
*Hymn to be sung at the Funeral of
Dr Livingstone*
Published by Harrison & Sons,
London, 1874
Printed sheet, 20.2 x 12.8
THE DAVID LIVINGSTONE CENTRE
(225)

6.18
Admission card (and envelope) for
Edward Unwin to Livingstone's
funeral in Westminster Abbey,
18 April 1874
Printed card with black wax seal
and envelope
Each approximately 8.6 x 12.2
THE DAVID LIVINGSTONE CENTRE
(229)

6.19
'The Main Stream Came Up to
Susi's Mouth'
From *The Last Journals of David
Livingstone*
Engraver's woodblock
9.7 x 17.2 x 2
PRIVATE COLLECTION

6.20
'Forging Hoes'
From *The Last Journals of David
Livingstone*
Engraver's woodblock, 9.5 x 9 x 2
PRIVATE COLLECTION

6.21
'David Livingstone'
From *The Last Journals of
David Livingstone*
Engraver's woodblock
Approximately 13 x 10.5 x 2
PRIVATE COLLECTION

6.22
'Slavers Revenging their Losses'
From *The Last Journals of David
Livingstone*
Engraver's woodblock, 10 x 17 x 2
PRIVATE COLLECTION

6.23
Black tin travelling case used by
Livingstone
38.8 x 66.5 x 41.2
THE DAVID LIVINGSTONE CENTRE
(309)

6.24
Mail sack for the Cameron search
expedition
Cotton bag with ink inscription
Approximately 20 x 40
THE DAVID LIVINGSTONE CENTRE
(131)

6.25
Basin belonging to Livingstone
and used on his last journeys
Enamelled iron, 5.7 x 15.7
GLASGOW MUSEUMS (1900.159.t)

6.26
Matted locks of Livingstone's
hair
12 x 14.7
THE DAVID LIVINGSTONE CENTRE
(485)

6.27
Cast of Livingstone's left
humerus
Plaster, 36.5 (length)
THE ROYAL COLLEGE OF
SURGEONS OF ENGLAND

6.28
Moulds of Livingstone's left
humerus
Plaster, 21 x 9
THE ROYAL COLLEGE OF
SURGEONS OF ENGLAND

6.29
Section of the mpundu tree from
the shores of Lake Bangweulu,
under which Livingstone's heart
was buried
Tree bark carved by Jacob
Wainwright, 1873, approximately
100 (height)
ROYAL GEOGRAPHICAL SOCIETY
(0.3 [RGS 314])

6.30
Livingstone Medal of the Royal
Scottish Geographical Society
By P. Macgillivray, *c.* 1881–1890
Silver medal, 6.3 (diameter)
COURTESY OF THE TRUSTEES OF
THE NATIONAL MUSEUMS OF
SCOTLAND (H.1966.794)

238

Canopus

March 1871
Mer. Alt
...ella

° 28' 00

41. 30

19
51   32
27   28

* 82   32
  4 1   1 7
  9 0
  4 8   4 3
  5 2   3 7   5 4
  3   5 4   5 4

*) 131°   16   30
   65   38 . 15
   90
   2 4   2 2
   2 8   4 0
   4   26

...tas Mer. Alt.
° 4' 30"

error 0"

...do land Rt = Kasongo's 20 March

...ba at 9 A.M. camp —

4th April, 1871 Canopus

Noon   *) 83°   5 1   7 A.M. fair
81°   28.10
        4 1   3 2 . 3 0   28.40   73
        9 0   29.12

...chan...   4 8   2 8